SEARCHING FOR LOST CITY

Searching for Lost City

ON THE TRAIL OF AMERICA'S NATIVE LANGUAGES

Elizabeth Seay

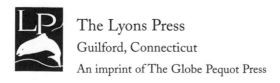

The Lyons Press
Guilford, Connecticut
An imprint of The Globe Pequot Press

The Lyons Press is an imprint of The Globe Pequot Press

10 9 8 7 6 5 4 3 2 1

Printed in the United States of America

Designed by Paul L. Schiff

ISBN 1-59228-195-8

Library of Congress Cataloging-in-Publication Data is available on file.

CONTENTS

Introduction

Lost City is a real place, back in the foothills of the Ozark Mountains. To get there, you must leave the plains of Oklahoma. Gradually, the hills approach and fold you in secretive valleys. The roads curve, and sight lines shrink. The trees multiply, approach the road, line it, and finally loop over the top, locking their branches so you are driving in a tunnel of green.

In these woods that cover northeast Oklahoma and reach fifty thousand square miles into Arkansas, Kansas, and Missouri, things that have disappeared elsewhere are alive. People who live here see bald eagles and black bears; outlaws and militiamen hide in the hills. The elusive thing I came to find—and I was a rueful naturalist, knowing that anything that thrives on secrecy can be killed by exposure—was a language. People had told me there were places in these hills where Cherokee was still spoken. As I eased around mountain curves, I rolled down my windows, as if a sound might be flung out of the forest, but I heard only wind, birds, and my own car wheels kicking up gravel.

I was looking for more than Cherokee. I was looking for any Native American languages that were still spoken. Once, more than three hundred Native American languages existed in the area of the continental United States—as different from each other as Turkish, English, and Chinese. Now, the number of languages has dwindled to about 150. I suspected that Oklahoma was a haven for some of the remaining tongues. The state, whose name is a Choctaw coinage meaning "red man's land," is the former Indian Territory, where the government drove out more than sixty tribes in the nineteenth century. The remnants of about forty still exist. While Native American tribes survive all over the United States, Oklahoma is home to the most diverse mix, with descendants of groups from New England, the South, the Northwest, and everywhere in between. Thus the state represents a microcosm of the continent.

As I drove through eastern Oklahoma, I glanced occasionally at a creased map on the passenger's seat. It was covered with Indian words, naming places in the state: *Ochelata, Talihina, Anadarko. Talala, Eufala, Okemah. Weleetka, Wewoka, Wetumka.* The persistence of these names on the map seemed remarkable. In most American places—Massachusetts, Oregon, Tennessee—Indian place-names represent tales from the past, faraway points on a time line—or nothing at all. They float on the map, free of their moorings in language. But in Oklahoma, it is still possible to follow the lines from the names to the namers.

I was an unlikely person to be drawn to Native American languages. Westerns always bored me. I have no Indian ancestry. I grew up in Oklahoma, but my white community looked east for inspiration. To most people there, Indians were just a history lesson: a shield on the state flag, a mass of faceless feathered headdresses in a glass display case, and the litany of the first five tribes in Oklahoma, their names as familiar and meaningless to a child as the names of Columbus's three ships: Cherokee, Choctaw, Chickasaw, Creek, Seminole; the *Niña,* the *Pinta,* and the *Santa Maria.* Indians were the girl I crayoned in first grade with a feather in her hair and the name "Princess Wildflower," the fry bread we cooked at day camp, and my blue pendant shaped like a thunderbird, the Plains spirit that brought the rain. Indians were a longhaired laborer standing at a bus stop and the feel of fifth position in ballet class, as I rounded my arms, stretched my neck taller, and turned my knees outward, aware that the Indian ballerina who taught the class was walking by.

Native Americans made cryptic appearances in my family's Oklahoma. They showed up in the cemetery down the street, in the lilting syllables on the maps, and on the highway signs we drove by when we went from town to town: ENTERING SAC AND FOX NATION RESERVATION. The landscape rolled by: golden wheat fields on one side and strip malls on the other, and three minutes later, another sign appeared: LEAVING SAC AND FOX NATION RESERVATION. We never slowed down.

It's hard to say whether we knew any Indians. If you go to a cocktail party in Tulsa and walk over to a group of people eating cheese puffs at the canapé table, you might well find out that three-quarters of them have an Indian grandparent, but they don't consider themselves Indian.

What I saw then were the outskirts, the off-putting fringes of the Indian world, the made-in-Taiwan pottery, the turquoise bolos, the chemically colorful headdresses, and the New Age seekers with names like Star Dancer, all arrayed around tribal life like strip malls on the edge of town. They were the shorthand version of the culture, a kind of pidgin, akin to the dialogue that movies used to depict Indians on screen: "Many moons I come back."

In school, I always liked the feel of other grammars—the ablative twist of a Latin word ending, the clarity that French's subjunctive gave to wishes, and the quality of other-ness that foreign languages carried. Even in something as mundane as XXIV—a set of numerals—you recognize a concept in a foreign housing (ancient, cumbersome, Roman) that is familiar and deeply strange at the same time. You know it and you don't. There's something exciting about other languages' combination of exotic and familiar, incomprehensibility and understanding.

But it never occurred to me to look for Indian languages in Oklahoma. I was already elsewhere: trying to read every book in the school library or daydreaming in the magnolia tree in our yard or, when I was older, cruising around the endless highways or rereading Keats's "Ode on a Grecian Urn," in part because I loved the words and in part because I had to write a paper so I could go away to college and start my real life. I moved to the East Coast and lived there for more than ten years.

Still, I wound up here, driving around rural Oklahoma, Indian country. What eventually drew me back didn't spring so much from memories of Native America as from the poetry I had read as a child, the foreign words I'd learned, and an idea I had developed about the value of language.

Authors Daniel Nettle and Suzanne Romaine write that in Micmac, a language spoken in Canada, some trees "are named for the sound the wind makes when it blows through them during the autumn, about an hour after sunset when the wind always comes from a certain direction. Moreover, these names are not fixed but change as the sound changes."

There is something about this notion that invites us to leave what Aldous Huxley calls "the ruts of ordinary perception" for a moment. Instead of classifying trees with known names, we imagine a place— and I use the word *place* loosely, as I could say *a time* or *a mind-set*— in which, first of all, we can actually hear the sound of wind in the trees, and second, we can see the trees in a new way, without the residue of the arbitrary syllables—*maple, chestnut, sycamore*—that we know. The Micmac methodology for naming is not as unfamiliar as it first appears: Many common English bird names reflect the sounds they make. But the concept heightens our auditory sensibility, gets us wondering if we could listen more, and reminds us that there are other ways of making sense of the natural world.

Learning new languages can bring unnoticed aspects of reality into focus. The Comanches have a word for the bump on the back of the neck, which is thought to be a place where the body is centered. The Muskogee-Creeks single out the particular kind of love that children and their parents and grandparents feel for each other, using a word that also means "to be stingy." There is an Iroquois word for the desire within each person to be kind and to do good, and a Muskogee-Creek word for the craving for something salty, not sweet.

These words convey information the way cups carry liquid, giving a shape to the contents. They exert what author Howard Rheingold calls a "subtle leverage" on the mind, helping you to see more, hear more, taste more. And they embody the accidental poetry found in the ordinary speech of another language.

I can't say that I understood all this immediately. I had to travel deeper into a vague interest in order to discover the subterranean flare of passion. But even before I learned any Native American languages, I enjoyed the way language can open—or close—certain doors of perception. I had an appetite for word-pleasures and word-insights. From the beginning, I had a broad idea, with a simple equation: More languages equals more possibilities for thinking.

As an adult, when I became aware Oklahoma had two dozen Native languages left, I began to realize that I had grown up in the equivalent of a rain forest of linguistic diversity—and thus of ways to look at the world. At my office in New York, I found myself studying old maps of Oklahoma, seeing the names of its towns as clues to a mystery I had never recognized. I wondered if we had been deaf to dozens of poetries, if Oklahoma had a kind of wealth it had not recognized—a treasury of languages, as hidden as the oil that lay there untapped for millennia.

Ochelata, Talihina, Anadarko . . . Haltingly, faintly, the names on the map bring to life the world of the old Indian Territory. Between the 1830s and the 1890s, dozens of tribes were sent there. Groups came from Georgia, Alabama, and the rest of the South to the state's eastern forests, while some upper Plains tribes wound up in the flat center. The southwestern tribes, like the Comanches and Kiowas, were confined to Oklahoma's share of the arid landscape where they had made their last stand. In that continent in miniature, they contemplated forming an Indian state.

Oklahoma is a forced melting pot, a multicultural refugee camp. Its towns include Konawa, "string of beads" in the language of the Seminoles; Koonkazachey, the name of a Kiowa-Apache chief; and Kosoma, "stink," named after a swamp by Choctaws from Alabama. The settlers in this world didn't come up with the optimistic names you find on most American frontiers, such as Hope or Harmony. They had no illusions about Independence. More often, you find homesick renditions of places they had left, like Wewoka, "roaring water," reprising Alabama in a drier country. You find the exhaustion of Broken Arrow or Keota, "fire gone out" in Choctaw, which memorializes a clan that arrived with pneumonia and died.

But the names on the map represent something encouraging, too: the continuation of Indian communities in a new place. Each town marks an effort to bring community life forward, the way the tribes brought the coals of their old fires on the trails of tears.

Cherokees used to begin traditional stories with a phrase translated as "in the great forever that was." It's like *Once upon a time,* but instead of placing us firmly in the past, it emphasizes the availability of myth and history to those who know where to look. These Indian place-names provide a link to the past that persists in the present.

So what you see on the map is not just Oklahoma. It suggests the dimensions of an American loss. Pontotoc, Oklahoma, is a secret sister city of Pontotoc, Mississippi, linked by the Chickasaws' path between the two places. The name *Anadarko* shares its origins with *Texas,* where some of the Caddos once lived, and Pottawatomie County's people created *Chicago.* Nowata was named by the people who named

Manhattan—the Lenni-Lenapes, known as the Delawares, who once included groups called the Raritans, the Tappans, and the Hackensacks. Now those links of migration and memory are largely forgotten. But when people ask what happened to the Native Americans who once populated the continent, Oklahoma provides one answer: Some of them came to Indian Territory. A whispered history of the United States is contained in their words.

In 1534, on the sixth of July, Jacques Cartier was hunting for a way to sail west to Asia. One of his boats was in a bay near Newfoundland, wending its way along the coast of what appeared to be a large landmass when, Cartier reported, "boates of wilde men" approached, "dancing, and making many signes of joy and mirth, as it were desiring our friendship, saying in their tongue *Napeu tondamen assurtah,* with many other words that we understood not." It isn't clear what the words meant, though one French translator rendered them as "We wish to have your friendship." The Frenchmen, feeling outnumbered in their single boat, tried to turn the natives away, but speaking French didn't work. They shot off their guns and struck out with lances, frightening off the men they called wild. This early exchange of words led to the first rough and tentative trade between the two cultures; the natives returned with skins the next day.

This moment of misunderstanding is a reminder of an era when North America was full of languages. Throughout the sixteenth, seventeenth, and eighteenth centuries, explorers of the New World kept encountering new languages and collecting odd bits of speech. As Cartier traveled, he compiled a vocabulary of a language now known as Lawrentian, listing words for hatchet, brass, sword, red cloth, and—optimistically—gold. Spanish settlers and missionaries produced grammars for several Mayan languages in the 1550s. John Smith, the English settler who encountered Pocahontas in Virginia, brought a list of Powhatan words back to England, organized into useful phrases such as: "In how many days will there come hither any more English Ships," and "Bid Pokahontas bring hither two little Baskets, and I will give her white Beads to make a Chaine." Roger Williams, the founder of Rhode Island, published a "key" to the language of the Narragansetts, the people from whom he purchased the land for his colony.

These days, it is hard to envision the former diversity of Indian cultures—hunters and planters, roamers and city builders, ice dwellers and seafaring canoers. Similarly, it is hard to comprehend the variety of American Indian languages that once existed, with more than fifty language families. The languages of Western Europe, by comparison, fall into just three families—Indo-European, Finno-Ugric, and Basque.

Some Spanish observers blamed the devil for the cacophony of tongues, calling it a plot designed to slow the Natives' conversion to Christianity. It was widely thought that the multitude of languages was a legacy of Babel. Some thought that Native Americans were a lost tribe of Israel; others thought they were Asian, Norsemen, Welshmen, or refugees from the lost continent of Atlantis. Later, Thomas Jefferson, who made a hobby of collecting vocabularies of Native American languages, wrote: "Among our Indians the number of languages is infinite which are so radically different as to exhibit at present no appearance of their having been derived from a common source." Even now, the language diversity of North and South America—which haven't been populated as long as Europe, Asia, and Africa—remains a mystery. Though the American tribes likely came from Asia, the languages are not like current Asian tongues. That may reflect the diversification of a single language over more than ten thousand years or a series of migrations. Other factors probably helped: the isolation of tribes over a vast expanse, the scarcity of empires that could impose one kind of speech, and cultural preferences for maintaining the identities of small groups.

The last idea may seem strange, because the movement of the past millennium has been toward the primacy of a handful of large languages—what linguist John McWhorter calls the "tall building" languages of English, Chinese, Arabic, and a few others—in Western Europe, America, and Asia. To a modern observer, the dominance of big languages appears to be an inevitable, universal force. But for most of human history, since language arose as much as 150,000 years ago, languages have been flowering into multiplicity. Every time groups split, their pronunciation, vocabulary, and even grammar begin shifting apart. British and American English today are kept static by the standardization of the languages in dictionaries, classrooms that teach "proper" speech, written literature, and television, but even here the languages have changed. Often, groups even create new ways of speaking in order to promote solidarity. Speakers of France's Verlan slang say common words backwards; researchers in Papua New Guinea—an island with more than eight hundred languages— recently watched the members of one village decide to adopt a new word for "no," solely to differentiate themselves from another village where the same language was spoken.

Whatever the cause, Native American languages became strikingly diverse. Some have rhythms and stresses similar to English; others have rising and falling tones as Chinese does. Some have fewer distinct sounds than English; others have far more. Some sound musical, others, guttural. And there are far more striking variations in their grammars and vocabularies.

A lot of the differences among languages lie in what they force their speakers to specify. For instance, in English, when a teenager says he was out with a friend and doesn't want to say whether that friend was a boy or a girl, he has to resort to a series of increasingly awkward repetitions of "my friend" or "the person I was with" because English forces him to choose between *he* and *she;* it does not have a gender-neutral third-person pronoun other than *it.* As linguist Roman Jakobson says, "Languages differ essentially in what they MUST convey and not in what they MAY convey."

By contrast, some Native American languages have a gender-neutral pronoun for talking about a third person. In other tongues, a speaker may be forced to include even more kinds of information—where the people she is talking about are in relation to her (are they in the same room?); whether they're socially higher or lower; or whether they are to the north or the south of her. Euchee, one of the languages still spoken in Oklahoma, has ten "genders" that include distinctions based on relationships and sex; for instance, a speaker would use one kind of *she* for an older woman who is a relative, another *she* for a younger female relative, another for an unrelated Euchee woman, and still another for a non-Euchee person—or an animal. Rather than saying *it,* she may have to specify whether the object referred to is flat or round or cylindrical or liquid.

Muskogee-Creek speakers don't simply use a past tense but choose among four pasts: the distant or mythic past; the past five to twenty-five years; the time between yesterday and a year ago; and the very recent past. Caddo speakers don't state a fact without expressing how they know it. As easily as we make *has* into *hasn't,* they attach a particle to the sentence *It has rained* that notes whether they saw it rain, whether they were told it, or whether they are inferring it. Other languages automatically mark statements as personal remembrance, things the speaker can't vouch for, or things the addressee ought to already know.

Native languages explode Western Europeans' assumptions about the parts of speech. Anyone who tries to follow the old-fashioned sentence diagram will be baffled by languages in which nouns routinely do double duty as verbs or sentences consist of one long word. "Single Algonkin words are like tiny imagist poems," said linguist Edward Sapir. As you study these languages, you can't help but notice how useful it would be to have some more grammatical nuances—say, a particle equivalent to *either* that signals a list of three or more things, or a way to clarify English's vague *they* by distinguishing between genders, between people and objects, or between two and many. People have the idea that the languages of small, premodern groups are primitive in some way, but grammatically they are often more sophisticated than English.

But all this linguistic diversity is little known these days, because most of the languages encountered by those early settlers are gone. The Taino language that Columbus heard is gone. John Smith's Powhatan is gone. The language Cartier tried to capture in his vocabulary is gone. It appears to be in the Iroquoian family, and it has left behind at least one word, which meant "settlement." It is pronounced: *Canada.*

Americans have grown accustomed to hearing other languages—nothing surprises us about hearing Spanish or French. But the Native American languages? We think of them as ancient artifacts, embalmed on maps, from Canada to Massachusetts, or melted into English—persimmon and petunia, skunk and squash, tomato and toboggan. The South knows about bayous and hominy; Palm Beach retirees talk about hurricanes, barbecues, and hammocks. But in those places, the languages that created the words have disappeared.

Some linguists predict that there will be about twenty Native American languages left in the United States by the middle of this century. The healthiest languages are in Arizona and New Mexico; there are as many as 150,000 Navajo speakers. California has the most languages in a single state, at fifty, though most have few speakers. Alaska and Washington and a dozen other states have several languages apiece. Hawaii may have several thousand speakers of Hawaiian. Some of the American Indian languages outside U.S. borders—in Central and South America, as well as Canada—are used by millions of people. But most of this country's languages are dwindling away.

With time running out, I decided to find out what was left of these languages in Oklahoma. I used my map to drive through the state, looking for a community where a Native language was still spoken. It took me nearly three years to travel over the seventy thousand square miles of Oklahoma, enough land to fit most of New England turned sideways.

Oklahoma doesn't have the culturally traditional, language-rich reservations of Arizona and New Mexico or the isolated communities of Alaska and Canada. But its linguistic diversity and compressed history made it a rich site for investigation. And, of course, it had an added attraction for me: It was my home state. As we grow older, we lose our own cultures; we lose the landscapes we know. I wanted to visit the Oklahoma I had lost by never knowing it.

You might think America would reserve for its Indians the most god-awful place it had left, but in fact Oklahoma isn't bad. It's bright, sunny, and full of birds. The main reason the United States sent the Indians there was that it was relatively free of settlers. (No one knew about the oil yet.) Oklahoma is an administrative leftover, a pan-shaped vacancy, handle jutting west, which was left after the surrounding states were defined: Kansas on top, and Texas below. Just below the center of the United States, Oklahoma contains the ecological features of many regions. In the east are oak and hickory forests like those of Arkansas and Tennessee, climbing over the remains of ancient mountains. In the west, the land flattens out, the bone-beige fields of the Plains begin, and some patches are pared down to desert. As I drove, I felt I was crossing the nation itself.

I inquired at the gas-station smoke shops where tribes sell tobacco, the glittering casinos, the floodlit powwows, the white frame
country churches, the neat government houses on land allotments,
and the tents where old men huddle in peyote ceremonies. What
would become of Comanche, with fewer than a hundred speakers left,
Ponca, with thirty, Otoe, with four, Wichita, with two? Language is a
hard thing to see, and so its story lies in its habitats—the people who
use it and the places where it echoes. This book is a stitching of tales
from those travels.

But the physical journey was only one part of the quest. I also
wanted to understand the meaning of this loss, to know how we got
from the era of three hundred languages to the era of twenty, and to
see what is lost when a language is lost.

Whether small languages are worth preserving is a live question,
not just in Oklahoma but around the world. Scholars agree that 50 to
90 percent of the nearly six thousand languages now spoken—Harsusi
in Oman, Saami in Finland and Russia, and Ainu in Japan—are likely
to disappear during this century. The causes are mostly the same as
those that have reduced Oklahoma's languages: Nations mandate a single language; the destruction of forests shakes tribes out of isolation;
the linkage of local economies into one global system provides incen-
tives to speak dominant languages and draws young people into cities;
and television, radio, and the Internet bring English into every home.

A few languages, like Gaelic, Maori, and Hawaiian, have been
brought back from near extinction, but most remain at risk. It is hard
to create the conditions of isolation and commitment in which a language can acquire new speakers. If whole countries, with millions of
speakers, can lose their languages, then what hope do smaller tongues
have? The movement of the world's small languages is toward silence.

It's hard to judge the value of other people's languages—which are,
by their very nature, hard to appreciate. They make strange artifacts.

(What would you put in a museum of languages? Not a sarcophagus, an ark, or a chalice. For cultures without writing, there is not even a manuscript.) How to measure the value of keeping around Cherokee—or, for that matter, Ainu, or Aramaic? How many languages do we need? If languages are worth preserving, how many dollars are people willing to spend on the effort? When languages are lost, how are we to mourn their silence?

To answer these questions, I found the journey took more than a map of the state. It required me to ask people not just whether they had a language but why they had a language. And it required me to renew my own romance with words. Languages exist in the fragile, intangible, cerebral spaces that communities make for them, as big as a city, as small as a single mind. You have to leap into unreal, envisioned places to understand what language means; imagination is a kind of tool for the voyage. To get to a lost city, you have to find another way inside.

CHAPTER ONE

"Where Do I Find Lost City?"

As WE DROVE ALONG a road with gentle curves, Hastings Shade looked beyond me and said, "Over there," and I looked out the window in anticipation. "See that road up there in the grass." I could see a kind of flattening in the hillside. "That's a boundary line." I squinted but couldn't see anything more. We drove on, looking for clues to a hidden community.

Shade, the deputy chief of the Cherokee Nation, had promised to take me to a place where people still used Cherokee. At this point, I knew very little about the status of the Indian languages. I had heard rumors that they were still spoken back in remote parts of the state: There were said to be Comanche speakers in the western part of the state, Choctaws in the south, and Cherokees in the east; just under the surface of the cities I knew, people lived their whole lives speaking Muskogee-Creek.

1

My own benchmark for a healthy language was simple: a group of girls chatting in the bathroom. At a meeting of Native-language groups at the University of New Mexico in Albuquerque, I was standing in front of one of the sinks in the bathroom when two girls came in. They were from either the Hualapai or the Havasupai, I wasn't sure which. One tribe lives at the top of the Grand Canyon, and one lives at the bottom. These small, isolated tribes have kept their languages, and these teenage girls had been making a presentation at the conference. They came in, talking in their language, and they kept chatting as they went into the stalls—talking through the metal walls—and changed out of their fancy skirts into jeans and T-shirts and then came out and washed stripes of paint off their cheeks.

The language passed over me too quickly, as impossible to capture as the memory of a flavor. Only a vague impression remained. How to describe a foreign language? It is more difficult than describing music. You can examine its structures in a textbook, but the closest you can get to its reality as it passes is simply to say, as with music, the way it sounds. As I singled out words, it was as if I were trying to catch a waterfall with a little cup, knowing the best I could do was dip out samples.

The girls might have been discussing how the presentation had gone or what they might do for lunch or who was in the audience, but they didn't have to think about their language. That was the point. They felt themselves to be in their own country.

But scenes like that were hard to find in Oklahoma. As I began traveling around the state, I was surprised at how obscure its tribes and their languages had become—how lost. They were lost enough that there was no state body devoted to Native-language policy. Lost enough that when I typed tribal names into my computer, my word-processing program proposed that I change the Seminole to "semiannual," Seneca to "séance," and Osage to "dosage." Lost enough that

2

white people didn't find the notion threatening. Lost enough that no one even thought about translating the in-flight service into a Native language on the airplane I took to Tulsa, as the wheels came down and the couple next to me put their blue American Airlines pillows on the back of the seats in front of them and began to pray.

I found books you could use to learn a language and classrooms where men and women listed simple words—bluebird, sugar, corn, sleep. I knew there were cultural centers where Indians costumed in loincloths smoothed long wooden bows and if asked would offer a forced greeting; there were nursing homes where old women would lean over an anthropologist's microphone and pronounce the words. But none of this constituted a living language, an everyday mode in which a mother and daughter moved around a kitchen chatting or two guys greeted each other with a joke.

I moved toward the Cherokees because their language was said to be the most widely spoken Native tongue in the state and among the top five in the country. The Cherokees don't have a reservation, since Oklahoma abolished reservations before statehood, retaining their outlines only on road signs and tribal governments' maps. But the fourteen counties where they've settled do have room for seclusion.

At first, the public face of the Cherokees appeared overwhelmingly assimilated. Tahlequah, the tribal capital, might have been any Oklahoma town, from the churches advertising on billboards to the glittering lines of traffic in front of Wal-Mart, Reasor's, and Hollywood Video. The tribal government, known as the Cherokee Nation, had a business complex that resembled a corporate office park, with its comfortable conference rooms, WELCOME signs in gold lettering, charming, southern-accented receptionists, and phone-mail systems in which I tended to get lost, holding to the sound of a mournful Cherokee hymn.

But eventually, a Cherokee public-relations director sent me to Shade, the highest-level administrator who could speak Cherokee fluently. I found him at a park by Rocky Ford Creek, making a blowgun out of cane: heating it over a fire, straightening out the kinks against his knee, and knocking out the natural segments inside with a length of rebar. His grandfather had taught him how to use it to send a dart of black locust wood toward its target. He boasted that "I could walk down the creek there and have dinner by the time I get home" and sold me his book, a Xeroxed bundle titled *Myths, Legends, and Old Sayings.* Years later, I noticed an old-fashioned whip made out of a flayed hickory branch in another Cherokee's house and was told that Shade was the maker. He knew how to make jigs for catching crawdads (walnut wood, soaked for two weeks) and how to speak Cherokee, and I got the feeling that the two skills were linked.

Shade had grown up in a small Cherokee community, and when he offered to guide me there, I jumped at the chance to go to a rural place. His community had an odd name that further piqued my interest: Lost City.

On the morning of our drive, I met Shade at the tribal complex. As I waited for him, I browsed around a gift shop full of Cherokee kitsch: cornhusk dolls wearing traditional prairie skirts, beaded barrettes spelling out NOEL, shot glasses and polo shirts with a Cherokee Nation seal, paintings of soulful wolves, a buxom porcelain Indian maiden with her buckskin dress slipping off her shoulder, and books that read like manuals for a culture—how to dress, cook, and heal like a Cherokee. In the background, a pop group sang "Kiss Me."

I bought a copy of Robin Coffee's book *The Eagle and the Cross.* A local newspaper had quoted the poet as saying that when he wrote, "I ask myself, 'will it break their heart and kick their ass at the same time?'" This seemed reason enough to get the book, but in addition, his description of an Oklahoma landscape I had known since childhood touched me. The poem was addressed to his mother. Part of it went:

> Redbuds bloom in early spring
> A butterfly above the trees
> Caught in the wind
> Struggles to get free
> One of the most beautiful things
> I have ever seen
>
> We have never spoken
> To each other
> In our Native tongue
> We speak
> A foreign language
> Like
> A scar upon our voice

I looked up and spied Hastings Shade emerging into the hall with an old woman. He was dressed casually, in jeans and a jeans jacket, and he looked morose even though he was making a joke; there was something about the squint of his eyes and the downturned lines around his mouth that made his face look sad in repose. He was telling the woman, who wore her fine, white hair in an old-fashioned bun, where we were going, and she recalled that some local group, perhaps the school, had once sold T-shirts that said WHERE DO I FIND LOST CITY?

We took his Dodge Stratus. Also in the car: binoculars, a bunch of business cards bound with a rubber band, a bright-striped blanket, and a long bow, made of the *bois d'arc* wood that had been considered fine bow material for centuries. It took only half an hour to get into the rolling countryside. The Ozark plateau is dissected by creeks and the rifts they have cut, and Lost City lies in a wide valley around Fourteen-Mile Creek.

When Europeans came to the United States, Cherokees lived in the southern Appalachian lands—geologically similar to the Ozark plateau—around Tennessee, western North Carolina, and Georgia. Most of the Cherokees were forced to leave their homelands in the 1830s and were marched to a reservation covering much of what is now eastern Oklahoma. Gradually, parts of the lands were chipped away and given to other tribes, and toward the beginning of the twentieth century the government divided up the Cherokee reservation and allotted 110 acres to each Cherokee.

As we drove, Shade told me a little bit about the community where he had grown up. He was sixty-two. When he was a child, he said, the area was predominantly Indian, "more or less one big family." Many people spoke hardly any English at all. We kept driving, past a fence with a PRIVATE PROPERTY sign, and he muttered that once, when this land was all Cherokee, he had walked straight through it.

We turned down a road that had once been wagon traces and drove along with the windows open, listening to birds. Shade kept up a mellow, soothing monologue in his deep southern drawl. "Yep, my old stomping grounds, all this area right here," he said. "I grew up here and went walking and hunting and running around barefoot . . . There's a deer, whitetail, good sign, they say . . . yep, we're looking at the fall, when leaves begin to change . . . or the grass gets sleepy, if you want to coin a phrase . . . or set a time frame . . . Yep, this is all new." We were passing fences and low, simple ranch houses and satellite dishes, birdbaths and plastic swimming pools. "All of this is new." A hand-lettered sign that said GOSPEL SINGING pointed up a dirt road.

Shade pulled over at the side of the road and pointed to a flat slab in a clearing. "This was my grandmother's kitchen," he said. "We lived right down there. Every now and then I tell my wife, 'I'm going home,' and she knows where I'm going."

I was beginning to realize that he was limning a picture of loss. Many of his family members had died, and their children had left for jobs in bigger cities. Meanwhile, whites had come to this open countryside to run farms and ranches in the lush and rolling hills. Not far away, a group of French monks had built a Benedictine monastery, saying the land reminded them of rural France. Shade told me that on the road where he had grown up, there were once five houses. Now he counted thirty-three houses—many of them owned by whites.

He estimated Cherokee was spoken in ten of the houses on that road. While older people still used the language at home and at church, there was hardly anyone under forty who even understood Cherokee. "My sons speak, but only when they have to," he said.

The road straightened out just after a hand-drawn sign that said LOST CITY GARAGE, and soon we came to a graveyard and a school—home of the Lost City Indians, according to the sign. Shade pulled into the drive, saying "that's new" to one of the buildings, and parked near the graves. They looked new, too, with stones of polished granite and regularly placed bouquets of plastic flowers. The wind had scattered their pink petals through the grass as if they were real.

Shade pointed past a building painted with Big Bird and Barney, saying that he had learned English in the school that stood on this spot when he was a child. "We were told we would never amount to anything anyway," he said. When he was thirteen, a teacher had answered a question by saying: "What do you want to learn for? You're never going to be nothing more than a drunkard when you grow up." He quit high school, though he later got a GED and eventually became a teacher.

He didn't pause for me to comment but went into a joke: "Yep, this was a small school then. We had running water . . . we run and got it."

He hoped that someday the school would offer a Cherokee-language program. "This is where the learning has to start," he said as he whirled the car around and drove out, continuing down the road. The only person we saw was a white boy riding a horse, wearing a Confederate-flag T-shirt. He waved to us.

We paused at an intersection of two roads with farmhouses on three corners and took a right. "So is this the way to Lost City?" I said.

"This *is* Lost City," Shade replied. "There used to be a store on this corner but it's gone." We drove silently for a moment, passing farmhouses decorated with pumpkins for Halloween. As a Cherokee-speaking community, then, the place really was nearly lost.

And yet the past didn't seem far away to Shade. As we passed empty fields, he kept pointing out things I couldn't see. "I see it because I know it exists," he said. "If you don't see it, you'd never know." He conjured up a culture in which people knew how to hunt with a homemade blowgun, to gather lengths of honeysuckle vine for baskets, and to read the weather forecast in a spider's web. They knew where to find huckleberries, blackberries, mushrooms, greens, nuts, and hidden springs. They told stories about the time "back when the animals could talk," feared the raven mocker and other animal agents of the spirit world, and knew the names of their ancient clans (his was the wild-potato clan). He evoked a world in which Cherokees once knew as many as 130 different bird names, from the horned owl, which meant "wizard" or "spirit," to the mockingbird or "head-eater," which explained how the bird got all his voices.

I asked why a modern student would need to know all those birds and their names in Cherokee.

He turned the question around and asked: "Well, what's most important to you?"

"Me," I stuttered. "I guess . . . at different points in my life, different things," I said, stalling. "But certainly it's always important to have people you love around you, family . . ."

"Okay," he said. "I know what birds are here, which ones are used for medicine, and from the birds I know what season it is. I know from them what the weather is going to be. And if the weather changes, how is it going to affect my *family?* It's all part of one big picture."

Shade's mental world suggested the larger context in which languages exist. The Cherokee names encoded information about the birds: impressions of what they ate, where they nested, how they sounded, and what they meant—carrying the shadows of bird-spirits Cherokees had worshiped, each with its own fables and aspects. In the past, all this could have been useful not only for hunting but also for explaining the world around them. Biology and cosmology lay in the names. The world described in Cherokee bird names is not exactly the same as its English counterpart, and it is that Cherokee complex of Appalachian landscape and hunting lifestyle and whippoorwill mystery that gives the words their value.

One sociolinguist, Joshua Fishman, has described the relationship between language and culture as "indexical"; the language "associated with the culture is best able to express most easily, most exactly, most richly, with more appropriate over-tones, the concerns, artifacts, values, and interests of that culture." Some Indian languages have specialized vocabularies for types of baskets, others for acorns and the foods that can be made out of them, others for shamans. Some California Native languages express direction in terms not of north and south but the upriver or downriver flow of water. When people have no language to bridge the gap between generations, they diminish their ability to decode their history. When you lose a language, then, the size of the loss is somewhere between a list of bird names and a conception of the world.

We passed Fourteen-Mile Creek, a sparkling rivulet, and climbed a yellow-gray gravel road to a cheerful site on a small rise, where the light trickled down through oak trees and honeysuckle vine ran wild. We pulled up in front of a white church. The country church, along with the school and the graveyard, was one of the most active institutions left in Lost City, Shade said. It held services every Sunday, and while the main service was in English, a group of old women sat in a room in the back to conduct a Bible-study session in Cherokee.

A sign above the church's door said SWIMMER BAPTIST CHURCH, and below it were four of the thick, curlicue-garnished characters of the Cherokee alphabet. Shade got out of the car and I followed him up to the little church, studying the letters. Shade said the characters ᏍᏗᎪᏱ, *s-di-go-yi*—which sounded more like *sti goy*—meant "the little place." It was not only the name of this church, he said. The original "little place" had been a meeting place in the old Cherokee lands. The settlers here—some Cherokee towns had moved together to found new communities—had aimed to bring the old place forward, to signal the continuity of a tradition. In that respect, the "little place" was like so many places on the Oklahoma map, named after predecessors in older lands.

Shade tried the door of the building. It was locked. We walked back to the car and then drove on out. "You get what you came for?" Shade asked me.

I said a meek, "I think so," though I knew I hadn't.

I had seen the Cherokee alphabet before in a bilingual hymnbook that a Cherokee man in Tulsa had shown me. At the time, I thought little of the encounter, because the man wasn't fluent and had inherited the hymnbook from his father, but I noticed the English names of the songs Cherokees sang: "In the Sweet By and By." "We're Marching to Zion." "Heaven Beautiful." These lyrics—perhaps sung on Sundays at the "little place"—told of a lost place and a promised place. They were songs of exile. I half hummed a song as I looked out the window:

> By the waters of Babylon.
> There we sat down.
> And there we wept,
> As we remembered Zion.

How was it that I could feel that longing, too? I didn't have spiritual leanings or hopes of finding Indian ancestry. Perhaps it was as simple as understanding the desire for home. Cherokee country reminded me of it. Back when I had first seen Hastings Shade making his blowgun out of cane, he had been standing at a spot on a creek where a spray of pebbles widened the stream, as if a great hand had sprinkled them down for the crossing. The light-stippled, roughed-up water struck me as deeply familiar, and I recalled that this eastern Oklahoma terrain had formed my own idea of summer. The camp where I had learned to ride a horse and to canoe was not far away; there had been childhood trips on the Illinois River, which cut through the Ozark plateau on its way southeast from the Rocky Mountains to the Mississippi, and I had swum on the dammed-up lakes nearby. The landscape was resonant: the gnarled, wiry oaks splattered with pale blue lichens, the hot, viney woods, the modest mountains, the redbuds in Robin Coffee's poem about his mother tongue. I hadn't cared for these things much as a child, but it seemed to me now that I missed them. This was the terrain of the past itself, from which adult life seemed a kind of exile.

It occurred to me that Lost City was a deeper ideal as well: a unity of people, place, and language, where the songs of the past made sense and the gestures of living were filled with meaning. I had come thinking I would simply hear a language spoken. It seemed easy enough.

But to look for a language was to look for a lost city in the larger sense, a thriving community with the ability to name its surroundings and retain its memories, a place where language and culture kept each other alive, where ancestral voices echoed in the words.

I asked Shade if every Cherokee settlement was equally fragmented: Was there another place where people of all ages still spoke Cherokee? Somewhere, though not in Tulsa, a world that more closely matched the Cherokee language might still exist. Shade suggested I might search further east, deeper in the hills. He didn't tell me how to find it, and so I wandered uncertainly for a while, but later I would discover he was right.

For now, as we drove back through the empty fields, Shade told me a story about how Lost City got its name. The tale went back to the very earliest settlers in the area; he thought it might even be a story from the Osages, who inhabited eastern Oklahoma before the Cherokees arrived. Slowing down, he pointed across a field and said, "Near some falls there was a camp of gypsies. *Anidolido,* 'roamers,' we called them. Time went on, they lived there for a while, and people just got used to seeing them there. One day they were gone. It looked like they were fixing breakfast. Everything was on the fire, but there were no people. No bodies or nothing," he said. "Maybe they became people that live on forever, *aneyhiya.* They must have had a reason or they knew what was in store for them."

I looked through a stand of trees at a clearing. "How do we know that happened?" I said. Later on, I asked other Cherokees if they thought that story was true, and I got cryptic answers like, "That sounds like Hastings Shade." I heard also that the name might stem from a land swindle, and that the loss in Lost City occurred when whites began moving into the area and burying their dead in the cemetery, causing local Cherokees to flee elsewhere.

"Is it true?" Shade said. "Who knows? There's nothing here."

12

CHAPTER TWO

Lost Causes

THE COMANCHE LANGUAGE and Cultural Preservation Committee meets at the Museum of the Great Plains, a tribute to extinct cultures in the region. The first thing you notice is a replica of a giant sloth, a Jurassic mammal that resembles a car-sized chipmunk. Nearby are a big skull with tusks like a curved forklift and a diorama of prehistoric men confronting a mammoth in a pit. The museum then jumps a few millennia to the buffalo robes and beaded cradles of the Plains Indians and after that to the gun belt of a marshal on the frontier.

The status of the Comanches in the back room is unclear. They once reigned over the southern Plains. Now they are down to about seventy speakers of the old language, and they are plotting to keep it from becoming another artifact in the gallery of extinctions.

I hadn't expected to get here—to a small language's last stand—quite so fast. But as I pushed outward from Cherokee country to the rest of Oklahoma, looking for language communities, I quickly discovered some depressing facts: Among the twenty-five or so Oklahoma tribes that at the time had living languages, sixteen had fewer than a hundred speakers, and most of those speakers were over seventy years old. These language communities were not altogether gone, but they were cities of the elderly.

As far as many linguistic scholars are concerned, such languages are lost causes. They are, according to the depressing categorizations of ethnologists, *obsolescent*—a term with the gentle inevitability of a waning moon—or *moribund,* death-bound, suggesting Roman legions marching off a cliff. One linguist, Michael Krauss, measures languages' health by dividing them into four categories, ranging from Class A, still spoken by all generations, to Class D, languages spoken only by very aged people. Most of the languages in Oklahoma are Class C languages, spoken by people old enough to be grandparents. Krauss expects the Class C languages to be gone by 2060.

According to one commonly accepted benchmark promulgated by linguist Ken Hale, languages today need not only the support of a nation-state but also at least one hundred thousand speakers to pass from generation to generation. These numbers may seem high. But today, it's getting harder to maintain the kind of isolation and cultural commitment that keep a language vital, and the larger world pattern shows small languages—Manchu in China, Lufu in Nigeria, Yaaku in Kenya—gradually aging out of existence.

Comanche is part of a large and ancient language family called Uto-Aztecan that once was found from Oregon to Panama but now includes just a few healthy languages, like Mexico's Nahuatl. Most of the members of this family are obsolescent (fewer than a hundred speakers) or moribund (fewer than ten), according to charts created by linguist Lyle Campbell. And some are even worse off, marked with the sad little cross he gives extinct languages: "† Gabrielino † Fernandeno *California.*" (The rosters of languages have an abbreviated eloquence. My favorite on Campbell's Eastern Algonquian list is "† Massachusett *Massachusetts,*" a line that suggests a concise history of displacement.) As "obsolescent," Comanche is marked for disappearance within decades.

But it seemed churlish to point all this out to the Comanches. Despite the long odds placed by academics, the Comanche Language and Cultural Preservation Committee was moving toward the goal stated on its Web site: "To restore the NUMU TEKWAPUHA [Comanche] as a living language once more and to take our language of heritage into the Twenty-First Century." The group had created a master–apprentice program, which paired up old speakers and young learners and encouraged them to speak Comanche together several times a week.

I didn't see why having a small number of speakers had to be a mortal blow. Many bands of just a few thousand people have passed their languages along for centuries, particularly in isolated places such as Australia and the South Pacific Islands. Gullah persisted for nearly two centuries in the remote, culturally cohesive area of the Sea Islands off the southeastern United States. Other factors—the speakers' settlement patterns within a larger community, their numerical importance in relation to other groups, and their own attitudes toward the language—can make a big difference. Many tribes have created new speakers by starting immersion schools. In the past two decades, New Zealand's Maori have stabilized their language at about ten thousand speakers and Hawaiian has made a comeback. Several small North American tribes have managed to maintain their languages with relatively few speakers, including Arizona's Hualapai, Montana's Crow, and Canada's Cree and Ojibwa. Indeed, the basic job of keeping a language alive is simple: Just keep adding speakers.

Isn't it unfair to proclaim a language a lost cause if its speakers don't agree? Can an outsider pronounce a language dead? As I drove to visit the Comanches, I wondered what exactly life is for a language.

To get there, I headed away from the green hills of Cherokee country toward the southwestern Plains. As I drove, the land gradually flattened into fields, alternating green winter-wheat and tan fallow patches. In the east, I could always see a little ruffle of hills, but west of Oklahoma City, past a series of turquoise puddles known as the Canadian River, I would be in the stark western plains—the basin of an ancient sea, where plants had folded themselves into the seams of the earth and become oil.

I took a northern route that was not direct, passing Bear's Glen, one of the places where Washington Irving stopped on his trip through the area in 1832. Back then, travelers came to this territory, a sparsely populated area of the Louisiana Purchase, the way they'd now visit some remote hinterland of Mongolia or Peru. What is now Oklahoma had hosted various tribes for eleven thousand years, starting with a culture that had left spear points by the bones of a mammoth near present-day Anadarko. During Europe's Middle Ages, a Caddoan civilization built mounds in southeastern Oklahoma. The explorers Coronado and De Soto traveled over the region and found a few tribes. But as late as Irving's visit, this territory was still unknown to whites. Osages, Quapaws, and other nomadic groups roamed over the land.

In a book called *A Tour on the Prairies*, Irving described his camp site near the Arkansas River as broad and sandy, "intersected by innumerable tracks of elk, deer, bears, raccoons, turkeys, and water-fowl." It lay in "rich bottoms, with lofty forests; among which towered enormous plane trees." He enjoyed his travels in Oklahoma—"encamping in some beautiful place with full appetite for repose, lying on the grass under green trees—in genial weather with a blue, cloudless sky—then so sweet sleeping at night in the open air, and when awake seeing the moon and stars through the tree tops."

I took a turnoff and stopped at Bear's Glen. Some of Irving's trail was under water; the junction of the Arkansas and the Red Fork Rivers was long ago dammed to form Keystone Lake. (Oklahoma has dammed up so many of its creeks that it claims more human-made-lake shoreline than any other state.) There was no sound but the soft wash of water on the shore. Irving had made his trip sound fun; at one of the Arkansas campgrounds, he described a group of Osages sitting around the fire, telling stories and doing imitations of the nineteen-year-old European count who accompanied Irving's group. But my tour of Oklahoma more often reminded me of another Irving story, the tale of Rip Van Winkle, who sleeps away a hundred years and then returns to a place that has changed beyond his understanding. The core of the story is the horror of surviving your time.

The other major account of this terrain was written by Thomas Nuttall, a botanist who traveled on the Plains in 1819. He had a terrible time: The water was "always stagnant, and often putrid," he wrote. The insects "filled even our clothes with maggots." The "dazzling light of the prairies proved oppressive and injurious to the eyes." The local Indians stole his pocket microscope. His conclusion, after two months in which he nearly died of malaria and went days eating little but beaver tails, wild honey, and wormy elk meat: "I could not help indeed reflecting on the inhospitability of this pathless desert, which will one day perhaps give way to the blessings of civilization."

And yet Thomas Nuttall's journals suggest that a kind of original nostalgia accompanied even the earliest white pioneers. "This wilderness, which we now contemplate as a dreary desert, was once thickly peopled by natives, who, by some sudden revolution, of which we appear to be ignorant, have sunk into the deepest oblivion." He added, "The aboriginal languages of America, hitherto so neglected and unjustly consigned to oblivion as the useless relics of barbarism, are, nevertheless, perhaps destined to create a new era in the history of primitive language." He wrote this before Sequoyah's alphabet was in use, before the southeastern tribes were expelled from the South. Nuttall's words reminded me that Americans had been mourning Native American languages even when many of them were healthy.

Indeed, Indian culture is perhaps the most American of lost causes. As early as 1600, Europeans were coming upon deserted villages; their diseases had spread into the country ahead of them. Look at the letters of the first white settlers, and you find them traveling abandoned Indian traces and marveling at the mounded graves of the dead. If the Indians were *pre-lost,* defined as lost the moment they were glimpsed, then no one alive bore any responsibility for saving them. And yet the tribes persist; the elegies were premature.

The town of Lawton offered few clear signs of Comanche life. I drove by Fort Sill, an army base originally established for guarding Indians, and suffered along the longest, densest strip mall I'd ever seen, with a dense forest of signs on poles lining the road. I picked out a few names—the Big Chief restaurant, Zapata's Cafe & Cantina, the Comanche Pawn & Gift Shop—but then I had to blink, dazzled by the hard glints of light from Huffy's discount liquor, Kar Kleen, Chili's, Fong Village Chinese restaurant, and Quick Lube. In front of me in traffic, there was a pickup with a matted collie in back who kept trying to stand up and slid around stupidly, and later there was a big, fenced flatbed packed with relaxed young army recruits, all shaven down to their pale heads, wearing camouflage and leaning against each other.

My first sight of the language committee seemed less than promising. When I arrived at the Great Plains museum, I faced two dozen people, mostly old ladies in jumpsuits, lodged patiently at folding

18

tables. What was more disturbing: The Comanche language committee spoke English. Only occasionally did these older ladies—who had the mellifluous names of their era, like Lucille, Rosalie, and Gloria—throw Comanche phrases into the conversation. They broke in and out of it as they chatted about their illnesses and memories and who was getting married or divorced. Hot Plains sunlight streamed in through glass doors; outside was a wooden stockade where cowboy reenactors dressed in dirty buckskin were demonstrating bullet making.

Modern language revivals often start with a committee. When a language grows small enough, a group of elders can take over processes normally left to the anarchic evolution of language. For instance, the Comanches had stopped coining terms for modern items like "telephone" and "dishwasher" by the 1960s, and so the committee took on the job of creating new words. Other tribes debate whether they want to write their languages down—a disturbingly untraditional idea when a language has been transmitted orally. The Comanches already had an alphabet developed by an academic.

Some groups also have to pick a standard dialect. Enshrining one kind of speech as the language is controversial—as it might be if, say, English came down to six speakers: two Mississippians, two British Cockneys, and two Jamaicans. If you could take only one dialect to a desert island, which would it be? That was a real question for some tribes.

Upon its founding in 1993, when there were fewer than two hundred speakers left, the Comanches' committee envisioned an immersion school, but there weren't enough speakers to staff it. So the committee, led by Ron Red Elk, decided to make its own teachers through the master-apprentice program, as well as community language classes, summer camps, and preschool classes. In the meantime, the committee tried to promote the language in an assimilated tribal world: A picture dictionary offered the Comanche word for "umbrella," and a CD-ROM allowed a user to click on a word and hear an elder saying it. At the tribal Halloween party, they handed out treats to children, asking for a Comanche word in return, and in their newsletter they published translations of songs like "Joy to the World."

As I got to know them, I realized how novel—in a way, revolutionary—these elders' efforts were. Once, old people had been accorded high status, in part for a very practical reason: They were the guardians of the tribe's most valuable knowledge. In an oral culture, they were the tribe's librarians, pharmacists, scholars, and storytellers. In an age of science and modern entertainment, they risked becoming irrelevant, as their knowledge and stories were seen as outdated. But the elders realized they had something that no one else in the world had: the memory of a world when everything was done in Comanche.

The great-grandparents of Comanches alive today were among the nomadic, horse-mounted warriors that once dominated a 250,000-square-mile stretch of the Southwest. They had a macho culture that was virtually created by the arrival of horses on the Plains in the 1700s. During a short period in the eighteenth and nineteenth centuries, the Comanches gained a reputation that reverberated into the twentieth century. They call themselves the *nuhmenuh*, "the people," but the name they were saddled with—*Comanche*, borrowed now for attack helicopters and Jeeps—is derived from a Ute word for "adversary."

It has been fewer than 150 years since the whites chased down the last band, killed the horses that defined their culture, and virtually exterminated the buffalo they had depended on. Thus the people I met were the survivors of a recent cultural disaster. They had come a greater psychic distance than the Cherokees in a shorter time. Their grandmothers' grandmothers knew how to put up a tepee in under thirty minutes and carried their children in cradleboards. One Comanche, Rosalie Attocknie, told me stories she'd heard from her late husband's grandmother about going on horseback raids and pulling white settlers' clothing off the clotheslines. Another, Vernon Cable, showed me a picture of an old man with a deeply scarred face and told me about his great-grandfather, a Mexican captured by the Comanches at eight years old. People still felt strongly about Texas, heart of the Comancheria, part homeland, part enemy territory. "Texas," Gladys Narcomey said to me. "That's where our home is." She had spent nearly all of her seventy-seven years just outside Elgin, Oklahoma. She sent me a poem of hers that began: "Texas! When my aged Aunt heard your name, She wept."

Only now, explained Margrett Oberly Kelley, a tall, poised fifty-year-old with a serene face, do Comanches have the time and leisure to promote their culture. After the trauma of resettlement in Oklahoma and integration into white society, she said, "What we are doing is much like what people who survived Auschwitz had to do: piece themselves back together to start over. Now that people do have jobs and casinos and have a little money to do the ceremonial events, you see a little bit of the culture coming back."

All this was helping encourage some Comanches to remember their language. I began talking with Ken Goodin, who was three-eighths Comanche but looked completely white, his eyes as blue as his turquoise bolo. He wore a white shirt with snaps, a white cowboy hat, snug jeans, and boots. His hair and mustache were white. "I wake up in the morning and go into the bathroom and decide whether to be a white man or a Comanche," he said. "I look at myself in the mirror, and if I say *onehundreddollarbidnowtownowtowwillyagivemetwo*, the white man's auction talk, then I'm going to be a white man that day, and I go out on my tractor and talk hay talk with the farmers." He worked as an auctioneer for extra money, having retired from his job as a fireman, and he also farmed his own allotment, an activity he described as very white; most land-owning Indians, he said, lease out their tracts. He went on: "And if I look at myself and say"—he sang a

few bars of a Comanche hymn, one that his grandfather made up—
"then I'm going to be a Comanche that day."

He hadn't spoken the language since he was a child, but now that
he was hearing it again, some words were coming back to him: language as recovered memory. (I had seen Internet rumblings about the
idea of using Western hypnosis to reclaim forgotten languages,
though I found no cases of it.) "I can be driving my tractor," Goodin
said, "and a word will pop into my head and later I'll ask my wife or
someone and realize my mother used to say that word. They're just
asleep up there, all these words."

Still, a lot had happened in the long, hard century between the
past of tribal memory and the present. The Comanches had been
taught in school that their language was primitive and bad, and they
had stopped teaching it to their children, and some people had
stopped using it themselves. They had begun to think of themselves
as outdated. So switching back to Comanche was difficult for many
people. I noticed this when I spoke to one master-apprentice pair,
Gloria Cable and her daughter, Billie Kreger. Kreger suggested that
her mother tell me a story, and Mrs. Cable uttered a few sentences
haltingly. As Mrs. Cable faltered, her daughter, watching closely,
broke in to prompt her.

I wondered if she was telling it completely. A researcher among
the Cup'ik in Alaska had found that speakers, influenced by English,
had started telling stories without certain affective suffixes—convey-
ing shades of emotion like "poor/dear" or "that darned" or "shabby
old." It was a small example of how the color can drain out of a language when it isn't spoken much anymore.

A language doesn't go from present to forgotten in an instant. My own grandmother sometimes loses a word and—without
missing a beat—throws a synonym out in its place. "That thing that
we ate was delicious!" When you get older, the complexity of your

language diminishes. You lose words, and you simplify constructions. You tell the same story again. You can lose whole topics as vocabulary disappears. So the language that's available grows a little less complex.

Gloria stopped and folded her hands on her voluminous navy sweatshirt, which featured a birdhouse and the words GREAT GRANDMA LOVE FOR GENERATIONS. Kreger, a big, hearty, forty-nine-year-old with short hair and an efficient manner, told the story in English.

"It was about a prairie-dog town that was there on the open prairie. And here comes Coyote. Coyote's hungry, and, coyotes being tricky as they are, he thought of a scheme to trick them so he could get something to eat. So he tells them, 'We're going to have a big dance. Lock up your homes and come on out.' And they came out and danced, and Coyote sang songs for them. Then he said, 'It's even better if you close your eyes when you dance.' They closed their eyes and danced around him, and he had this big club, and he'd knock them on the head as they'd go by, and he had built a big fire so he could roast them. Now one little prairie dog opened his eyes and said, 'He's killing us! Open your eyes and run!' and they all tried to run to their houses, but they'd locked them up. So he killed a bunch of them. And he had his fill of prairie dogs that day."

Mrs. Cable nodded approvingly.

Her daughter said, "It isn't the same, in English, the way he says 'close your eyes.' Can you explain what he says, Mother?"

Mrs. Cable shook her head negatively. She turned to another friend and continued a conversation in English, "Yes, I lost my appetite."

"I know it."

"She's in the hospital now."

Her daughter said to me, "The old people speak Comanche, but they need encouragement, because they got so used to talking with each other in English."

Indeed, it wasn't enough for older Comanches to awaken the language within themselves. Old people discourage innovations and slang. They forget words. They talk about old-people things. And they unknowingly allow the language to lose one of its big attractions for learners: the hope of company. As fewer people speak a language, fewer want to speak it. How many Americans have improved their language ability in the hope of meeting Japanese women, flirting with Italian men, or impressing a Spanish lover? Any language you can't use in bed is in trouble. The Comanches didn't want to lose sight of their main goal: to pass along the language to new learners.

That was why, when Richard M. Codopony Jr. walked into the room and tried to ease into the crowd, people noticed him. At thirty years old, he was their heir. There were a few other young people in the master-apprentice program—even one seven-year-old. But Codopony was a particularly committed learner, and the tribes' hopes for another generation of speakers seemed to rest on his shoulders.

Five nights a week, Codopony was learning the language from Carney Saupitty Sr., his seventy-five-year-old uncle. I went to watch them work at Codopony's home in Apache, a small town named after some prisoners of war (including Geronimo) who were taken to Fort Sill in 1894 and later settled on land nearby. Apache was a small country town; I drove by the house several times in the dark. When I walked in, Codopony showed me to a plump couch, where we chatted awkwardly as we waited for his uncle to walk over from his house.

Codopony had round, dark eyes and pale skin; his mother was white. The range of emotions he showed generally ran from distantly polite to tentatively friendly. His features had a set, designed stillness, so that when he did break his repose to smile, it was startling and nice.

I am shy, and I don't like bothering people, as I obscurely worried I was doing on this night and many nights to come in Oklahoma. As a journalist, I usually offered the lure of publicity, but here no one seemed to care. So, sitting there, I felt my motivations stripped down to my curiosity. Some linguists used to call their Native sources "informants," and I felt guiltily like I was asking for a betrayal.

I reflected that the language-preservation efforts were simply news—something Oklahomans might want to know about. On this land that I crossed and shared and claimed, there were a million different struggles for existence. Their stories were Oklahoma's stories—and America's.

But what if my very presence was endangering something, exposing their magic or distorting their image, creating the latest western fantasy? I didn't have an answer, and I suspended the question, thinking that maybe when I understood more, I would know what to do.

When Saupitty arrived, he looked at me sharply as he sat down on one of the couches and asked how far I went in school. "M.A., Ph.D.?"

"Just a B.A. so far," I said.

"Sorry. I only talk to Ph.D.'s," he replied, chuckling. Saupitty wore his white hair in a ponytail and had on a bolo tie, a denim shirt, tan pants, and a cap that said SUMMIT RACING on the front. He was garrulous, opinionated, and confident, sitting straight up with his chin thrust out and dropping ten-dollar words into the conversation with a soft southern accent. He said proudly that he'd had more education than most people his age: He'd worked his way through junior college, and had enough talent in chemistry to go to a midwestern university, but he didn't have a lot of money, and working and going to school was just too hard, so he left. He had worked a number of blue-collar jobs, such as painting aircraft at a military base, but he told me, "I could've done better in my life if I'd had the gumption to stick with it."

Saupitty looked at me piercingly and then turned to the serious work of the master-apprentice meeting. He began a story in Comanche, sitting erect in a traditional pose, hands on his knees, looking straight ahead.

As Saupitty talked, in a march of staccato syllables, Codopony began concentrating, sitting straight, with his eyes shut. The story went on for five minutes, and then I stopped thinking about time myself, except that I knew this was the longest time I had ever heard an Indian language spoken.

Juanita Pahdopony, a Comanche artist, had described the language to me as "economical." She said, "If you're a nomad, you come from a people who do not take a whole lot with you, and you would learn to cut down on your stuff—not a whole lot of adjectives, or words." When I mentioned this later to Codopony, he called the language "matter-of-fact" and "descriptive." It named a skunk with a term that loosely meant "smell goes around from place to place" and called a turkey "peeper," to describe the way it peeps at a person from the foliage.

When Saupitty finished the story, the two had a conversation in Comanche. Codopony broke into English: "I should tell the story? The same one?"

Saupitty joked: "Unless you have another one in mind."

Codopony repeated the story back in Comanche, faltering only once, and Saupitty listened, eyes closed, punctuating the pauses with a short, soft "ah!" Occasionally a truck growled by on the road outside.

They began another story. Saupitty talked, and this time Codopony responded in the pauses, sometimes with a rather English-sounding "hmm." After a stream of language, they stopped, apparently midstory. Codopony said, in English: "Okay, so when that hide peeled back, that's when he knew something bad was going to happen."

Saupitty said: "It was *dead*. They killed it." Then he broke into Comanche again. Finally, Codopony explained to me: "Some Comanches killed a buffalo. When they butcher it, they cut the hide down his back, over the hump, and this time when they were pulling the hide off, the buffalo stood up, and the hide was hanging off his side like curtains. So the medicine man went over and hit him on the head with his shoe, and the buffalo died.

"The medicine man told them not to eat the buffalo. It wasn't a good sign, but the rest of the group didn't listen. So they ate all that, and he didn't eat but stayed up and kept a lookout, and the enemies came, and he tried to wake them up and tell them, but they wouldn't wake up, and the enemies killed them while they slept."

Codopony looked at me. "I guess they ate too much," he joked tentatively, as if anticipating my lack of understanding. Later, he said that the story had a simple lesson: "It's about taboos. When a medicine man says, 'Don't do it,' don't do it." I wondered if it was meaningful that Saupitty had chosen to tell a story about ignoring one's selfish desires, taking notice of the spirit world, and obeying traditional authorities.

Saupitty turned to me. "We have mystic stories, and that was one that actually happened," he said with a flare of enthusiasm. As in Lost City, I felt the proximity of another world, as if a window had been opened. But it quickly closed as he looked down. "Now we lost it. We're too modern."

Codopony had his own way of keeping the Comanche world alive in his consciousness. He had stopped listening to the radio and cut down on TV. "Popular culture interferes," he said. "You have to give up something. What am I going to get out of *Married with Children* or *Friends* compared with the language? One is entertainment, and the other is my culture." He allowed that he did rent movies for his children. But, he said, "At this point I don't even go see my friends anymore." Most of his peers hadn't learned much about Comanche culture, and his knowledge embarrassed them. His wife, Anita, was white, and their three children spoke English, but Codopony used Comanche words with them occasionally and hoped they would learn more.

I wondered aloud why Codopony was so different from the rest of his generation, and he said that he had spent a lot of time around his grandparents when he was growing up. Though his parents lived outside Oklahoma, he came here during the summers, and his grandparents used Comanche to talk with their friends and to tell him bedtime stories. By the time he was thirteen, he was asking them to teach him how to say new things. He added, "I've always felt more comfortable with people who were older."

He moved back to Lawton when he was a young adult and began speaking Comanche with anyone he could find. Now, he and Saupitty were working through a dictionary compiled in the 1950s by a white man, and they corrected the dictionary as needed. Codopony showed me his beat-up copy and I opened it at random, noticing where he had crossed out the book's "to tame a wild thing" and penned in "break a horse." Already, he knew Comanche words that no one else—not even the language committee—could confirm.

Someday, he said, he might teach the language; in college at Cameron University in Lawton, he wrote a lengthy paper on language acquisition called "A Better Way to Learn Comanche," and teachers suggested he enter a master's program. But when he led one high-school class, he was discouraged by the students' lack of interest. For now, he was working to support his family, training horses and moving inventory in a Comanche tribal warehouse. "I can't understand how people don't want to learn it," he said in his measured, neutral voice. "I'm disappointed with the lack of interest by younger Comanches."

These emotions came out more vividly in his paintings, which hung around the house. One showed Comanches in blankets with scowling faces of fire-engine red, floating against a black night sky that shaded to red. A scroll winding among them bore the script the Comanches used. Codopony explained that the phrases were questions about what would become of the language. His angriest work was a multimedia sculpture built around what looked like an unearthed skeleton. The skull was agape, covered with tangled, long, dark human hair, and gagged with an American flag. Below were a bone breastplate and a blue buffalo nickel, and the whole scene was bound with thick twine. Codopony said he did the work after reading somewhere the sentence *Who is to say that taking away a culture's language isn't as violent as war?* The hair on the skull was his own.

A self-portrait on another wall showed the long braids he once had. In it, his braids were bound in red cloth and his body was wrapped in a bright-striped blanket that had belonged to his grandmother. He stared out of the frame with a challenging, even supercilious, look that I hadn't seen on him, suggesting that he was painting a prouder Comanche self.

Codopony and Saupitty talked for a little more than an hour, and then broke up for the night. After I said good-bye and turned to go out, Saupitty spoke to me again: "I'm a rare bird," he said, looking at me for a reaction. "Soon there will be nothing left but one of those old Indians with a spear, hanging his head, you know?"

"I know," I said, recognizing his reference. The Indian with the spear was a statue in the Cowboy Hall of Fame in Oklahoma City. The statue, which showed a tired Indian slumped on a horse, was created by a white man in 1915, and it was meant to represent the bittersweet triumph of Manifest Destiny. It's called *End of the Trail*—which, of course, Oklahoma was. Saupitty seemed to be admitting the whole effort was a lost cause. But then again, that's what white people had thought a century ago. In retrospect, it seemed that the sculptor had lamented a dying culture too soon; the Comanches were still here.

I saw Saupitty again, at a language-committee meeting: He stalked in, greeting no one, and sat down by himself. I walked over to him. "Hi. I'm Elizabeth. Remember I met you . . ." He indicated he couldn't hear me, shaking his head. He was wearing the same SUMMIT RACING cap. I noticed in the light how his white braid was turning yellow at the end, where it was tied with a thick, tan rubber band. His face was impassive. I started again, louder.

He said, "I can't understand you. You'll have to speak in sign language." Staring me in the eyes, he made a flurry of hand signs. I tried to improvise signs as I talked, but all I really knew was "me" and "you." Later, I wished I'd known that the Great Plains Indians had a sign language for all the different tribes. The sign for "Comanche" signified a snake going backward; the right hand ripples while moving slowly to the right.

But I was not succeeding; his intention was to throw me off the trail, not to help me crack his code. It made me feel unreal, incommunicado, acting in some obscure Uto-Aztecan verb tense that signifies the impossibly distant. Perhaps his refusal to speak was a trace of a time when the languages were alive. People told me stories about grandparents who moved behind the protective barrier of their own language when outsiders came around. Now, the barrier was silence.

We were interrupted, to my relief, by the meeting's secretary, who told us to get in line for lunch. Saupitty said something to her in Comanche, and she told me, "He knows I don't speak Comanche so well, so he always talks to me in the language." She shook her head.

I thought of the speakers I'd met—of Saupitty's crankiness, Codopony's paintings, and Ken Goodin's random recoveries of language. The language drew the alienated, old, and alone, existing in groups of ones and twos. It was the opposite of language's social purpose, and I feared for its possible end, the stasis of words on a page.

The best hope was Codopony, but I had no idea if his family would ever catch up to him on his solitary path into the Comanche world. Gradually, Saupitty and the rest of the language committee would drop away, and then he would be by himself—a community of one.

Still, that afternoon, everyone seemed to have a good time. Over lunch, everyone chatted in English about fishing, softball, and stories of old times, when some Comanches liked to eat uncooked liver right out of the buffalo. Then, without announcement, one ruddy-faced man in a gold knit shirt pushed his chair back from the table and began to sing a Comanche song in a professional-sounding baritone.

Other Comanches followed suit, and Lucille McClung, a wiry woman in a purple jumpsuit, outdid some of the others by singing two songs, gamely negotiating the swings from high to low notes. At the end of one, she laughed. "I got to start out high or they'll just kind of fade away."

"We are anyway," another old lady said, picking up on the joke. "We are fading away."

They chuckled and kept the songs going. I thought of a speech by one of the sociolinguists who studied declining languages. Joshua Fishman, a New York sociolinguist who has taught his children Yiddish, made a long and widely quoted speech at a 1995 symposium about the notion of revitalization. We have to ask, he said: "Is reversing language shift a lost cause?"

And he replied to his own question: "Well, perhaps it is." But, he went on: "All of life is a lost cause. We are all sitting and dying right in this room. . . . We all know the road leads only downward into the grave. There is no other way it will go. Those that have hope at least share the benefits of hope, and one of those benefits is community."

The last time I saw Codopony, he was talking Comanche to his horse in a corral. The tribe sold mustangs to tribal members for twenty dollars, aiming to help young people connect with Comanche history, and Codopony was breaking the one he had bought—"calming him down," as the Comanche language put it. I had followed him out to a corral in the countryside. We were on smooth plains with clumps of foliage tucked like garnish in the creek beds, and behind us rose the Wichita Mountains, a jumble of ancient, badly eroded granite, older than the Appalachians. They looked bombed out in places, and parts had indeed been used for artillery practice.

I watched Codopony climb into the ring with sweet feed in his hand, joking that these horses were so short they made him look tall; he was five foot eight or so, stocky and muscular. His horse was a brown male—in Comanche, *ko-dek-ma*, a cognate of *Codopony*, which means "brown eyes." The two other horses in the ring skittered to the other side, but the brown male stayed calm as Codopony fed him and then ran his hands over his gums, haunches, chest, and legs. "In animals, the back leg would have its own term," he mused out loud to me. I was watching safely from a lawn chair outside the corral.

As Codopony stroked the horse, he murmured to him in Comanche, saying that he was a good horse and that no one was going to hurt him. A few minutes later, he took a length of rope and twirled it in the air, testing to see if the horse was spooked. He threw it on the ground and laid it on the horse's back. He had owned the horse for a good six months, and the animal knew him. "My gift is I'm not afraid of them," he said, pushing the horse backwards with an exhortation in Comanche.

When I asked how he learned to take care of horses, he said, "I'm Comanche." During their glory days, Comanches had developed extensive lists of horse colors, actions, and diseases, as well as the terms people used to talk to them. Horse talk was part of tribal tradition, passed from man to man, and Saupitty had taught Codopony many words. There was even a Comanche approach to horse training and riding, which involved "making the horse as comfortable as possible" and leading him with body language. Codopony planned to teach his horse to respond to voice commands in both Comanche and English, so that other people could ride him. "He'll be a bilingual horse," Codopony joked in his calm, horse-talk voice.

As he worked, a smooth edge of cloud flowed across the sun. A storm was approaching; we could see vertical rain to the west on the Wichitas.

Codopony kept talking softly as he approached with a blanket and threw it over the horse's back. When the horse stamped impatiently, Codopony called him *pu-ku-tsi su-wat,* or "stubborn," a word once used for crazy warriors who did daring things to gain respect. With a careful movement, Codopony put the saddle on the horse's back. The horse shifted in place, ears switching back, but stood patiently as Codopony worked a bit into his mouth.

Codopony lit a cigarette, sheepishly admitting he never rode without nicotine. The horse stood still as he put his foot into a stirrup and hoisted himself on. As the two of them walked stiffly around the corral, I wondered if any language had a word for the horse and rider moving together. Codopony put the horse through his paces in Comanche, telling him to walk and trot. After a while, they stopped in front of my lawn chair. Codopony was having fun, looking more like the Comanche self I'd seen in his portrait, direct and confident.

It was possible he was the last person speaking Comanche to a horse, and I said so. He thought it over and shook his head. That probably wasn't yet true, he said. But he had only about thirty or forty people left to speak it with and most of his friends were elderly. "My friends are dropping left and right," he said. "I was born too late or too early." He was too young to live his life surrounded by the language, but too old to be ignorant of its existence. "I feel screwed either way," he added.

We could hear thunder, and the clouds were blue-black. The yellow fields glowed intensely in a celestial light that broke through in places. The wind blew cooler. The gray screen of rain approached, and out in a field, the whine of a combine stopped abruptly. We heard thunder—"the clouds crying," as the Comanches said it. I stood up anxiously, and watched as Codopony dismounted. He began unsaddling the horse, praising its work.

As I listened to him talking to the horse, I thought that it should seem lonely, but it wasn't; horse talk was earthy, warm, and even companionable. So what is life for a language? I was hearing a language declared to be dying. But it was hard to characterize this instance of speech. A language does not fade to silence simply; it becomes more secretive. Its cult becomes tinier. It emerges in shorter flashes: the horse talk; the man recalling his mother's words in the roaring solitude atop his tractor in a field; the women singing in a museum.

As I drove away, all I could see was the three horses huddling, mutely nuzzling each other, in the first raindrops, as if no one had ever been there. Birds rose crazily, the wind blew, and the trees went tossing around. Codopony had told me the Comanche word for "lightning" contained the term "red," but it looked blue to me. When it hit, it lit up the whole countryside, and it looked like a different land. For a second, I could see everything, and I kept the visual memory on my inner eye as my car crept up the highway toward Tulsa.

CHAPTER THREE

The Code Talker

I MET CHARLES CHIBITTY, the last Comanche code talker, at a powwow southwest of Lawton. It was several months after I visited the language committee, and I hoped to see Comanche used in the life of the community. The powwow was a mesmerizing pageant of trembling feathers, glittering beads, and jingling, bell-covered dresses, all circling under the sky in the soft heat of June, and I stayed for two days. But in all that time, I hardly heard any Comanche spoken. The language committee had a table where a few people handed out flyers and syllabaries, but the attention was on the dancers and drummers.

An emcee kept the powwow moving with a gentle English rap that drifted out over the ring. Occasionally, he worked in a mention of the *nuhmenuh*, the Comanche people or thanked the people who ran the little food stands at the edge of the arena for supplying fry bread, burgers, and balls of flavored ice to the singers. "Smell that barbecue. That's Kate's Barbecue. Mm-mm. Mercy. Thanks to Kate's

Barbecue. And thanks to Prairie Flower for the snowballs. We want to thank you, Prairie Flower. Anyone know how to say 'snowball' in Comanche?" He laughed gently.

I wandered around the edges of the arena as the dances continued, and by Saturday night I had heard that a kind of celebrity was there, "a warrior's warrior," one Comanche said. During World War II, Chibitty was one of seventeen Comanches who were trained to transmit U.S. military messages in their language, a "code" the enemy never cracked. (A larger and better-known group of Navajos used their language to send military messages in the Pacific, an event documented in the movie *Windtalkers.*)

Now Chibitty occupies a peculiar space in the local celebrity culture. The United States has showered him with military medals and a Citizen's Award for Exceptional Service; the French government has made him a chevalier of the National Order of Merit. The walls of a room in Oklahoma's state capitol building display a mural of him lying on the Normandy beach, talking on a military telephone. Chibitty makes public appearances all the time: shaking the hand of the governor, smiling in a feathered headdress on a DISCOVER OKLAHOMA! poster, or handing out dream catchers at a local gymnastics competition.

Chibitty occupied a prestigious place in a lawn chair near the drummers' circle. When I introduced myself, he nodded and motioned to a thin, brown-haired girl to clear out of the seat beside him. She did so without reluctance, and though she was just eleven, her movements were deliberate and graceful. Once or twice, she fixed her serious, blue eyes on me, and then she lounged in front of us, reading a Harry Potter book. "This is your granddaughter, right?" I said.

"This is my daughter," Chibitty corrected me.

I was confused for a moment, wondering if I had misheard him over the drumming and singing of the powwow. Chibitty was stocky and square-shouldered. He had been a boxer at school and on military teams, "packing dynamite in both fists," as the military newspapers put it: half a dozen knockouts in his army career alone. At just under five foot six, he still had that compact, powerful build. His dark gray hair grew to his shoulders; his skin was lined but not loose, and his eyes held mine steadily as we talked. Later, I confirmed that this was the granddaughter he had adopted after his daughter died, but I would have believed he was young enough to be her father. Over the powwow's noise, I could gather only bits of what he said, and we made plans to meet a few weeks later at his home in Tulsa.

Traveling in Oklahoma had left me with a deepening sense of loss. Among the thirty-nine official tribes in the state, nearly a dozen didn't have any language at all.

The Trail of Tears, the long march the Cherokees made to Oklahoma, is well known. But every tribe that came to Oklahoma had its own trail of tears, and some groups had been essentially on the move since the 1700s. Since the time of Cartier, wars had extinguished whole tribes while pushing the remainder into the middle of the country; new diseases disrupted Indian communities; and in the nineteenth century the United States launched a policy of forcing Indians to move west of the Mississippi. The groups that got to Oklahoma were the remnants—as small as a few hundred people—of tribes that had been slowly harried out of existence. The Illini, for instance, covered the Midwest with as many as ten thousand people before the seventeenth century, but over two hundred years they were slowly diminished in wars and moves to Missouri, Kansas, and finally Oklahoma. In 1854, remnants totaling eighty-four people merged with other reduced bands to become the United Peoria, Kaskaskia, Wea, and Piankashaw of Oklahoma. They grew as large as two thousand by 2000; "to paraphrase Mark Twain, rumors of our extinction are greatly exaggerated," their Web site said. But the tribe had lost its linguistic community long before I got there.

Other tribes had come to Oklahoma with their languages intact. But their tales were grim, following the same outlines as the story of Indian assimilation into mainstream culture. Between the 1880s and early 1930s, the United States dissolved many Indian reservations, subdivided the land among tribal members, and sold unallotted land to non-Indians. The government also abolished tribal governments. Thus a number of tribes, particularly in Oklahoma, lost their communal land base and the integrity of their communities.

At the same time, the tribes lost their ability to subsist economically without dependence on outsiders, forcing more people to speak English. The Plains tribes were hit hard by the loss of their horse-wealth and their freedom to roam, as well as the extermination of the buffalo herds, while the eastern tribes, the farmers and hunters, saw gradual restrictions of their hunting rights and their land base. Finally, the United States ran schools that aimed to make Indians abandon their language and their culture. While New Deal bureaucrats tried to end the most coercive policies, the devaluation of Indian identity persisted in schools throughout the late 1960s.

At times, the languages seemed to be receding as I raced toward them. I kept arriving in places where a language was recently gone. I called the Ottawas—another once-powerful midwestern tribe—a few months after I'd heard that their chief, Charles Dawes, was an active promoter of their language. When I asked for Mr. Dawes, the woman who answered the phone at the Ottawa tribal headquarters seemed surprised.

"Well, you know, he's passed on," she said.

Me: Oh! I'm so sorry to hear that.
Her: Can I help you?

Me: Well, I was wondering if there's anyone who speaks the language.

Her: Well, there's Charla Dawes.

Me (thinking she said Charlie): But he's passed on, right?

Her: No, there's Charla, his daughter.

Me: Oh. She's probably pretty young, right? I mean, does she speak?

Her: She don't speak it too well.

Me: So I'm calling too late.

[silence]

Her: Well, what did you want?

Me: Just to find out if there were any fluent speakers of the language.

Her: No, we don't have any.

Initially, I was reluctant to take in evidence of loss. I knew that I might be having trouble finding thriving languages simply because I was an outsider. At various tribal headquarters, secretaries kept information buttoned up as tightly as gatekeepers at Fortune 500 companies. When I contacted them, they grilled me about what I was up to. "I'll give your number to someone, but we are very traditional and we don't like to give out information," said a woman at the Kickapoo tribal headquarters. The Kickapoos, for their part, had faced broken treaties, political conniving, the cession of their reservation, and the forced schooling of their children in the past century or so. I had heard that they had kept their language going, but I was never sure, because no one ever called me back.

For a while, I kept walking into English-speaking gatherings, thinking, *This is not what I'm looking for,* and walking out again. I occasionally heard encouraging confirmation that if you looked in the right places, you could find secret communities of people still speaking their languages. My ride with Hastings Shade, the Comanche powwow where no one seemed to be speaking, and various amateur language classes all seemed like missteps that I would correct later, with time and the right approach.

But at the same time, I feared that the idea of lost communities of speakers might be a fantasy, a kind of urban legend fueled by wishful thinking. In New York City, I worked across the street from the World Trade Center, and for weeks after the towers fell, people used to say that there might be survivors living in the underground mall, beneath the rubble. "You know, there's an Au Bon Pain down there, with muffins and bread and things," someone would say. It was such an appealing thought that we half-believed it for a while.

Chibitty, by contrast, represented a rare, triumphant moment for a native language. Then eighty years old, Chibitty was a link to a time when Comanche was considered a prized asset, a national resource. For those Comanches who shouted into the radios in Normandy, laid down telephone lines in the Belgian forest, and marched into Germany, speaking their language must have been, for once, a display of honor, a proud flexing of muscles. I hungered for a success story to counter the sadness I felt closing in on efforts to preserve the languages.

When Chibitty returned my call to set up our meeting, he didn't say hello: He just said "Chibitty." The first syllable was *chai*, like the tea, and in his soft Oklahoma accent it came out *CHAH-biddy*. It took me a moment to work out the word. When I asked him why he did that, he said, "Oh, everybody knows Chibitty." He mentioned that he might be busy, as he was getting ready to travel to a speaking engagement. "I gotta make a dollar for me and my little girl," he said. He added that most people who took his time paid him for it, but if it was a hint, I let it drop.

Chibitty lived in a middle-class neighborhood of policemen and teachers. When I pulled up at his flat-roofed ranch house, I recognized it by the stickers on the back of his Mercury Tracer. They read: LAREDO'S 6TH ANNUAL MEMORIAL POW-WOW HONORING CHIEF CHARLES CHIBITTY and PROUD PARENTS OF AN HONOR ROLL STUDENT AT HOOVER ELEMENTARY and ANYONE CAN BE A FATHER . . . IT TAKES SOMEONE SPECIAL TO BE A DADDY! The entryway leading to a recessed front door was lined with American flags and brightly painted cow skulls.

Chibitty met me at the door with a solemn handshake and led me back to a long, low living room. His gray hair cascaded down over his black T-shirt, and his straight, military bearing seemed incongruous with his casual white shorts and tennis shoes. The room was like a big trophy case, walls lined with photos, medals, boxes of commendations, trophies, and knickknacks. He had spoken to plenty of journalists over the years, so he seemed to have a show-and-tell routine down. For a while we wandered around, he, picking up spears, helmets, and file folders, I, following, holding out my tape recorder like an offering. He sang me the powwow song written by a Comanche in honor of the code talkers, using a strong, steady baritone to pound out syllables I couldn't understand. (This was not to be confused with the code-talker song sung in a video about Chibitty; a white Texas woman freelanced it for him, singing: "Comanches talking on the radio, / In their native tongue so the enemy won't know.")

Chibitty unfurled a battered red flag—big enough to be a bedsheet, with a giant black swastika in the middle—that he and his buddies had brought back from Germany. It had faded to a mellow cherry color, and he said he'd been offered a thousand dollars for it but wasn't selling. He showed a videotaped TV segment on the code talkers, pointing to the screen occasionally with a military sword. In one corner of the room was a feathered headdress mounted on a bayonet.

Scattered around the room as well were his daughter's things: a Tom Clancy novel, a few Jessica Simpson and Britney Spears CDs, a poster for the movie *Pocahontas*. As he told me his well-practiced war stories, a bird in a cage on the floor burbled continuously and a dog barked from the backyard. It all seemed a bizarre mix of cultural signifiers—but it was no stranger, I realized, than the wandering thread of his life.

When Chibitty was born, in 1921, most Comanches spoke the language. Oklahoma had been a state for fourteen years. Just forty-seven years before, the last bands of Comanches had come straggling onto the reservation around Lawton. Chibitty showed me an old photo of himself as a baby, swaddled and strapped to an old-fashioned cradleboard.

The government was trying to train the Comanches to assimilate, and his generation was hit hard with the message that the language was backward. In grade school around Fort Sill, Chibitty said his punishment for speaking Comanche was having to pick up trash for hours. At seventeen, Chibitty was sent to an English-only boarding school for American Indians in Lawrence, Kansas, and he never really lived in a Comanche-speaking home again. It was a transitional moment: In 1940, a linguist reported: "Most old people over 60 speak little or no English, while most young people under 30 speak little or no Comanche." Chibitty was determined to succeed in the prevailing culture. When he went home for a visit, around Christmas in 1940, he heard that the army was recruiting Comanches, and he talked his mother into letting him sign up.

The code-talking idea wasn't unprecedented; an army officer in World War I had overheard a group of Choctaw soldiers talking and used them to send messages across German lines. Meanwhile, during World War II, the Marines were training 450 Navajos to transmit and receive messages in the Pacific, though the Comanches knew nothing about it at the time. It was said at the time that Comanche men, coming from a culture of warfare, were eager to join. It's hard to tell if that was universally true, but many Comanches honor their soldiers as warriors in the line of tradition.

Chibitty and the other Comanches were sent to Fort Benning, Georgia, in 1941, for training in the transmission of messages. First, the Indians worked to come up with terms they could use in a code. They developed words for modern and military terms that didn't exist in their language. One of Chibitty's training officers, Hugh F. Foster, a retired major general of the army, described the process to me later. "I would say 'overpass' and they would jabber in Comanche for a while until they came up with something, and I would write it in my little notebook using my own phonetic system. Then 'underpass.' 'House.' 'Hospital.' "

For "tank," they used their word for turtle. When they discussed "machine gun," one of the soldiers said the sound reminded him of his mother's sewing machine, so they made it "sewing-machine gun." A bomber became a "pregnant airplane." For Hitler, they used a word that meant "crazy white man." They came up with a military vocabulary of about 250 words.

Their language play contained a series of apparent contradictions: They were practicing the kind of modern adaptation the language needed to survive, but they were also creating a lexicon so exclusive that Comanches outside their group wouldn't understand it. Their ability to speak their language was the source of their recognition, but it was also their ticket out of a Comanche world. Their code was meant for both communicating and disguising meaning—like the trappings of Indian identity, both recognizable and obfuscating.

Chibitty showed me an old Fort Benning newspaper with a write-up of the Comanches just after they entered training. It began: "Fort Benning's red men are having quite a lot of fun playing the white man's war games. War paint and feathers have changed to khaki, and the tomahawk has given way to the Tommy gun. Even a tough top sergeant says they're making good soldiers, and that's big heap praise in any military circle." Chibitty didn't remark on the tone, but he did say that one time, while he and some other Comanches were shooting pool, a sergeant walked in and told them not to speak their language. Chibitty said his reply was: "You want us to stop? Let's go outside." He added, with a big smile: "The guy didn't go out."

The Comanches were trained in the technology of communication: operating the field telephones and switchboards that would be used in combat zones, laying lines for the phones, climbing trees and poles to attach the wires. Major General Foster described Chibitty as he was then. "He used to box with the team for his company. He's a little pint of peanuts. Stocky. All of the code talkers also had other jobs, and he was a telephone lineman, and their job was to lay wires through the woods and valleys, and it's strenuous work, walking cross-country carrying a heavy line."

Several Comanches were disqualified, but fourteen went on to Europe. Chibitty landed on Utah Beach a few days after D-Day with the Twenty-second Regiment of the Fourth Infantry Division. He said his first message back was: "We are five miles inland. The battle is getting worse and we need help."

Chibitty followed the Twenty-second Regiment through France and Belgium. Teams of Comanches had to be available in several locations to receive each other's messages, so Chibitty trudged between headquarters and the front lines. "Sometimes the Germans would sneak in and tap onto the telephone lines. Some of them could speak better English than I could," he told me.

Chibitty was too sharp to forget what he had already told me, but he mentioned three times on separate occasions that he saw Private Mullins, "a little white guy from New Jersey," get hit by shrapnel two feet from him and die. He remembered walking on a road through

Belgium's dense, rugged Huertgen Forest as snow fell in big flakes on the scattered bodies of Americans and Germans along the road. Later, he said, he watched tanks come up the road, now covered with snow, and wondered what had happened to the bodies. Nearly thirty thousand American soldiers died or were wounded in the Huertgen Forest. It stuck in my mind, the image of him on a long march through the woods.

He wasn't famous until much later. The Comanche code talkers received no special honors until 1989, when the French government gave them medals recognizing them as knights of the National Order of Merit. By then only three were left. After that, Chibitty and the others received recognition from Oklahoma and various groups—from the tribes to the local chapter of the Daughters of the American Revolution. In 1999, the Department of Defense recognized the code talkers in a special ceremony, but by then only Chibitty was left.

After Chibitty had told me a bit about the war, I began to ask about what happened later, following the thread of language into Chibitty's private life (which is, after all, where language lives). I wondered how the lesson of his first twenty-five years in Lawton and in the army—that "speaking Indian," as he put it, could be in turn honor and shame—had played out in the civilian world. We walked into the back of the living room, and he switched on a lamp; the afternoon was wearing on. We sat down on his couch, and he began talking, in his ruggedly poetic way.

After the war, Chibitty lived out a philosophy he had developed in the army: He could maintain a Comanche identity while also succeeding in the white world. He headed to Tulsa and married a Shawnee-Delaware woman he'd met back at boarding school before the war. He said there were good work opportunities in Tulsa. He was not unlike many Indian soldiers who returned from the war. A Bureau of Indian Affairs relocation program in 1952 encouraged still more young people to leave reservation areas for urban centers. After Chibitty worked for a while as a mechanic, he was offered a job as a union glazier, an installer of windows and mirrors, and that became the foundation for his prosperity.

Chibitty pointed out the people in a long line of pictures on his wall. One photo showed the family in black and white: Charles, Elaine, and their two children, Pamela, born in 1949, and Charles Jr., born in 1951. He said, "There's my wife when she was a Grand High Lady Shriner of North America, the first Indian ever to reach that title." Chibitty, too, was a member of the Shriners, a nationwide fraternity with the trappings of a secret society; the members wore red fezes and called each other by titles such as *Imperial Sir*. He joined the Masons and the Elks as well. As we talked, he studied the picture of his wife, posing with a pensive face in a black-and-white studio photo. "Boy, I had a pretty one," he said.

"And here's my daughter doing the Lord's Prayer in Indian sign language," he said, moving along. That act is particularly Oklahoman: It merges Indian and Christian identity into a feminine ritual that is still performed at beauty pageants and powwows.

Beside that picture was a head shot of Pamela taken later. She had fine cheekbones and long hair down her back and was made up like a cover girl. Her beauty was striking, and I told him so.

He said, "Yes, she had a modeling deal." He went on, "She was first-runner-up Miss Teenage at Edison High School. When she went on stage she was dressed up in a full Indian outfit and she's up there talking about her old grandma and what they did, and a little bit later there was Indian music, and then when that modern music hit, she come out with her tap-dancing deal on and she tap danced. And when she come out only first runner-up, that crowd just booed and booed and booed. The girl that won boo-booed in her ballet dancing. *She* shouldn't have won.

"Of course, my daughter was Indian. Well, she cried, but I said, 'At least you had the crowd behind you.'"

Pamela Chibitty was also named a Comanche tribal princess, winning a contest held every year for girls who could demonstrate they knew their language and customs. She and Chibitty later traveled around doing exhibition Indian dancing together, both at powwows and at predominantly white events. (The modern powwow itself evolved out of ceremonial dances in Oklahoma around the turn of the twentieth century—it gave reservation Indians something to do and white people something to see—so the flow between being Comanche and acting Comanche was more natural than it might seem.) Chibitty moved on to point out a picture of Pamela in a white buckskin dress with fringes. "Now I got that buckskin dress made where it could fit this one," he said, indicating a picture of a girls' basketball team. I could just make out his adopted granddaughter, Lacey, in the photo.

"Is she Comanche?" I said.

"She's a Seneca," he said. "Probably got a little Irish in there but we just put Seneca down." Later, when I asked again about her ancestry, he said she was only a small part Indian: "If she has a nosebleed, she might lose it."

I couldn't find out much about Lacey's birth parents, because the legal details of her adoption were sealed. Pamela Chibitty had adopted Lacey and then died, suddenly, in 1991. She had been out in a remote part of the state when her appendix had ruptured. "They 'coptered her in toward Pawnee, but it was too late," Chibitty said matter-of-factly.

Chibitty and his wife, Elaine, took in Lacey, as well as Pam's older sons, Chebon and Acee. (She was divorced.) Three years later, Chibitty's wife died. At that point, the Seneca tribe petitioned to get Lacey placed with a Seneca family, but Chibitty fought them in court and won.

For a Comanche man to raise a mixed Seneca-white child recalled a long Comanche tradition of adopting children of other ethnicities. Often a Comanche would adopt one to replace a dead child of his own. "White people when they pass away, their kids got nobody, the tribe would go in and take those kids and raise 'em up. It's the same thing like I'm doing with my daughter," Chibitty said. This was a generous way of putting it; sometimes, in the nineteenth century, the kids were captives, and the Comanches had killed their parents. One of the Comanches' most famous leaders, Quanah Parker, was the child of a white woman captured as a girl and raised in the tribe. Juanita Pahdopony, a Comanche artist who had described the language to me, said that the Comanche phrase for "I love you" also meant "I claim you."

Chibitty gave Lacey the Comanche name *NAI-vee-quan-ah*, which he said meant "beautiful fragrance," though they only used it at Comanche ceremonies. It had been Pam's Comanche name.

As we spoke, I heard the dog's barking get louder and then heard the shouts of kids in the backyard. They were bouncing on a trampoline back there. "Ah, that's my daughter," he said. I asked if she considered herself Seneca or Comanche.

"We go both ways." He explained that they went to Seneca tribal events.

And down in Comanche country?

"She's a Comanche. Everybody knows her down that way, too," he said. "When my wife took ill, went into heart surgery, I made a promise to her that I would raise [Lacey] the best way I could and that she wouldn't be in need of anything and that I would raise her both white and traditionally combined.

"She knows all about Indian ways and stuff like that. I been talking to her in Comanche. She's just picking it up a little bit at a time, like I did when I was raising up."

He looked over at me. I had my tape recorder going but was also scribbling notes. "You should take shorthand," he said, teasingly. "My wife, she took shorthand; she was a professional legal secretary." I made some flustered reply and then got back on track.

"So you're teaching her the language?" I said.

"Soon as she gets more interested," he said. She was busy with school and also took tap-dancing, ballet, and gymnastics lessons. "Right now she's playing and growing," he added. "She's a gifted and talented child at school. She's on the honor roll. I'm real proud of her. She knows my relatives but I told her we're going to go back to hers, too.

"Me, I like to visit, but I'm up in age now," he said. "I want to visit with people at the dances. And if I put all my stuff on, I dance and get sweated up and then by the time I go back and get dressed then everybody'll be gone. I had my time of dancing. I was a champion dancer for years. From nineteen forty-five to up to when I was fifty-five years old I was still fancy dancing like that. That was what I learned to do since I was learning how to walk. They got straight dancing with no feathers—it's more dignified—but me, I liked to cut up." There was a picture of him crouched in a dance pose and wearing a headdress on a shelf by the TV.

"Are there any particularly Comanche values that you try to teach her?" I asked.

He said, "The only thing I try to teach her is that you can be just as Indian one hundred percent and carry your tradition, whether it's Seneca like yours or Comanche like mine, and still go to school and get the white-man ways just as good as the whites. Me, I think we're just as good as anyone else and could be better if we had the chance.

"Because my daughter and my son, they proved they could go both ways one hundred percent. My daughter went to OU [University of Oklahoma] and was executive director of the Native American

Coalition of Tulsa," he said. "Everybody knew who she was even here in Tulsa."

He turned to a picture of his son, a young man dressed in dancing regalia. "My son turned out to be a lawyer and he was a top Indian dancer, too," he told me. "My son, he played Will Rogers High School football, and we insisted he go to two years of another school after that, but we said, 'If you stay in [beyond that], we'll help you financially any way we could.'" His son got a B.A. and then a law degree from the University of Tulsa.

Chibitty went on, holding my gaze: "He told me when he was a young boy still in junior high and we was watching that black-and-white TV, he said, 'Daddy, I'm going to be a race-car driver, and I'm going to be a lawyer, and then when I make money, I'm going to take you fishing in Old Mexico.' He used to see them catching all that big bass down there.

"And I said, 'All right, I'll be looking for it.'

"He was racing cars here at the fairgrounds, and then he turned out to be a lawyer. He said, 'Daddy, this Indian law is a whole field by itself.' And he'd fly all over the United States, Alaska and such, and help all the Indians. When they'd have their problems with state and federal law, he'd straighten it up. And there got to be pretty good money in it.

"Then one time, he had to leave court at Shawnee and was going to Norman. The girl he was going to marry was going to OU there. West of Tecumseh, a big truck hit him in 'eighty-two September."

Later, I looked up news accounts of his son's death in the highway accident. He was thirty-one. "All that education and everything," Chibitty said. "That was one of the hardest things I could take."

I whispered that I was sorry, and we sat for a moment. It was getting darker in the living room as the sun left the windows, and I was startled when Chibitty spoke again. "This is him up here," he said, looking up at the back wall. Next to the son's picture hung a sign from an office door: CHARLES CHIBITTY JR./ATTORNEY AT LAW.

Lacey came in from the backyard and looked at us, sitting there. I noticed again how pale her skin was, with a sprinkling of freckles. Tall and slim, she wore shorts and a T-shirt, and her fingernails were painted black. She gave a polite smile that revealed braces. After we were introduced again, I asked her if she spoke Comanche.

"I've learned a little bit," she said cautiously.

"Well, we go to powwows and stuff like that, and I holler at her," her father put in.

"So what would be an example of something you've learned in the language?" I said.

"*Gi ta*," she fired back. "That means 'no.'" She and Chibitty cracked up.

"Can I have some money?" she said to him.

"I'm about broke," he said jokingly.

"I need thirty bucks. Hey, guys, come back in." She motioned to a shy group of kids who were standing just outside the door. I wondered if they were scared of Chibitty or me. A minute later, they all ran out again, and Lacey ran after them. She appeared comfortable in Tulsa. It was hard for me to see how, in the absence of a tribal community, she would ever become fluent in the language.

I asked if Chibitty had taught his son Comanche. Since Chibitty's wife was a blend of Shawnee and Delaware, they couldn't have spoken it at home.

"I taught him some. And I made him a tape," Chibitty said. "I would say *Kee ma*. Come here. *Kee ma. Kee ma.*" He spoke as if teaching me. "Come here. Come here. *Kee ma*. And *Kaa ra*. Set down, *Kaa ra*. And *Deuh ka*. Eat. And you can use that together, *Kee ma Deuh ka*. Come and eat. So I had a whole bunch, nearly a hundred words, and he'd listen to it. He was making a speech at the university up at

Wichita, Kansas, and there was one Kiowa man up there, Harvey Ware, I know him and his wife from way back a long time ago. The man went over and said to him, 'Do you speak Comanche?'"

He smiled at the memory. "And I had taught him to answer, in Comanche, 'I don't speak Comanche but my father is helping me.' So he was picking it up pretty good."

He didn't know what had happened to the tapes. Pam's other two sons had grown up—they were twenty-six and thirty—and moved away. "As far as talking Indian, I don't think they're interested in it," Chibitty said.

He himself didn't use the language much anymore, but he still remembered everything. "When I make speeches at schools, and I ask if anybody's Indian and some of them raise their hands, I say, 'If you've got a grandpa or grandma or some uncle who still speaks the language you belong to . . . ask them to talk to you, because we're losing our language awfully fast.' It's like me, well, I'm from Lawton, Oklahoma. We all talked Indian there all the time. And then I moved over here to make a living. Now there's a few of us here that's Comanches. We get together and we talk, and I'm still one of the last, maybe the last, that could sit and talk Comanche all day long and don't have to use English."

I sat silently for a minute, retracing what had happened. It seemed that the language itself was now a code, a secret communication that in time would have no one left to decipher it. The code talker was fast becoming one of the last talkers. And even his success story was also a sad story.

Probably parts of his story were typical: the cultural dislocation, the forces drawing him into the mainstream. These were the battles of a whole generation. Other parts were his alone. Chibitty had worked hard to raise children who would gain honor from their Comanche identity. Yet all his successes had been provisional, ended by random tragedies. I didn't know what it meant; all I knew was that's how it happened. That's how the code talker's heritage came down to Lacey, all his lines to the future cut but this one thin cord.

When I left, I gave him a business card with my phone number, and he thought for a moment, then dug a card out of his wallet and handed it to me. It was a little worn and more than a decade old. It said DANCING MOCCASIN / INDIAN DANCERS / SPECIALTY DANCES: WAR DANCE EAGLE DANCE SHIELD DANCE HOOP DANCE. CHARLES CHIBITTY / PAM CHIBITTY. Then he stood outside, his strong, boxer's arms loose by his sides, as I drove away.

Later, I called him to check on his wife's title. "Did you tell me your wife was Grand High Lady Shriner?" He said she was. He was proud that she was the first Indian to hold the title and that she had won on her first run for it, too. He flew up to be with her at her installation ceremony in Toronto. He said he woke up early the morning of the ceremony, and, while his wife was sleeping in the hotel room, he went down to the lobby for some coffee.

"When I come down that morning, I had a T-shirt on, and one old lady says, 'Hey, you. Come here,' and I worked around there for about an hour and a half just moving chairs and getting stuff ready. I didn't say nothing. That little old lady said, 'Thank you, mister,' and I went on. That night at the reception, I had my tux on. And feathers, too, and that little old lady, she stopped and said, 'Oh my goodness, oh my goodness, I didn't know you was the Grand High's husband!'

"I said, 'Don't mind me, lady. I been a peon all my life,'" he said, slyly. "That's what I told her."

CHAPTER FOUR

Orphan Child

SEQUOYAH HIGH SCHOOL stood high on a lonely hill. Along the driveway into the school, there was a fork in the road and a sign that said: GOOD BEGINNINGS NEVER END. It was an appropriate message, because the roads led to both the past and the future of the Cherokee language—to the story of both a bad beginning and a new beginning. I took the left fork one day, traveling into the past.

I hadn't intended to come back to Cherokee country so soon, but the campus of this old school was essential to understanding what had happened to many American Indian languages. The picture of loss was growing more vivid—yet also more confusing. Chibitty, who had left his community and faced some of the benefits and losses of assimilation, told only part of the story.

To say that a language gets "lost" (odd word—as if the language were misplaced accidentally) doesn't describe the process by which languages vanish. It is hard to imagine a person forgetting something so deeply ingrained in the mind. Most people assume the disappearance of languages is part of a natural process of evolution, as people start using a dominant language or their grammar shifts; indeed, languages do change naturally until Latin becomes French and Chaucer's tongue becomes ours. If that were the whole story, language loss would be sad but inevitable.

But the story of Native American languages has another element, one that changed the life of every old person I met, whether Comanche or Ponca or Cherokee: a large-scale effort to force Indians to speak English. Boarding schools like Sequoyah's predecessor, Sequoyah Orphan Training School, pushed several generations to unlearn their languages. That was why I found myself wandering around Sequoyah High School on a chilly spring day with Sadie Parnell, an eighty-four-year-old Cherokee woman who'd gone to school there sixty years before.

Parnell started school in 1924, when she was not yet six. She and her older sister had been living with their grandfather in a rural area near Vian. She didn't think of herself as an orphan, but her mother was dead, and her father had abandoned the family. Her grandmother had died, too.

She lived with her grandfather in a two-room log house near a creek. Her grandfather farmed a patch of cotton and tobacco, and she remembered watching him tuck his long black braid, with only a few strands of white, under a plain black hat when he went to town to sell and buy goods. She wasn't old enough to go very far with him; nor did he allow her to go along when he went to collect medicine plants for teas and salves. But her grandfather did take her to stomp dances, a traditional ceremonial gathering. Parnell, who said she was called by a name that meant "white girl" because she was fair, recalled the safe feeling of falling asleep on a pallet underneath a wagon while the adults danced all night around a fire that sent sparks straight up into the darkness. Her grandfather spoke very little English, and she learned none.

That life ended one summer day when her grandfather came home from a trade trip to town. He told Sadie and her sister— a third sister was living with another family—that an agent from the Indian-affairs bureaucracy had approached him on the road and convinced him that the girls would do better in life if they got an education at Sequoyah Orphan Training School. About a month later, her grandfather put them in the wagon and drove them to Sequoyah.

Parnell found the tall brick buildings grim and scary; they had once housed an insane asylum. After the family spent the night camping at the edge of the school grounds, her grandfather enrolled the sisters, and a matron took them away. The woman led the girls to a dormitory, stripped off their flour-sack dresses, bathed them, and cut their hair above the shoulder. They never saw their old dresses again. They put on clean uniforms—a middy blouse, a blue pleated skirt, and a tie, black for the bigger girls and red for girls like Parnell. Then they were led into their classrooms. Parnell was in first grade. She sat and cried quietly all morning as the tide of unfamiliar sounds washed over her. Once, the teacher said something to her in English, and when Parnell didn't respond, the teacher took out a ruler and spanked her.

At lunchtime, the children formed a line and marched out of class. Across the campus, Parnell saw her grandfather watching to see how she was. She ran to him and asked him to take her home. He replied that this was the best place for her and her sister, and she let him walk away.

Parnell said she had a hard time learning English at first. She let other girls who were bilingual tell her what was going on in class. But every time she answered a question in Cherokee or got caught whispering to her sister in the language, she had her mouth washed out with soap. Eventually, she began picking up English. By the time

Parnell was ten, she and her sister spoke English to each other even in private.

Along with English, they learned math, geography, history, and other standard subjects. When they weren't in class, the students had chores. Boys were taught to milk cows, grow vegetables, and repair farm equipment. Girls learned sewing, cooking, cleaning, and nursing. Parnell cleaned dishes, wiped tables, and folded clothes in the laundry.

For most of the time she was there, the school was run in military fashion. Every morning, the students got up at 6 A.M. to the sound of a whistle and made their beds. They marched downstairs, lined up at a long, double washbasin down the center, got a ration of tooth powder, brushed their teeth, and washed their hands and faces. Then they marched outside and did calisthenics for thirty minutes. They marched to the dining room, marched to class, and marched back to the dormitories. At night, a bugle played "Taps" as they fell asleep. Most Indian boarding schools were run along these lines; when the code talkers joined the army, their officers noted approvingly that they were already trained in military procedure.

On Saturday nights, they watched cowboy serials on a big screen in the auditorium, and on Sundays they had church and then went out to the main lawn for dress parade, a drill session. Sometimes, too, Parnell's grandfather came to visit, walking the thirty miles from Vian. He spoke Cherokee with her, and his last visit was the last time she spoke it.

Parnell was inside a system designed to eradicate Native languages. From the 1880s through the 1920s, the United States placed Indian children in day and boarding schools that aimed to erase traditional ways from memory. In 1877, the Indian Office supervised 48 boarding schools; by 1897 there were 145 boarding schools with 15,026 pupils. The removal of children from their families was mandatory in many Indian areas, and sometimes families were threatened with suspension of their food benefits if their children didn't attend school.

The aim of the schools was reflected in the motto of Carlisle Indian School in Pennsylvania, one of the first to be founded: "Kill the Indian, Save the Man." The schools' founders sought to transform children from group-oriented tribal members to self-interested citizens, from nomadic hunters to tradesmen and employees. Teaching Indians to act like typical Christian white people of their time involved training in everything from vocations to the liberal arts to table manners. One school bureaucrat, Estelle Reel, wrote in a report to the school community that every girl should be taught "how to cut bread into dainty, thin slices and place [them] on plates in a neat, attractive manner."

Eradicating the old languages was a key part of the curriculum. At one Carlisle school commencement, the Reverend A. J. Lippincott said, "You cannot become truly American citizens, industrious, intelligent, cultured, civilized until the INDIAN within you is DEAD." In an era when frontier wars were fresh in people's minds, it was believed that Native American cultures were inferior, representing earlier stages of the development toward civilization. The ideology of the time assumed that a few Indo-European languages were best suited to clear and complex thinking; meanwhile, the establishment of a modern industrial society required workers with generic sets of abilities, including reading and writing English.

All around the world, nations were creating boarding schools that aimed to integrate indigenous groups into modern culture: Canada created them for its Native American tribes, Australia for Aborigines, and Scandinavian countries for the northern Saami people. Later, the Soviet Union made schools part of its effort to turn Siberian tribes like the Chukchi into proper Communists.

Not every child who went to an Indian school got his or her mouth washed out with soap. But some of the alternatives were even worse. Here are some of the recorded punishments for kids who spoke their own languages in America's Indian schools:

> getting spanked
> getting beaten
> getting whipped with a strap
> getting locked in a closet
> carrying stepladders on one's shoulders
>   for several hours
> being kept out of dances
> being forced to hold quinine tablets
>   in one's mouth
> wearing a sandwich board on which
>   a message about the language
>   was written
> standing face-first in the corner of
>   the school room
> getting demerits restricting outings
> getting forced (for boys) to wear
>   dresses or to do laundry
>   with the girls

The schools were not the only things that hurt the Native American languages. Much damage had already been done. Later, wars led young men away from their hometowns; postwar relocation programs and economic hardships brought Indians to urban areas; and inter-marriage among tribes created households where English was the common tongue. But the schools had the most direct impact, working on an emotional level to link the languages with shame, disgust, and stupidity. Ironically, it was the dropouts, the least schooled, who retained the most of their languages.

The removal of language has become particularly noticeable in recent decades, now that people of Parnell's age are grandparents. As I had seen in my visit to the Comanches, the function of grandparents in Native cultures has traditionally been to transmit the past. If no Indian grandparents know the past, there is no history.

While Parnell's experience was similar to that of many Native children in U.S.-run schools, the institution of Sequoyah Orphan Training School isn't fully typical, partly because it served mainly orphans and partly because it was founded by the tribe itself. The Cherokees who came to Oklahoma started creating their own versions of European-American institutions before the Civil War. By the 1850s, they had day schools and seminaries, courts, and a Constitution. The Civil War caused intertribal warfare and general lawlessness that destroyed the fledgling Cherokee state and killed hundreds of people. By the beginning of 1863, there were hundreds of war orphans; as many as one-quarter of Cherokee children were parentless. The tribe opened the Cherokee Orphan Asylum in 1872. At that time, most teaching was conducted in Cherokee.

But the U.S. policy of dissolving reservations ended the Cherokees' sovereignty and deeply changed institutions like the school. Most Indian governments were disbanded in the years leading up to Oklahoma's statehood. (Cherokee political leaders were named by the U.S. president until 1970.) In 1914, the school was officially sold to the state of Oklahoma, and from then until 1985 various branches of the U.S. government operated the institution. The school gradually came to serve nonorphans, and however Cherokee-centered it had been at the beginning, it turned into a typical government-run Indian school.

One day when Parnell was about twelve, the school superintendent called her and her sister together. He said the Indian school agent had come through and left a message that their grandfather had died a few weeks earlier. The news hadn't been worth a trip to the school. Since their grandfather had already been buried, the superintendent said, there was no point in their going home.

Parnell attended the school until she graduated with the class of '37. As a teenager, she tried to rebel—she was punished for rolling her stockings below her knees and not keeping her hair at regulation length, and she even once climbed out of a window and ran away, but she was caught early the next morning and whipped. Still, she stayed in school long enough for its lessons to take effect. She forgot the Cherokee language. After she graduated, she thought she would pick up the language again. She trained as a nurse, and she heard plenty of patients speaking it in the hospital where she worked. But she found she couldn't understand much of what they were saying.

She married another Cherokee who didn't speak the language. He had been to another local school that inculcated the prevailing attitude—that speaking Cherokee was painful, shameful, or simply outmoded. School provided a kind of aversion therapy that meant they associated the language with pain.

In the 1960s and 1970s, Parnell tried to learn Cherokee again. She took a course and memorized the Cherokee alphabet. She told me: "The first thing I did when I got up in the morning every day was to start my alphabet and see if I could remember what I had learned the day before—just from memory to write it or to speak it." But her studies didn't stick. Somehow, Parnell said, "It completely slipped away from me."

Not every child who went to school forgot the language completely. But there was more than simple memory involved in Parnell's loss. Sometimes a traumatic experience can create mental blocks to remembering things. Parnell was taught not to speak the language, and then when her grandfather died, a last essential tie to the language was broken—the tie of love and community. She saw no more point in speaking it, and the language died in her. Her story showed how intricately the language was tied to the social life where it was used.

Now Parnell lives alone in a big white ranch house at the top of a hill. Her late husband, a rancher, left her in comfortable straits. When I went to see her, the nose of my car eased among the staring cows, nearly shoving them aside as I drove up the long driveway. She came out, walking with quick, strong steps, grabbed two hulking rottweilers by their collars—"Down, Panzer! Detrick!"—and led me inside to a plush easy chair. She had a short shock of straight white hair and firm, thick arms, ringed with loose bracelets. As we discussed her story, she didn't smile much but looked at me with an intense, dark-eyed stare, bringing to mind the unafraid teenager she had been.

Her living room was full of knickknacks, and I complimented her on a doll collection I saw on her shelves, with Scarlett O'Hara and Princess Diana prominently displayed in glass cases. "Thank you," she said in her terse, direct way. "I never had dolls when I was small." I looked around. "My pride and joy's back here, right in the corner." She pointed to a big Indian-maiden doll in a buckskin dress and headband, with staring black beads for eyes. The TV was on, and a western was playing at low volume. I saw a dusty street, heard gunshots. Once or twice I saw cowboys surprise an Indian maiden in a buckskin dress like the doll's.

Parnell is plenty vigorous, and she agreed to go with me as I drove to the school. She lives close enough to the campus to see its high water tower from her front door. "I've always heard a saying that when you grow up you always come back to the place where you're raised," she commented. "They say you come back to your home." Looking back, she was glad the school had given her somewhere to go. "After my grandfather died, I had no home," she said. But she was still angry about having lost the language. "They wanted to civilize us," she said. "And I guess we became civilized."

The former orphan training school has changed a great deal. The era of government-run Indian schools slowly petered out after the 1920s. In the 1970s, the Cherokee Nation was reborn after the federal government reaffirmed Indians' right to self-determination, and in 1985 the Nation took over its school again. Now Sequoyah takes Native American students from all over the country. Many Cherokees come, but there are also Pimas, Utes, and Navajos. Sequoyah is technically a private school, but no one pays tuition, with funding coming from the BIA, the Cherokee Nation, and the U.S. Department of Labor. The school even has a Cherokee class.

I had been to the school once before and even gone inside to speak to Don Franklin, the school historian. His office was near the gym, where a thunder of basketballs interrupted us and we could hear the thump and the squeak of shoes on the gym floor and the bass boom of "We Will Rock You" being played in preparation for a game. I noticed the lineup of the freshman Lady Indians: three Ashleys, two Amandas, a Keely, and a Kelsey. They were playing the Oktaha Tigers. Franklin, a heavy, blond guy who resembles Chuck Norris enough to have received that nickname from the kids, let me page through his old copies of *Oklahoma Indian School Magazine*, which carried the article "How Indians May Use Their Leisure Time" and a report by a student that began: "The Indians lived in wigwams. . . ." Most of the teachers are Native, but there is only one fluent speaker at the school—Jim Carey, the Cherokee teacher. When I asked if others knew the language, Franklin thought for a moment. "A bus driver may speak it," he said.

Later, I walked up and down the halls, lined with cheerful posters and red and white lockers, looked at a case of band trophies, and eaves-dropped on the singing coming from a Cherokee-gospel class. I recalled the old hymns about the promised land. Some traditional Cherokees went to stomp dances—as Sadie Parnell's grandfather had—but Christianity was just as deeply embedded. After the class, a heavy boy with a friendly, open face came out, humming an old, sad song called "Orphan Child." Written in Cherokee, it's one of the tribe's best-known songs, suggesting that being an orphan is in some way a quintessential experience. "I hear a grieving voice from those who have lost their parents," one line says.

Eric, the boy who was humming, was sixteen. He wore tennis shoes, baggy pants, and a windbreaker. He said he had learned some Cherokee, but they taught the same thing over and over in the classes he'd taken: "Days of the week, months of the year," he chanted in a bored tone. "I sing a lot better than I speak." He told me he was Choctaw, Creek, and Cherokee as well as a tiny part Natchez. "They came out of Louisiana," he said. "Dad's great-aunt was one of the last speakers. They got exterminated in the seventeen hundreds or some-thing and mixed with the other tribes," he said cheerfully.

The day I came with Parnell was a Sunday, and we drove around a quiet campus. She had been back one or two times before, but she muttered things like "Well, I'll be darned. Everything is changed" in her deep voice as we drove around. The trip reminded me of driving to Lost City with Hastings Shade. Only here I knew what had hap-pened and what wasn't there.

Where the agricultural fields had been, there were now empty lawns and a new, red track where a few pairs of girls were speed-walking, swinging their arms out confidently. Most of the old dorms were gone, but Parnell recognized a mowed, central field where some little towheaded boys wearing enormous baseball gloves were messing around with a ball. "This was where they used to have dress parade," she said. Every dorm had a company and they marched like soldiers on the parade grounds, vying to walk the straightest line in the most perfect formation. "People on the highway would stop and look at us." Now there were just skinny boys laughing and running in the fields on a warm afternoon.

Across the street from the school, there was once a graveyard, and as we drove out of the campus, heading back toward Parnell's house, she began talking about the graves. "There was a girl, her name was Sadie, Sadie Jumper," she said. "She died. She had her little Girl Scout uniform and pin on when they buried her."

"How did she die?" I said.

"Some sickness." Sadie shook her head. "She was buried right there." The headstones had been bulldozed, and Economy Storage Co. had set its little containers on the scraped dirt. "They just done away with it," she said.

That bothered her particularly because she has never found her grandfather's grave. Since she wasn't informed in time for the funeral, she never found out where he was buried. The best lead she ever had came from the woman who owned the house where he had died. The woman had been pregnant, and she worried about the baby. "Indians are real superstitious," Parnell commented. Another contact told Parnell that people had carried his body on their shoulders around a fire in an old-style religious ceremony. But no one knew where he was buried.

Parnell leaned back and laughed. "Soon's it gets a bit nicer," she said, "I'm going to head back down to the sticks and see what I can stir up."

She still visits old Cherokee cemeteries around Vian with a guide-book called *Our People and Where They Rest*. But she admitted she probably will not succeed in finding the grave. Nobody had the money to buy a headstone, so the grave may have had little more than a big rock at the head and a smaller rock at the foot. And the chart of grave locations doesn't help her much, because it's hard for her to decipher the Cherokee words.

Sequoyah's campus was more than a place haunted by the past. The sign that said GOOD BEGINNINGS NEVER END came at a junction where you could take a right, and if you drove up the road, you could find a teacher reading a story to a little boy in Cherokee.

Inside a small classroom, a teacher named Lula Elk sat in a corner with Kenny, a three-year-old in a red shirt that said ELMO on it. The book they read—Dr. Seuss's *Are You My Mother?*—was actually written in English. But Elk, a small woman with round brown eyes and a blanket of smooth hair down her back, translated each page into Cherokee as she turned it, telling the story in a low voice, as the boy followed the pictures. In the story, the mother-creature leaves the nest and the child-creature goes looking for her, approaching a cat, a hen, a dog, a car, and even a bulldozer-like machine called a Snort. As the child-character called to his mother, Elk singsonged: *"Eh-ji, Eh-ji."*

The walls of the dingy but cheerful classroom were decorated with handwritten slips of paper listing Cherokee words like "door / *s-du-di.*" Copies of Sequoyah's syllabary and pictures of animals with Cherokee names hung on the walls. The children—there were seventeen enrolled but only a dozen present—were not supposed to use English, and the rule appeared to work, although the effect at this moment was silence. Another Cherokee speaker, an older woman named Ella Christie, was consoling a little girl who was sick.

When I found them there, I felt I had come a long way from the old orphanage. With this class, which was then a pilot version of an immersion school, Cherokees hoped to use the institutions that had damaged the language to bring it back. They planned to slowly expand their immersion school to go through sixth grade by 2012, with about twenty students per class.

Children have a remarkable chance to become fluent in languages during the early years of life, before they are three or four. Their brains' synapses are on the increase, and the brain, geared for rapid learning, has a high metabolic rate, allowing children to develop an uncanny grasp of any language to which they are exposed. During their first year, babies learn to control the parts of the mouth that produce speech. They also tune their ears to the sounds of their parents' language. Every infant is born with the ability to make all possible linguistic sounds. But within the first year of life, the infant's brain begins developing perceptual filters that impair the ability to hear sounds not used in the native tongue. This is why adults have so much trouble mastering the sounds of a foreign language—even when they know the grammar, they can't reproduce the accent.

Around the first birthday, babies understand words and then begin to speak them. Around eighteen months, children learn faster and string together words. Around the age of three, children begin to speak faster and acquire all the complexities of their language. About everything after that is fine-tuning vocabulary and learning complex sentences.

While older children can learn languages, their brains are not nearly as flexible. Metabolic activity in the brain slows after the age of four, and little-used synapses slowly disappear throughout childhood. It is unclear how fast the decline occurs. Parnell, for instance, switched languages entirely between six and eight—though only after being immersed in English in an unusually rigorous environment. Scientists don't agree about whether there is a critical period in which language must be learned or what that age might be. Some say four, some say eight, some say twelve or fourteen, and some say the decline is slow and imperceptible, going from childhood through adolescence and adulthood. But it is clear that learning the grammar and sounds of a new language is more difficult for adults, and that hardly any adults can achieve the kind of fluency that allows them to be mistaken for native speakers.

Specialists in prosody, or the study of rhythm and intonation, say that the rhythms and tones of language—the difference between *Greenland* and *green land,* or between *The child I knew drew pictures* and *The child, I knew, drew pictures*—are internalized early as well. Babies hear intonation before they understand words. Intonation is central to understanding a language, particularly one like Cherokee, which, like Chinese, uses variations in tone to convey meaning. It can also communicate subtle emotions—shame, guilt, sarcasm—that may vary slightly in different languages. Children also are primed to learn subtler social cues about demeanor and affect, the typical expression on one's face while speaking, the range of emotions displayed normally.

There are psychological factors that help children learn better than adults, as well. Infants learning language are motivated by the need to communicate important matters: They need food. Second-language learning depends on the sheer will of the learner. Children tend to be less afraid of making mistakes, and they often haven't absorbed cultural notions about one language's superiority to another.

So on one level, the immersion class showed a promising direction for the future. A number of groups around the world have had some success in bringing back their languages through immersion programs. Hawaii has sharply raised the number of children who speak Hawaiian with the help of a network of preschools and immersion schools that go through twelfth grade. In New Zealand, networks of day-care centers and immersion schools have played a big role in stabilizing the Maori language. Navajos offer bilingual schools and immersion programs that allow children to learn entirely in Navajo for several years. The Yupiks of Alaska, the Blackfeet of Montana, and the Mohawk in Canada, among others, have started more children on their languages through immersion classes.

At the same time, the Cherokee class demonstrated the toll that the old anti-Cherokee attitudes had taken. There were a number of ways the legacy of the past limited the success of the new program. Most obviously, there weren't many speakers left to teach it. That meant it was small; even at its largest, the school would serve 160 children. Cherokee classes were offered at the high-school level at Sequoyah, and the Cherokee Nation was promising more immersion classrooms, but only a few other public schools even exposed children to the language.

The Cherokees were also introducing the language in local Head Start programs. But when I visited, Head Start offered only five to fifteen minutes of language a day, though there were plans for an immersion center. Just eleven of the more than two hundred early-childhood unit employees were fluent in Cherokee.

In theory there were thousands of Cherokee speakers—the estimates of the 1990s ran as high as fourteen thousand, with a thousand estimated speakers in North Carolina. But the Cherokee Nation could hardly find any speakers, or at least any who were qualified to teach. In a survey of three hundred people, it found that only about 15 percent spoke Cherokee at a conversational level or better, and just 1 percent—that was three people—had attained the highest level of fluency, which included Cherokee reading and writing. No one under forty was considered even "conversational." What's more, the survey's authors acknowledged its sampling was unrepresentative and it was likely that the percentage of speakers among the 115,000 people in the Cherokees' fourteen counties was much lower. No one would give me an estimate of speakers, but when I asked Dusty Delso, the tribe's executive director of education, if there might be ten thousand Cherokee speakers left, he said, "No way."

The bulk of the Cherokee membership was now culturally white. All you needed to enroll in the Cherokee Nation was a single ancestor on an early-twentieth-century roll, so there were hundreds of thousands of legal Cherokees whose identity was based on only a fraction of blood; rumors swirled that someone who was only one four-thousandth Cherokee had recently joined the tribe. In the 2000 census, three predominantly Cherokee counties ranked among the top ten counties in the United States where residents said they were of two or more races (the highest percentages were in Hawaii).

A related difficulty—and another legacy of harsh school systems—was that almost by definition, most of those who did speak Cherokee could not or would not teach in a school. To teach Cherokee in a Head Start program or a public school, teachers needed to meet state certification standards (which required college degrees and training in early-childhood education), as well as passing a Cherokee Nation test. But—again following impeccable logic—most of the remaining speakers didn't have college degrees in early-childhood education. Most speakers had retained their language by resisting or avoiding schools.

The Cherokee Nation didn't need to follow state certification requirements for the tribally run immersion class that I visited. It was trying to train new teachers by offering full scholarships to any speaker who would go through a training program at the local Northeastern State University. But that would take time. In the meantime, the Cherokees had trouble finding people who were comfortable in a classroom. "Even if you waive the credentialing, you can't find people with the energy and patience to put up with children day after day after day," said Gloria Sly, who oversaw the immersion program as interim director of the Cultural Resource Center.

Elk, the youngest teacher in the immersion school, was in her early forties. She had managed to keep the language because she grew up in a remote area and kept speaking the language with her grandparents. The continued presence of her grandfather, whom she said "wouldn't talk English," had been a kind of counterpoint to the public schools' English lessons. She had worked her way from running an in-home day-care center to Head Start to the immersion job, and she was planning to take more college classes. But she was a rarity, with her relative youth and bilingual credentials.

In finding and recruiting Cherokee speakers, the tribe also faced a problem that had been perhaps exacerbated by the English-only programs of the past: the wide and long-standing divide between assimilationists and traditionalists. It was part of the Cherokees' distinctive heritage to have both tremendous modernizers—the minority who built a legislative and judiciary system, orphanages, schools, newspapers, and presses in the nineteenth century—and a determined tradition of opposition. Antagonism between the camps had existed at least since the nineteenth century, when mixed-blood Cherokees began creating a modern republic. The pride of place in Tahlequah's old town square went to monuments commemorating the assimilationists' legacy—the arrival of the first telephone, the founding of the bilingual *Cherokee Advocate* newspaper in 1844, an eight-foot-tall Statue of Liberty, and a Confederate war memorial.

I sensed the diversity of Cherokee life in my travels. Among the tribes I visited, the Cherokees were the most likely to be businessmen who played golf at Tulsa country clubs, the most likely to make me feel underdressed when I went to interview them. Now that these Cherokees had decided to revive their language, they were working through people with advanced degrees, professional PR managers, and consultants.

And yet, at the same time, the Cherokee Nation included also the most backwoods, the most toothless, the most furiously private people in Oklahoma. Even in the heart of Tahlequah, I'd occasionally meet someone from an old-fashioned world. Once I chatted with a man who was selling silver and beadwork at a table on the sidelines of a powwow. He was about fifty, with a scraggly ponytail, a small, quirky mouth, and an evasive, shy look. I asked him if he spoke Cherokee, and he answered, in rough English: "It's my language." His words had chipped-off edges like the arrowheads they sold at the next table. Behind him, a dour grandma with her hair in a tight bun was eyeing me. She was selling beadwork and dolls that looked homemade, in contrast to the professional silver and turquoise at the other booths. I didn't have to ask if she knew the language, but I asked him if his family spoke. Where was his community?

"It's just me," he said slowly and smiled. "Me and a few ducks and a dog."

Another time, a woman I met at a language conference told me about a barbecue where I could meet speakers, but when I called on the way there, she seemed to have changed her mind. I heard her telling someone, "This woman wants to hear the language," and among the muffled responses I could hear over the line, a man said, "Well, tell her to stop and ask people on the street in Tahlequah," and there was laughter. She said to me, "We were speaking it earlier, but now we've stopped, and there's no point in your coming out here." I didn't have directions, so I didn't push her.

The two sides of the Cherokee Nation coexisted uneasily; I had met a tow-truck driver who admitted he was part Cherokee but didn't participate in their national holiday, which he said was "just a bunch of drunk Indians." I noticed the way administrators at Head Start said "Kenwood is an Indian community," and the way people from the backwoods talked about going to "Cherokee Nation"—as if it were another country. What I was seeing was the layered complexity of the area: Some Cherokees were colonized, some put on colonial airs; they were as genteel, poor, divided, deep, and haunted as the South itself. (Indeed, at some level they *were* the South. Its most loved traditions—from its folktales to its river-loving Baptists to its corn pone and succotash—had roots in the southeastern tribes that were among the first slaves and the last slave owners.)

Boarding schools like Sequoyah did not create the rural–urban divide, but their poor treatment of Cherokee culture fueled and supported the logic of resistance to assimilation and to the modern Cherokee Nation itself. Between 1907 and 1975, the Cherokee Nation's chiefs were appointed by the federal government, and even after the government began electing chiefs again, the assimilated types who emerged as leaders were seen as serving a white agenda.

As many as ten thousand Cherokees—including many of the most rural, traditional communities—belonged to an alternative political organization called the United Keetoowah Band. The UKB, which required one-quarter Cherokee blood for membership, had a larger percentage of speakers among its membership. But the Cherokee-language survey didn't interview people who were not enrolled with the Cherokee Nation, effectively excluding any speakers registered with the Keetoowah Band from its tally. Some Keetoowahs (pronounced *ke-TOO-wah*) also complained that some speakers failed the Cherokee Nation language-certification test because of dialect differences and that with the pilot program in highly assimilated Tahlequah, no funds were allocated for busing in the rural children who were most likely to be able to practice their Cherokee at home.

Back at the Cherokee Nation's Cultural Resource Center, Dr. Sly was skeptical about problems with dialect and noted that the test's emphasis on biliteracy—reading and writing in Cherokee—was a problem for some test takers. Meanwhile, Dr. Sly said, some critics still hadn't accepted that Cherokee could be taught in classrooms. They believed it should be taught at home as it had been in the old days. "But it can't be taught there," she added with her characteristic snap. "Daddy and Mommy don't speak it anymore!"

Her point reminded me of Sadie Parnell: Why indeed would you need an immersion school if you hadn't lost the linguistic bond between mother and child—if, indeed, the Cherokees hadn't at some level become cultural orphans? The old boarding schools had used hundreds of staffers and millions in government funds to move children into English, the dominant language. Getting Cherokee back, once lost, would require even greater efforts—if indeed it could be done. And this time, the federal government wasn't making it a priority. As Sly said: "The amount they used to eradicate the languages is not there to replace it."

At the same time, I felt the picture wasn't complete. Given the complexity of the Cherokee population, it seemed that school classes might be only one front for the transmission of the language. What if Cherokee Nation was missing something: some holdout homes where the parents still spoke Cherokee? The presence of one exception—the young teacher, Elk—suggested there were still communities like that. And the best chances for the language had to lie in these places, settlements where language was an integral part of a social bond, where traditional life continued unbroken, and where language was a live line between the generations. In search of these places—the real lost cities—I would return later to Cherokee country, following a chain of chance contacts.

As I watched Lula Elk read, a long chain of pointed darts protruded toward my face. I had nearly tuned out the other little boys shooting each other, using few words of any language other than the universal "Pow!" and "Bang!" I moved the darts away gently and turned around: "Bang!" a little boy said. He was shooting me.

I picked up a shorter stick of plastic darts and warded his off. We played until the plastic darts fell apart. "You broke it," he said accusingly in English. I felt guiltier that he had spoken English.

Then he put it together again and I warded him off with something that looked like a small shield until I realized it was some sort of recording device called a "Little Linguist." I hastily put it down.

I felt that my English-speaking presence was contaminating the class. The all-Cherokee environment was that fragile. As I waved to Elk and edged toward the exit, a little girl started running around, pointing to signs on the walls with Cherokee writing. "What does *this* say?" she said to an older teacher. I backed out the door.

After I left the school, I found myself thinking about Sadie Parnell, and I wondered if people still carved headstones in the Cherokee alphabet. I drove to the Cherokee Heritage Center, which happened to be nearby. It wasn't open, but I talked to a woman standing outside calling for a cat named Tut. He came running up. Around his eyes were sexy-looking natural black lines. I asked if stone carvers used the alphabet, and she said, "Yes, I bet there are some, because, you know, the Cherokee language is coming back."

On my way back to Tulsa, I drove by the school again, and again passed Economy Storage, site of the former graveyard. Don Franklin at the school called the defunct graveyard "the forgotten club." Then I drove on by the school, and a few minutes later I came to Greenleaf Cemetery. Greenleaf was the place where the municipality moved stones from lost graveyards—some came from a town flooded by a dam, and others were from the old graveyard, across from Sequoyah. Thinking of Parnell's grandfather, I stopped my car and got out there.

It was getting gloomy, with rain patting on the granite and slapping on the tin. I'm a minor cemetery buff, and this was one of the poorer cemeteries I'd seen, the field fenced off with sagging wires. The stones weren't very old, and yet it was all decrepit. It's easy to forget that decay is measured not in time but in ability to maintain things, which represents some combination of work plus money plus caring.

These were the gravestones of the poor: The oldest were granite, carefully chipped to headstone size, with key-scratched words in the Cherokee syllabary and numbers like 1882–1923. Then there were hand-lettered slabs of concrete with single names—M O S E and M A S O N—and rough hearts, drawn with a stick when the concrete was wet.

Some were tin plates with names written in black marker. It was thin institutional tin, like we see sometimes in military cemeteries. There was one that said: UNKNOWN FROM #30 AMBER HALL NO. 49. 8-11-42. Another said: WHITEWATER INFANT. This was the horror of institutionalization: Those who buried these people here did not know them.

Sometimes the tin plates were gone, rusted off, and there was just a tin stick. Sometimes there was a single brick.

Some gravestones were actual stones—chunks of granite covered with pale lichen and moss. My overeducated mind found them picturesque, but they also reminded me of Parnell's story—these were the kind of stones that her grandfather would have had.

Each monument told less than the one before, as if counting the stages of the movement toward forgetting, oblivion, pure loss from all human memory. The verb *to silence* is a trendy term that is rarely used literally. But sometimes people really are silenced. When they have no language to bridge the gap between generations, to allow the past to speak to the present, their history is silenced in a profound way. They become orphans.

One side of my family was from the South, and as I grew up I quickly became aware of slavery's reverberations. When we visited the old family land in Panola County, Mississippi, I understood the significance of the little graveyard where the tombstones of sharecroppers lay toppled beside the cotton fields. But it was not until I was much older that I knew that the county's name, *Panola*, was the Choctaw word for "cotton" and that before my ancestors were there, the Choctaws were "removed," in the bureaucratic language of the time. Even in the history-obsessed South, these things had been virtually forgotten, because there was no one left to tell the tale.

The blank, eroded markers seemed a visual symbol of this loss. There were no witnesses, no signs that anyone was there. Missing: the record of the death. Missing: the cemetery. When the grave site is lost, the death itself is lost. There is nothing left even to mourn.

CHAPTER FIVE

Plan B

NOT EVERYONE LETS GO of their dead. There are people who freeze-dry their dogs. There are Web sites devoted to fortune-cookie messages. There are societies for the preservation of railway depots, barbed wire, blast furnaces, terra-cotta (Friends of Terra Cotta), comedians' gag files, string figures, and Hackensack's water-filtration plant. The Smithsonian has fifty-five thousand drawers full of beetles, not to mention recordings of the sounds of insects' wingbeats, the movement of the intestines, and the heartbeat of Laika, the Russian dog launched into space. Record-storage company Iron Mountain Inc. houses about two hundred million cartons of paper. A Cassini probe on its way to Saturn carries a DVD-ROM with 616,403 people's signatures.

Some people are even trying to put disappearing cultures on a hard drive.

I realized there were alternatives to the graveyard as I joined a group of people around a breakfast table littered with high-tech audio equipment: a Philips CD player, a Compaq Presario 1200 with a CD-ROM drive, a slender portable microphone, and tiny, transparent speakers. The shine of the disks and the delicacy of the little keyboards lent a kind of authority to the project: We were mustering the best we had, the most sophisticated products of our time, to preserve a language. The guy operating the archiving equipment, Brian Levy, gave me a handout that said, combining countercultural defiance with mainstream technological optimism, "How can we defy the injustice and the senselessness, which is too much of the history of the world, through digital technology?"

Levy fiddled with some equipment, and a hypnotic song emerged: a fast drumbeat, a rattle adding a layer of rhythm, and an old man's voice, singing a few phrases over and over. An elder from the Caddo tribe had recorded himself singing peyote songs. "If you close your eyes, it's almost like he's there," Levy mused.

Levy called the project "Plan B." Plan A, of course, was natural transmission of the language to a new generation, but in the Caddo tribe only about twenty-five people were left to speak the language, and they were nearly all over seventy. So Levy, a white thirty-one-year-old, was trying to record as much of the language as he could.

Several times a week, Levy went to the house of eighty-six-year-old Wilson Kionute to tape him talking, singing, or telling old stories. Kionute had no wife or children and could interest few other Caddos in listening to him. So he was passing his legacy—his knowledge of the language, his stories about the culture—to a young outsider. Or, more accurately, to the video- and audiotape archives. In their sessions, Levy tried to think of everything anyone could possibly talk about in Caddo: names of animals, trees, birds, horses, car parts, Memorial Day ("when you put the flowers down"), as well as expressions for talking about hunting, fishing, driving, and watching baseball on TV, stories about the creation of day and night and how the tortoise got its squares, sex acts. "What if a Caddo wakes up in a hundred years and says, 'I wonder how the Caddos said 'jerk off'?" Levy said. "Well, it depends how you do it . . ." He was locking all these data on the language in a trove of recordable CDs and digital audiotapes.

Listening to the tapes, I thought of Richard Codopony repeating Carney Saupitty's Comanche stories and of Charles Chibitty and his adopted granddaughter. This was the strangest yet of the ad hoc adoptions that transmitted each language.

I first met Levy at a conference in south-central Oklahoma. I had gone there in the hope of finding someone who would help me reach a thriving language community. But at the conference, as always, people were talking about languages in need of rescue. In Oklahoma, the Euchee, Otoe, Ponca, Kansa, Osage, Quapaw, Pawnee, Wichita, and Plains Apache tribes were all down to twenty-five or fewer speakers.

Those who work with small tribes employ euphemisms like *less commonly taught* or *sleeping languages,* aiming to keep spirits up. In a conversation I had with Linda Jordan, a researcher who was working to protect Cherokee, she evoked the power of positive thinking. "I've had this insistence that we have to think about these languages as living languages. My dad should have died last August but stayed alive until November. We treated him as if he was alive. These doctors would treat him as if he was dying, but we fed him; it kept him alive." As for bad news on the languages, she said, "If I were to internalize it, it could hasten the languages' death." I didn't point out that she had chosen as her analogy a terminal case.

When I first walked into the building, a meeting house at an old church campground, I heard a linguist talking about a practice called Self-Immersion. It brought to mind Richard Codopony and his horse. "If you have nobody to practice with, practice with yourself," said the linguist, Akira Yamamoto, who was the head of a language-preservation group called Oklahoma Native American Language Development Institute. "Home is the ideal place for total immersion," he continued. You could wake up and greet the sun in your language; you could talk to yourself in the mirror as you brushed your teeth; you could name your breakfast foods to yourself.

After the meeting was over, I wandered toward a couple of men in loud conversation. "How about if we keep this stuff alive in archival form?" one said. This was Brian Levy. He was dark-eyed, animated, and intense, and he spoke with the fastest Louisiana drawl I had ever heard.

The other man jumped in: "I'm not interested in pickling the language and putting it on some shelf in the Smithsonian," he began. This was Richard Grounds. With his thick ponytail and casual jeans, he looked scarcely older than Levy, but his booming voice and scholarly locutions gave him away as a professor. His tribe, the Euchees, had only six speakers left. But he said he would rather burn the tapes of the language than see them survive a tribe that no longer used the language.

They walked outside, and I followed them to the porch of the old bunkhouses, where we stood and talked as it grew darker and the light of a single bulb drew a muted crowd of bugs. I realized that they were articulating an important debate, one that was being carried on around the country as people tried out the last options for saving small languages. I decided to join them at Levy's house when they met in December.

The project of documenting and archiving disappearing cultures is taking hold all over the world. The Long Now Foundation in California plans what it calls The Rosetta Project, a "near-permanent" archive of a thousand languages that will include translations of Genesis chapters, word lists, sketches of languages' morphology and syntax, and audio files. All this will be stored on a micro-etched nickel disk with a two-thousand-year life expectancy. Elsewhere, National Science Foundation–funded researchers are creating a database of endangered-language data, and the Center for the Documentation of Endangered Languages at Indiana University is archiving recordings and making multimedia dictionaries. On the Internet, linguists and computer programmers chat about how to capture languages in Java fonts. Dozens of Web sites present bits of endangered languages, from tribally sponsored dictionaries to a "Hall of Vanishing Languages" to whimsical projects listing fifty ways to say "I love you."

Most linguists hope for what they call "re-vernacularization," the revival of a language as a spoken tongue. These new media seem particularly appropriate for orally transmitted cultures, because they bypass writing. No one has to create an alphabet. CDs and the Web media can store the precise sounds of a language, as well as videos that provide context for its use, and children can learn from them before they know how to read.

The idea seems far-fetched, but the major success story of language revitalization, the Modern Hebrew spoken in Israel today, was resurrected from a largely written tradition. Other groups in America have started bringing their languages back from books and recordings. Members of the Chumash tribe of California, whose last speaker died in the 1950s, have used tapes and books to study their language, and a group of Wampanoags in Massachusetts are learning a language that hasn't been written or spoken for almost 150 years, with the help of documents that include a 1663 Wampanoag Bible. Having studied the "dead" Latin language, I could imagine the utility of preserving some form of Caddo.

What's controversial about the notion lies in the interface with the people themselves. The basic problem is that recording a language is not saving it. Pressing a button seems so easy: RECORD. SAVE. STORE. But these are misleading words when applied to language; to preserve the outward form of something (as in *preserved fruit*) is not to preserve the thing itself. A stored language has the same kind of life on tape as the rows of Indian headdresses I used to see in museums' visible-storage areas. And the vision of a mass return to Indian languages has a certain Miss Havisham quality of wishful thinking.

Furthermore, "documentation" of languages has traditionally served the needs of outsiders. Thousands of linguists and anthropologists have come among the Indians to collect and record their fascinating case markers, their rare verb forms. The Marquis de Lafayette in 1786 sent George Washington a list of Native words collected by a German natural historian. The American Philosophical Society of Philadelphia began amassing monographs on Indian languages in 1815; Thomas Jefferson collected more than forty Indian vocabularies and grammars. The Euchees, Richard Grounds's tribe, have seen as many as fifteen outsiders collect vocabularies or do linguistic and anthropologic "fieldwork" between 1820 and the present. Linguists have flocked to Caddo, too, because of the way speakers run its sounds together, "as if you put the morphemes [the sound elements] in a microwave," Levy said. But the resulting tomes have disappeared into university libraries, and none of this recording activity has helped the languages survive.

Plan B, because it is well funded and often directed by whites, tends to become a new Plan A, grabbing funding and energy from actual language teaching. And what are you left with?

"I do not see the value of preserving language simply as a fossil record, a piece of data laying around for academics to process," Richard Grounds said. At the conference, he was talking too fast for me to take it all in, so I called him later to get the gist. "What even is the function, the possible purpose, of having a record of indigenous languages in this place?" he said. "It replicates the most basic colonial paradigm, which is to record and document that which is being wiped away and destroyed. It is precisely the same society that has for hundreds of years sought to destroy indigenous societies that is at the same time bent upon preserving the artifacts of the society that it destroyed.

"'We'll take it with us to the grave'—that's what the old people say. In war, do you leave all your goods for someone else to come and ransack? That wasn't their stance."

The Caddos were once a confederacy of bands scattered over Louisiana, Oklahoma, Arkansas, and Texas. Between the seventh and the fourteenth centuries, Caddoan chiefdoms were part of a civilization that stretched throughout the Mississippi River area and created population centers as large as thirty thousand. Their towns featured large mounds for temples, graves, and other buildings. The tribe had a far-flung trading network connecting groups from the Great Lakes to the Gulf of Mexico. They exported salt from riverside saltworks that were still in use when European explorers like Nuttall arrived, as well as pottery and bodark wood, the kind I'd seen in a bow in Hastings Shade's backseat. The imports excavated from their mounds included copper from the Great Lakes area, conch shells from Florida, and flint from southern Illinois.

The mound civilization had disappeared by the time the Spanish arrived, but the Caddos resurfaced as traders. When early Spanish missionaries and colonial administrators wrote back to Spain about the *"gran Reyno de los Texas,"* they were adopting a local word—*teijas*—referring to the Caddos and their allies. Later, the Caddos traded with the Spanish and French—for guns to supply to the Comanches, among others. After the Louisiana Purchase, white settlers pushed into the Caddos' territory, and the bands were gradually forced off their lands. They arrived in Indian Territory in 1859.

Their economic life in Oklahoma came to revolve around the town of Anadarko, whose name comes from their Nadako band of "honeybee people." Anadarko was once the home of the Indian agency, which handed out rations; it became a trade center for farmers and gave its name to an oil company that left. Now, its biggest employers are a utility company, the Wal-Mart Supercenter, and the local schools.

The four thousand or so tribal members who were left couldn't get a language class going for long. They had a couple of healthy speakers left, but few young people ever wanted to learn anything more than the peyote songs, and even the most committed teachers got tired of watching classes peter out. A few Caddos started a language class, interviewed elders, and began collecting words for a dictionary in the mid-1990s, but they couldn't get many learners to participate.

"Everybody wants to be interested, but actually nobody wants to be involved," Charlene Brown Wright, the head of the Caddo-language group, told me. She herself spoke Caddo only adequately, not fluently. "I'm not criticizing, because making a living comes first. You have to feed your family, and it's just kind of an extra thing."

She was pointing to the underlying problem, one that didn't lend itself to quick technological fixes: The Caddos' culture had never really recovered from the destruction of their old life.

The word *Caddo* comes from a band called the Kadohadachos that came from Louisiana and Arkansas, and it was a coincidence of land and language that brought Levy to the tribe. Levy was from Shreveport, Louisiana, which is in Caddo Parish. As a bright and unsettled teenager, Levy had wrecked a car and his body, leaving him with one leg slightly shorter than the other and a large settlement from a malpractice suit. When he graduated from college in 1992, he had a love for languages but no idea what to do with his life.

The way he told it to me, he had been brainstorming about his future, using a technique that his massage therapist–spiritual teacher had taught him, when he came up with a vision. "I went to sit in my bed at my grandparents' house, and bam! I get this image of an Indian at sunset," he said. "I got so excited I jumped for joy."

He began networking with experts on Native Americans and linguists, and refined his vision into a determination to work with the tribe whose homeland had become Caddo Parish. He started traveling to Oklahoma to work with the Caddos, and in 2000, they started a foundation called Kiwat Hasinay, or "House of Caddo Language." They were carrying out Plan A—the teaching of the language—with a dictionary, a phrase book, and language classes, but Plan B seemed like a good backup.

Levy cut an eccentric figure in small-town, churchgoing Anadarko. He rambled around with a perpetual five o'clock shadow, wearing loose, organic-cotton shirts and floppy all-natural sandals, playing Lenny Bruce CDs in the car and practicing Swedish and Japanese in his free time. He took Aikido lessons in Oklahoma City. The postman knocked on the door while we were meeting at his house, bringing a letter with a spidery return address from Japan.

But Levy found friends among the Caddos. He was funding Kiwat Hasinay—at the time, he estimated that he'd put seven thousand dollars into it—and the group had little other revenue. Also, his earnest commitment to the project impressed people.

It kept me interested, too. Ordinarily I am skeptical of visions sparked by massage therapist–spiritual teachers, but I was intrigued by Levy's enthusiasm and his manic, verbal energy. As he said of another linguist: "I admire passion wherever I find it."

When we met at Levy's house, Richard Grounds brought two women who were working on the Euchees' language project, Wanda Greene and Linda Littlebear Harjo, and as we listened to old men singing on the recording, Harjo spoke up: "Who did the drumming part?"

Levy said it was the singer.

"And he did the gourd, too? Oh my gosh!" she said, admiring a rattling sound I hadn't even heard. Harjo had listened for things that I hadn't known were there, and so she could reconstruct the scene in a way that I couldn't. The moment spoke to all the knowledge that remained outside of each recording.

Grounds sat and listened thoughtfully. He was not against all high-tech archiving; indeed, he was a reluctant technology specialist: He was leading the Euchees' project to create a CD-ROM that would preserve the language and culture. But Grounds made it clear that his project was mainly aimed at making the language accessible to community members now, while transmission from living speaker to speaker was still possible.

Indeed, Grounds's career could be seen as a strike against the placement of linguistic authority in nontribal hands. After getting a Ph.D. at Princeton Theological Seminary, where he wrote a thesis on the Euro-American heritage of colonial narratives in Florida, he joined Tulsa University's anthropology department, though he was on leave to work on Euchee projects. In his wallet, he carried a folded, battered piece of paper with a quote from Eduardo Galeano: "Blatant colonialism mutilates you without pretense: It forbids you to talk, it forbids you to act, it forbids you to exist. Invisible colonialism, however, convinces you that serfdom is your destiny and impotence is your nature; it convinces you that it's not possible to speak, not possible to act, not possible to exist."

The Euchees, also called the Yuchis, were in even tougher straits than the Caddos. They had only six fluent speakers left. Originally from Georgia, with a language not closely related to any other, the Euchees had never received government recognition as a tribe. Most were enrolled with the Muskogee-Creeks, though many with mixed heritage joined other tribes. Grounds was enrolled with the Seminole Nation.

Grounds himself didn't speak much Euchee; he had only heard it from his grandmother as a child. Still, he learned what he could from the remaining elders, and he tried to use what he knew to speak to his two kids. "When Allen was little, I found myself saying, 'Where are your shoes?' and I went to someone and learned the phrase. I never said that in English to the kids again," he said.

He had brought along a Euchee phrase book. I thumbed through it enough to glean pieces of trivia, such as the fact that peaches are the apples of Euchee—the reference fruit.

English	Euchee
apple	peach / big
apricot	peach / naked
orange	peach / big / orange-color
lemon	peach / big / yellow-color / salty

The Euchees sat quietly, with their arms folded, as Levy spoke. They discussed technical fine points that might mean the difference between preservation and loss, such as how close to put a mike to a speaker and what kind of batteries to use. We discussed the fact that elderly people don't like to put on earphones. We learned to run a cleaning tape for ten seconds, to put a windscreen around our tape recorder at a powwow, to use a pH-balanced, CD-safe pen to mark the disks, to store them in an acid-free box, and to migrate them to new media every few years.

Levy said to Grounds: "Now I remember you saying if it was between pickling and nothing, you'd just as soon have no tapes of Euchee left. You even said you'd like to burn them if the last speaker passed on. I don't know, do you still feel that way? Why would you want to burn the tapes, if even the elders now see that there might be some purpose in making something that will outlast their life on this planet?"

Grounds leaned forward. "Because I believe the language lives in the community," he replied softly. "If you don't get it from the people who have it, I don't think you have it. What you have is the correspondence between your language and the Euchee, but you don't understand that language, and you don't know that worldview, and you're not bearing that same tradition."

You might, for instance, learn Euchee numbers. But could you learn Euchee culture, too? There were subtleties in something as simple as teaching a child to count. You didn't just list the numbers. Instead, Euchees faced the children and held out their palms. "It's like giving a gift to a person," Grounds explained. As they counted, they had to bend their fingers, pinkie first.

Levy put on another recording, this time an old one made on reel-to-reel tape in 1956. A deep, authoritative white-male voice, like the narrator of a wartime newsreel, came on. "Examples in the Caddo Language," the voice intoned. "Caddo, for Caddo language."

"Hasinay," said the nasal voice of an old lady.

"Man," said the male linguist.

"Shu-moy. Shu-moy."

"Woman."

"Nap-ke. Nap-ke."

They went on, a man and a woman in stern dialogue, eliciting wrung-out drops of the language. It was hard to tell whether they represented salvation or just another tape to clutter up the shelves of the Smithsonian.

Levy repeated the Caddo words, perfecting his pronunciation, and remarked, "He knew to elicit everything imaginable." He was pointing to one of the implicit problems with trying to preserve another language: Outsiders don't know what questions to ask. People often told me about stumbling on unexpected kinds of information. A Comanche woman admired a black velvet dress trimmed with cowrie shells and learned from an elder that the dress traditionally could only be worn by a girl who was the only daughter in a family. A Cherokee student happened on one linguistic distinction when she found that a native speaker used a different possessive form for dogs and for cats. She inferred that Cherokees used different possessives to express degrees of emotional proximity; the speaker didn't like dogs. It was a subtle shade of meaning, but it was part of the linguistic complexity of Cherokee.

Levy added that if someone made an incomplete recording of Euchee, at least it would still exist in some form. "If you don't grab everything, Euchee will be different, but at least it will still be Euchee."

Grounds sighed. "I think there's also a significant difference. Hebrew was a written language for some thousands of years. The whole literary tradition of Euchee has all been spoken."

Oral traditions exist in the context of relationships. Unlike Western written literature, traditional stories are performances for particular people at particular times, and many elders didn't conceive of them as general information. A key feature of modern technology is its ability to make mass quantities, but many elders didn't want copies made. It wasn't so much that they feared digital burglars would start remixing the Caddo turkey dance without giving them royalties. It was more a matter of control. If ceremonial information was passed to people outside the tribe, it lost its sacred quality. You could get around that by limiting access to tapes to tribal members, but not every archive would agree to preserve limited-access policies *in perpetua*.

"There's power in this language," Grounds added. "I think it's something that's alive, and it only lives in the community."

Levy quietly switched off the tape of the Caddo and the linguist.

Greene, the other Euchee woman, spoke in her quiet, mellifluous voice. "I think the language is changing. I can tell from what I remember hearing till now, it's not as musical as it used to be." She

91

recalled greeting some older Euchees recently. "They were saying *fo-seh*, and when I said it back to them, mine was really nasal and it had a real Okie accent, and they just started laughing. *FO-SAY.* So I've been working on it, to not make it sound so Okie."

We laughed. Indeed, I saw the change as a sign of vitality: It meant Euchees were actually using the language.

As we began to finish up our session, we talked about visiting Wilson Kionute, the Caddo elder who worked with Levy. That reminded us of the world outside the room, the people whose voices were the rationale for both Grounds's and Levy's work. One of the Euchees' most active and loved speakers, Mose Cahwee, was in intensive care at St. Francis Hospital. Grounds noted that Cahwee knew an unusual amount about rare elements of Euchee culture, like the introduction of the peyote religion and the use of medicine plants. "He just has all this knowledge we haven't even talked about."

I asked Grounds if he planned to go to the hospital to conduct an interview. "When he gets back," Grounds said. "Right now he has a tracheotomy, so he can't speak at present, but when he's back to health we'll continue."

What looked like an simple solution depended on a series of frail people and frail relationships, and this human factor was the core of the problem with recording. "If you decide to invest six hundred hours of community time to work on a project for *gaka* [white] society, then I'm worried about the available powers of our precious community people themselves, particularly our elders," he said. "In a real sense to me, it's a trade-off."

He and Levy were working in real time, time measured in days of people's lives. The Caddo tribe had lost three speakers in the past year. If you found six elders, and you got each of them to tape two hours a day, two days a week, for two more years, you would have (2 hours x 2 days x 52 weeks in a year x 2 years x 6 elders) 2,496 hours, or 104 days. Could you pass on a language and a cultural heritage in 104 days? Would you use that to tape reminiscences, stories, vocabulary samples, or language lessons? Or would you have the elder use that time to teach the language to as large a class as possible? This was the arithmetic of cultural survival.

"If we can't get our own people to take effective steps now, there's no point in trying to initiate trying to reinstitute a language under artificial conditions," Grounds said.

Later that day, when Levy called Kionute again, we were at the Caddo tribal complex, a set of cinder-block office buildings in a rolling forest that resembled the Caddos' southern homelands more than most places around Anadarko. Charlene Wright was showing us the Caddo archival collection of 1968 recordings of powwows and videotapes with titles like *Mound Excavation Along Red River.*

Levy got off the phone and said Kionute, the Caddo elder, was too tired for us to go see him that day. We looked out over a valley, where the humps of treetops were silhouetted against an orange sky, and realized how late it was.

We began preparing to go, chatting about children's ease in learning the language. Wanda talked about a young relative of hers who pronounced words perfectly: "He's got that ear for that language," she said.

"Oh yeah, kids," Grounds replied. "They're better than DAT recorders."

"Do you think Richard was right? That it isn't worth trying?" Levy said later that night, after Grounds and the Euchee delegation had left. I had stayed in Anadarko, planning to go watch Levy tape Kionute the next day. We had gone to dinner and were driving back along dark roads where the only lights off the highway came from red flashes on top of transmission towers, phantom mountains. Riding in his car gave me culture shock; as we passed through the bland fields, Serge Gainsbourg and Brigitte Bardot were whispering a western fantasy on the car stereo.

I asked what he meant, and he went on: "Sometimes reality sets in a bit. It's a living thing that's dying, and I'm just trying to take snapshots of it." With few Caddos learning the language, even some elders had told him he was wasting his time. We passed Indian Hill Road and the sign for the Chisholm Trail, and he added, "It is a wacky thing to be doing this. I need to have my head examined."

And yet he loved working with the elders. The moments he caught on tape were so unique and so nearly lost, he said, that "it's a deep honor all the time; it moves me to tears at times." He liked being part of a mission to help save the small language. "I don't want to live in a world where the dominant society has eclipsed other societies," he told me vehemently.

I wished he wouldn't rant while he was driving, but I was touched by his ability to feel the loss and to let it drive him to action. Another reason I had wanted to stay longer in Anadarko, I realized, was that the day had stirred doubts in me, too. Some of Richard Grounds's comments hit close to home. "At the midnight hour there's a kind of colonialist nostalgia that sets in," he had said. "And now it becomes something that we pine for and belatedly seek to restore." That sounded familiar, and I wondered what stake we outsiders had in this project.

I told Levy that I thought the recording project was worth trying. He paused.

"We're just moving forward into the darkness," he said as we turned off the highway onto the road to Anadarko.

In my $24.95 room at the Anadarko Motel, there was a simple desk and a bed with sheets worn to soft threads, a thin, neatly folded towel, and a small book with a ribbon marking a page. I opened to the marked page and read: "And David made him houses in the city of David, and prepared a place for the ark of God, and pitched for it in a tent. Then David said, None ought to carry the ark of God but the Levites: for them hath the LORD chosen to carry the ark of God, and to men." Then there was a long description of a tribal lineage: Kohath, Uriel, Merari, Asaiah, Gershom, Joel—names of men long dead, come down thousands of years to this motel room in Anadarko.

Levy's Caddo contact, Wilson Kionute, had a voice that was hard to hear. It was small, and so was he, his body a skeletal frame for a red T-shirt and khaki pants. At eighty-six years old, he hardly ever went anywhere without a walker or a wheelchair. When he talked, he was all bright black eyes and large hands.

When we arrived at his apartment, in a building surrounded by open fields, we found Kionute sitting on the side of a bed pushed against the wall, his legs dangling toward the floor. He alternately leaned forward and slumped back against the wall as he spoke, his voice gathering strength and waning. He lived in the front room of a two-room apartment, with his bed, a few tables, and a TV at one end, and a kitchen area—a refrigerator and a table piled with boxes of crackers and old coffee tins—at the other.

Over the years, Kionute and Levy had developed a kind of familiarity. Levy, accustomed to their interaction and Kionute's weak sense of hearing, enunciated words loudly and kept a rapt eye contact with the old man. When Kionute tried to reach for something, Levy leaped forward to help him; he told me Kionute once bumped himself on the edge of a table. "His skin tore like paper," Levy said, shocked. As they spoke, Levy held his DAT tape player in his lap, tipping it toward Kionute and making tiny adjustments. Levy told me it had pleased him recently to hear Kionute refer to him as Brian; for years Kionute had called him *Tsah inkanishih,* "Mr. White Man."

On this day, we just talked in English, perhaps because I was there. I struggled to make sense of Kionute's mumbled reminiscences. When I told Levy how difficult it was for me to understand his voice, Levy said he might get dentures, and that would help. Dentures! This was truly an end for a language: depending on dentures to ease the passage of the last syllables.

Kionute had been raised with Caddo as his first language but was forced to stop speaking it in the mission school at Anadarko. "I ran away three times when I was just six years old." Now, he continued, "There's very few that can really talk Caddo language—you know, can understand it—and some of them don't even know what it means. And some of them, if you say something, they know what it *means*, but the meaning of something is how you use it."

He had spent most of his life around Anadarko, working as a laborer in local peanut fields. He had never married. The stories he told mostly revolved around the dilemmas that came from living in a white and Indian world at the same time: the cruelties, the little breakdowns of communication with whites, the sense that white and Indian mixed even inside individuals. His stories were short; you had to take them for what they were, meager threads to the past. Even with the best recording equipment, it was hard for him to articulate his world.

I asked him if there were hymns in Caddo, and he rummaged through knickknacks on a bedside table, looking for a tape. It turned out to be the drumming and singing of a powwow dance. He listened, nodding in pleasure.

Then Kionute recognized the voice of the singer and told us a soft story: "I was about seven, eight years old when I started goin' to them [powwows]. Growin' up, I used to carry the drum. I drummed for my daddy when he sang. I went through all that, and that's how come Daddy thought a lot of me. I wasn't joking with it. I meant what I was doin'." Kionute had grown up to be a member of the Native American

Church—the peyote religion—and also a Christian, "both the Indian way and the white man's way." Above the bed, I noticed a framed copy of the Christian "Footprints of God" story that ends, "there was only one set of footprints because I carried you."

"Daddy knew I was goin' to try to carry his ways," Kionute said. His brothers had become Catholics. One of his brother Jake's sons, Lyman, had rejected Catholicism and joined the peyote religion. "Lyman got a surprise out of that. We was havin' a [Native American Church] meeting, and Lyman, he broke down, and he says, 'You know, I wish I could have my daddy sittin' by me.' . . . Well, wasn't long, just about daylight, there come brother Jake. Lyman was wantin' that. He set down by Lyman, set down by his son. That's when my brother told him, 'It isn't that I don't like it. It's that I don't understand it.' He said, 'I guess I went to school too much, and I should have stayed with it but I didn't. But I still love you.'"

Kionute drifted a bit. He coughed, paused, and then regained strength. "I got all my feelings in that one way. You're talkin' about Caddo language, Caddo people. From way back, back in the 'twenties, when I got big enough to understand 'em, big enough, you might say, to know 'em, from that time on I learned my own people, what they are like. You might say I'm pretty well experienced with the Caddo people." He chuckled.

Levy asked, "How do you feel about how the language classes are going? How do you feel about all the stuff that Charlene and you and me—what we're trying to create?"

Leaning forward, Kionute said, sternly, "Let's just put it this way: It'll never come back." We looked at him, silenced. "But it's a memory. For the grandchildren."

"For your grandchildren," Levy repeated, nodding to me.

Kionute added, "The Cherokees, Choctaws, the Five Civilized Tribes, you get around them, they're almost like white people. But there's a history about them, and some of 'em still know something about it."

Levy prompted, "So are you wanting to leave behind the history of the Caddo people, the Caddo language?"

"Yeah, for my grandchildren," Kionute said.

"Are you glad we're making these tapes together?"

"You know what I've told you about that."

"You told me . . . that we just should do it on Mondays," Levy said uncertainly.

"No, I'm telling you about making this. You asked me if it's all right if you tape, and I said if you're going to make a benefit on that, then whatever your benefit, then you put some of it back in. In other words, if you're selling the *words*—"

"Oh, no, no, no—"

"—or writing a book," Kionute went on, "then that money has to come back, some of it has to come to the school, the language."

Levy said emphatically, as if they'd had the conversation many times: "Like I told you, that's what I'm doing. I'm not working for myself. I'm working for the school."

Kionute returned to his point: "You see, somewhere down the line, there's a history, you've read history in school." He looked at us until we nodded. "Okay, there's a book, and the language is in there. Someone reads that, and they'll begin to understand how life was back then."

Kionute's niece was coming over, and so we left him soon afterward. We backed out the door, nodding, thanking him, and leaving him sitting on the bed in his apartment. He watched us silently. He did not need to speak; he would not demand to be heard.

Driving back to Tulsa, I put on the radio. I scanned the stations: gospel, talk, country—"I still tremble when we touch"—an old-fashioned "Jingle Bell Rock," "Takin' Care of Business," and the news.

"Lucent expects a loss for the quarter and plans a restructuring. . . . Palm's second-quarter earnings are up 57 percent on sales of its hand-held organizers." This was the news, what we needed to know. It was picking out what was important, reinforcing it, putting it on the agenda for preservation.

I heard the loud and multiplied voices of our national culture: the talk-show hosts, the DJs, the Dixie Chicks, the president of the United States. Then there was Kionute, in his little apartment building sitting in the open fields of the Plains. His physical presence had stirred some quote in my mind. *An aged man is but a paltry thing, / A tattered coat upon a stick,* I recalled. *Unless* . . . I didn't look up the Yeats quote until much later. Unless . . . *"Soul clap its hands and sing, and louder sing. . . ."* His voice was so small, and yet it carried the memory of a people. The Caddo recordings were just evening things out, help-ing the fainter voices of our country survive.

I had always felt that cultural loss was a fuzzy concept. How can you mourn the loss of an abstraction? The encounter with Levy and Kionute helped me to feel the personal quality of it. As a journalist, I was accustomed to stilling my own feelings about loss, the way you might put a hand on the strings of a guitar. But this time, I let the res-onance spread.

When the Euchee elders said, "We'll take it with us to the grave," the image was not just a metaphor. The anger that surfaced in the recording debate was the anger of mourning: the tension between try-ing to keep something and letting it go. The imminence of loss was both a good reason to start taping and a good reason to resist. Archiv-ing felt too much like carving a monument. Voices on tape became a dead city where visitors could observe the empty grammatical structures, the useless walls of sentences, after the population had been wiped out.

The very invention of recording equipment was driven by a vision of death. Thomas Edison believed one key purpose for his phonograph was to preserve the "sayings, the voices, and the last words of the dying member of the family." The impulse persists: People now can buy tombstones with computer chips in them so that visitors can call up images of the dead. After the destruction of the World Trade Center, people created a Sonic Monument—a collection of "audio artifacts" of the building, voice-mail messages, tourists' video voice-overs.

There is something essentially twinned about the American mania for preservation and its sense of loss. The destruction and the nostalgia go together. And the pace of our archiving increases along with the pace of loss. Growing up always entails a loss of the past, but the sheer scale of the change now increases the sense of displacement. The news floods by, subdivisions replace countryside, and people move to new landscapes. (I myself had followed the common cultural pattern, moving away from Oklahoma at eighteen.)

These Native societies, entwined with their unique vernaculars, seemed to represent the struggle of everything outside the mainstream to survive. It seemed to me that the fate of the languages tapped a broader loss in common experience. In the poem "People," Yevgeny Yevtushenko writes about how "In any man who dies, there dies with him / His first snow and kiss and fight." The poem ends: "Not people die but worlds die in them." It was the private worlds that moved me, the ones that go away as we age.

It was the first day of astronomical winter, cold and clear. A gravel-carrying truck passed, spitting dust on my windshield. I drove through monotonous fields: This was not the sublime, open West but a moderate, nearly tamed land. Still, you could see beautiful things: the soft gray mist of twigs around trees; the frost-crisp fields, with white defining the furrows and the stalks; red mud staining old snow; a grass-grazed ice glaze in a ditch; fretted branch-shadows on the road; a dark bird in a bare tree. It was important to remember this day. This was how it was on the first day of winter, back when the last speakers were still alive. I understood the urge to write, to record things, obsessively, as if by describing you could keep them, as if by loving you could claim them.

A month after our meeting, Mose Cahwee, the Euchee elder whom Grounds had been planning to interview, died, reducing the number of Euchee speakers to five.

But the Euchees' own recording project moved forward, and they won a hundred-thousand-dollar grant to continue their work, hiring Levy as an archiving consultant. I found Grounds again at his office in the community center in Sapulpa, a suburb of Tulsa. Grounds taught a Euchee class to about a dozen students, from children to forty-year-olds, on Thursday nights. He prompted two elders, a man and a woman, to pronounce the words for him. (Men and women sometimes used different verbs in Euchee.)

I found him in a back office. He had just finished teaching, and the children in the class played around him as he fired up his Sony Trinitron. I asked how he felt about recording.

"I feel I'm stuck between both processes," he said. He still believed that learning from living speakers was better, but he noted that those living speakers didn't have the energy to teach everyone. "If we can make tutorial tapes, people can go home and practice. It's an extreme strategy only engaged in because of the age of the speakers." The computer screen glowed to life with old-time photographs and a series of icons. If you clicked on an icon, you found the dead Mose Cahwee, there and counting. Facing the camera, he held out his palm and bent his fingers, pinkie first, going one to ten. As we stared at the screen, two boys from the class came over, flicking around balloons on a string. One of them pulled at Grounds's arm. "Hey, can I play?" he said.

That spring, Wilson Kionute told Brian Levy that he didn't want to do the taping anymore. Levy said he never knew for sure why. Not long afterward, Kionute's apartment burned down. Rumor had it he was wheeled out with his wheelchair on fire. He went to live with some relatives.

Not long afterward, Levy left Anadarko. The failing economy had cut off the flow of income from his savings, and he needed to find work that paid. He called me almost two years later from Stockholm, where he had moved. He was immersed in Swedish and continuing with Aikido, and he was much happier there.

The Caddos carried on their language organization, and Levy continued to be involved, visiting Oklahoma twice a year, chairing meetings through phone conferences and emails, and editing a phrase book and children's book. But Caddo archiving was no longer his full-time work. From now on, he said, it would be a "lifetime hobby." He said: "What got me was that the immense task all fell on me, and my life was not meant to be that. There's such a limit to *time*."

He had created about 180 recordable CDs. One full set was in an underground commercial archive, Charlene Wright had three other copied sets, and one was at Levy's mother's house in Baton Rouge.

He believed in the importance of those archives. Still, he had gradually lost a small and intangible thing of his own: the belief that through them he had the power to save the language. "There is hope as long as there are speakers left," he said. "But the loss continues. The rest of my life I will watch this language slowly die. I have no choice."

CHAPTER SIX

The Kiowa Rules

ON THE DAY THAT I FOUND myself on the road to Anadarko again, fog surrounded the car. As the radio signals from Oklahoma City faded and fog closed in, I felt as if I were in a sensory-deprivation tank. I was driving west, but there was no sunset glow ahead, and the fog reflected my headlights back at me. The metaphor haunted me: The world I was seeking was invisible, too.

It was a year after I had visited Wilson Kionute and the other old Caddos, but the questions raised by Plan B resonated. To be moved by a hidden death was natural. But was any response needed beyond sadness? Was there anything—beyond shame over the American past—that made it necessary to prevent such losses?

One possible answer seemed to lie within the languages themselves. If we mourn a language, what we are really mourning is not so much the grammar as the passing of a worldview—everything from customs to beliefs to jokes—that tells people how to act and what to value, how to treat their parents, how to learn, how to age,

103

and how to approach death. To preserve a language is to preserve a philosophy of life that is deeply different from the Western European tradition.

The place we live is not merely a set of objects but also a matrix of ideas, memories, rules, and observances. We describe the world through scientific ideas and locations in space and time; we believe that phenomena can be reduced to physical causes, that people's behavior can be explained through psychological notions like "the unconscious." This is not to put scientific ideas on an equal footing with folk beliefs but to recognize that most of our everyday talk about the world lies in the realm of culture: The "heart" as the seat of emotion—and the concept of "an emotion" itself—are convenient but imperfect descriptions of reality. We use a set of cultural ideas to organize our thinking and operate a civic belief system based on notions like "civilization" and "democracy."

Likewise, other cultures are whole systems of ideas. But they are hard to see. For instance, Richard Grounds hadn't been able to explain exactly how Euchee ways of thought were different from ours—perhaps because he himself had been raised too far outside the language to know. Such things are literally ineffable, hidden behind the veil of language.

To understand another culture's ideas, as well as the way they connected to language, I decided to sit in on some of the Kiowa Clemente classes at the University of Science and Arts of Oklahoma. The course presented Kiowa and European philosophy together, comparing the ideas, history, and literature that guided the two worlds. In each class, the students read one Western selection—from Beowulf to Voltaire to Nietzsche—and one Kiowa story. In Kiowa, the course was called "two ways of thought."

As I drove by fields of a certain brown color, I thought of a conversation I'd witnessed as Alice Anderton, the linguist who ran Intertribal Wordpath Society, worked with a Ponca elder to develop a lesson plan. They were working in a schoolroom, and she was trying to write sentences like *The dog is white* in Ponca on a chalkboard. Anderton said, "How about yellow?"

After a pause, the elder, Parrish Williams, said, *"Zi."*

Anderton wrote it on the board. "What else?" she said.

"Well, you know there are some reddish- haired dogs, but they are also *zi,"* Williams said.

Anderton erased and rewrote her formula. They talked for a moment about gray, black, longhaired, and shorthaired dogs, and then Anderton said, "How about we get more colors?"

Mr. Williams said, *"Zi* is also brown."

Ever since then, I had thought of *zi* when I drove by the tawny fields; I saw them rippling like the coat of a strange animal.

The conversation intrigued me, because it pointed to the fact that languages divide up the color spectrum differently. Some languages seem to have as few as two colors—white and black. Some languages have only those plus red—the color of blood and some poisonous berries; others use the same word for blue and green. The field has been a ripe one for scientists who study whether language categories determine thought categories.

In the 1930s, a linguist named Benjamin Whorf hypothesized that language is a key shaper of thought. He wrote that the Hopi language didn't have past, present, and future tenses, and he suggested that "it is possible to have descriptions of the universe, all equally valid, that do not contain our familiar contrasts of time and space." The implication: "We shall no longer be able to see a few recent dialects of the Indo-European family, and the rationalizing techniques elaborated from their patterns, as the apex of the evolution of the human mind." Instead, they are "one constellation in a galactic expanse." His writing suggested that people's thoughts are limited to concepts that have language associated with them.

The notion led to a flood of studies on the juncture of language and thought. Cognitive scientists have been able to find some evidence that having a language that emphasizes the shapes of objects or the nuances of colors can sensitize the minds of the speakers to those aspects of reality. One linguist has argued that Chinese speakers have more trouble than American English speakers distinguishing between hypothetical events and real ones, because Chinese doesn't have a subjunctive tense.

It's important not to take this idea too far. We do think without language, visualizing, inferring, or counting. Translators—everyday commuters crossing from language to language—protest that their very existence shows that all ideas can find modes of conveyance in any language. While people pay more attention to those colors named in their language, there is no doubt that they can see colors that are not named. Meanwhile, scholars have disputed Whorf's interpretation of Hopi, noting that Hopis do in fact conceive of past and future, even if they describe it differently. Even the best-known notion about language and culture—that Inuits have more words for "snow" than other cultures—has been shown to be untrue. (It depends on how you count words for "snow"—we have *ice, sleet, slush,* and so forth.)

The links between languages and cultures have also proved shaky. Grammars develop in irregular ways over time, so that most of their major features don't have any cultural significance. Cherokees and Euchees, for instance, shared a similar lifestyle in the southeastern United States but had utterly unrelated grammars.

Still, languages make subtle contributions to defining each culture. Even translators allow that when they reword an idea, something is lost along the way. St. Jerome, the fourth-century scholar who first turned the Bible from Greek to Latin, noted: "Every single word has its own individual meaning; it may be that I have no word with which to render it, and if I skirt it with a circumlocution, I must make a lengthy detour. Add to these difficulties . . . the peculiar and, as I call it, indigenous quality of the language." That indigenous quality is the hardest thing to describe. It includes the resonance of shared memory and the definitions shaped by particular landscapes. A word is, as Oliver Wendell Holmes put it, "the skin of a living thought," a distillation, suggesting the culture the way a perfume suggests a flower.

Louise Erdrich has written about the subtle understanding she gets out of knowing that in Ojibwe, "the word for stone, *asin,* is animate. Stones are called grandfathers and grandmothers and are extremely important in Ojibwe philosophy. Once I began to think of stones as animate, I started to wonder whether I was picking up a stone or it was putting itself into my hand. Stones are not the same as they were to me in English. I can't write about a stone without considering it in Ojibwe and acknowledging that the Anishinabe universe began with a conversation between stones."

Things that stop traffic in Anadarko: a red light where no one is waiting, a train crossing town towing bins of gravel, and a man in a motorized wheelchair with an American flag flying from the back. Because Anadarko grew up near an Indian agency that distributed food and goods to many tribes, there is an unusual concentration, even for Oklahoma, of Indian themes: Indian City bowling lanes, Redskin Theater on Main Street, signs for Indian City U.S.A.: INDIANS—BUFFALO DANCING, one says, and then: TOUR THE ONLY AUTHENTIC INDIAN CITY. It was always difficult to tell what was new, what was old, what was authentic.

On a previous visit, I hadn't been able to resist following the signs for Indian City U.S.A. up one of the little hills that stood out so abruptly on the plains. Indian City U.S.A. was an unpopulated "village" modeling seven different kinds of Indian dwellings, from the

Apache wickiup to the Navajo hogan. Tame bison with tags on their ears sat quietly near the road, chewing cud like cattle. An expressionless old man in a cowboy hat led a group of seven on a tour, explaining the lodges and their accoutrements. He was Kiowa-Apache, and he seemed familiar with it all—when a woman on the tour commented that it must have been cold in tepees, he said that the moccasins he wore as a child were really warm. We stopped once at a burial rack, a framework of sticks with a shrouded figure on top. This was once common among the Plains tribes, he said. "Bodies are left on the rack," he explained in a small, flat voice: "It's a scaffold burial. This was used to release your spirit to the spirit world. Burial in the sky."

"Do the Indians still do it?" asked a woman.

"No," he said, adding that the Environmental Protection Agency forbids it.

Another time, when I visited the Caddos, I stayed at the Anadarko Motel. As I was checking out, Diane Mays, the proprietor, asked me to wait: She wanted to introduce me to someone, "A great Kiowa artist, nationally known. You've heard of Robert Redbird, right?"

I hung around for a few minutes, and soon a dapper old man walked in with his wife trailing behind him. As Mays introduced me, he sat down in a lobby chair, crossing his legs gracefully and letting his tweed jacket fall open to show a belt with a hunk of turquoise in the buckle. He had brought along a bunch of paintings, and his wife began handing them over the front counter to Mays as he began talking. "You wouldn't realize you'd find the top artist in America staying right here in town," he said. "I record. I'm a historian-artist. I document and portray ancient findings, ancient legends. I'm the only one left who was here in the old times. I don't do anything other than ceremonial paintings, because that's what I'm known for throughout the world."

He kept talking imperturbably as I examined his paintings. They were lovely and serious—spare compositions, with just a few shrouded, pensive figures and rich, textured surfaces. Often the figures floated against a sweeping, troubled sky, or a surface so flecked with color you barely knew where to look. "I've done so many wonderful things it would just boggle your mind," Redbird said. "I was an epileptic. Didn't have no future, nothing to look forward to. But I painted. Little did I know it was going to make me a very famous person." He pointed to a painting of three robed figures, their faces not visible. "See that right there? These are medicine men . . . That one there is blessing the water of life.

"Now, everything I tell you is real! I mean, even to this day, you can drink from that pot all throughout the night at a ceremonial till dawn, and that water will never go down. When the sun comes up and you drink of it, it will go down, but as long as that ceremonial's going on, it will stay to that level," he said.

Not knowing how to respond, I examined a white horse gamboling in a field. The horse was graceful and realistic, but what caught my eye was the field behind it, where jumbled colors suggested an array of wildflowers.

"Back in the old days, a white horse was very, very special. They were very rare. So if you caught a white horse, boy!" he exclaimed. "That was given to the elite warrior, so when you have all these warriors riding those horses and dressed in those red capes, boy, they're beautiful. Back in that time, they were like Elvis Presley. They were looked upon as a very celebrity-type person. Because they were death soldiers. They fought to the death. They were lucky if they did come back because they didn't care. Crazy men."

I asked if the field in the painting was a place he knew or a place he remembered or a place he had imagined. He said, "There's places out that way"—gesturing west—"that look like that. It's my interpretation of that. But it sure looks good."

The Kiowas had a vibrant art tradition, from the pictographic calendar records on buffalo hides that they'd used to record their history—a kind of indigenous writing system—to a series of drawings that warriors had produced in captivity. I later found that Robert Redbird was the son of a well-known Kiowa painter named Monroe Tsatoke, who used modern techniques to produce images of the past.

He went on. "You know what? I was inducted into the Motion Picture Hall of Fame with old Erik Estrada. I think it was not just my little part that I did in the movies as an authority on Indian lore and culture. I think it was more or less the performing arts. My wife sang, and my children played the guitars and instruments. We had a big old bus. We used to go to the biggest gospel jamborees in the country. We dressed in our Indian attire—our *regalia*," he said, teaching me the correct word, and he sat up—"Oh, I had that beautiful white war bonnet on, and I was singing: 'Hallelujah!' " His rich, tenor singing voice emerged. "Here was a lot of wonderful things," he said. "A lot of wonderful things."

"Do you speak the language?" I asked.

"She does," he said, nodding to his wife, a placid, round-faced woman, a retiring female bird to his red-plumed male.

She started to tell me about growing up in "the old way," as she put it: "We had a house and my grandparents had a tepee and we lived in both. My grandpa was a medicine man, and they were like doctors—"

"Boy, he's got a gleam in his eye," Redbird said, admiring one of his paintings.

She went on for a moment: "They took all the wild herbs, and they knew how to mix them to heal people. My grandpa's specialty was—"

"He's got a *gleam* in his eye," he continued. "I worked hard on that." We turned our attention to his painting, speechless.

"I'm a friend of kings," Redbird said. "Well, Prince Charles . . . entertainers throughout the country, celebrities of all sorts, even elite opera singers. Because I'm an entertainer. I'm always associating myself with June Carter or Tanya Tucker or Waylon Jennings or Johnny Cash, people like that. They may have celebrity status, too, but they're absolutely real people. Just like I am . . ."

His wife murmured to him, and he grumbled: "We have to go. It's okay. But I get tired. Everybody's tugging at me. Everybody wants me to do this, do that."

"He's a prophet not heard in his own land," the proprietor said.

"I don't care about that stuff," Redbird told me with a frown. "I'm glad to be home, glad to be living a normal life. But if they need me, I am a celebrity-status kind of person."

As I left the motel, I thought about the worlds Redbird had reimagined on canvas. I had no idea how true they were to their history, and all of Anadarko felt the same way, blending past and present in a series of incongruous re-creations. It was a bright, flat surface—like one of his paintings—that offered nothing but itself.

I was late to the Clemente class, having misinterpreted the directions, and after I made a dash into the classroom, I wondered if I was in the right place. Fewer than a dozen people were sitting at small desks, eating piles of pasty-looking food—white bread, white cake, orange cheese on a pale cracker. The people were of all ages, from the black-haired bundle in the arms of one woman to a big toddler on the lap of another to a smooth-faced young woman with perfect makeup to the grandmothers in their fifties. Only a few of the older people were talking. With a welter of late-for-class emotions, I nodded to the gray-haired woman at the front, who had to be Alecia Gonzales, the main Kiowa teacher, and she gave me a pleasant smile.

As with every element of Kiowa life, you had to know what was going on in this scene in order to see it. The moment I walked in, I was witnessing one of the strictly Kiowa elements of the course. Every class started with a prayer and then half an hour of eating and chitchat. The idea was to set a relaxed mood.

Nearly all of the students in the class I was visiting were Kiowa. But many of them were learning what it was to be Kiowa—at least at a conscious level—for the first time. "The kids themselves are trying to understand Kiowa-ness," the professor who taught the western part of the course, J. Sanders Huguenin, told me. "They're not sure what's what and how they're different." Their encounter with the Kiowa culture was more complex than mine: The meeting of European and Indian was internalized within them. The Natives they might need to talk to were their own grandparents; the country they wanted to explore was their past; and the identity they hoped to assume was both their own and utterly foreign.

I raised one big query early: I was looking for a community where the language was spoken naturally.

"Not here," Gonzales said. She noted that there were some people who were bilingual and could enjoy "fellowship in Kiowa," but it was hard for them to get together. "They're older, and we're fragmented now."

While Kiowa is taught in schools, Head Start programs, community classes, and even Oklahoma University classes, there are fewer than a thousand speakers left—Gonzales estimated that closer to four hundred remained. Gonzales taught Kiowa only at a beginning level in this class, sticking to words, sentences, and songs. Still, she said, "Kiowa language is a piece of everything that surrounds us, it's a piece of all that we are." The tribe was among the nomadic, horse-riding cultures of the Plains, and their loss, like that of the Comanches, was sharp and near.

She emphasized teaching through stories, a traditional concept. Kiowas used to learn simply by observing what went on around them, while the story "solidified" what they saw, as Gonzales put it. The class observed rules that governed the telling of traditional Kiowa stories; for instance, stories about Saynday, a mystical trickster-hero, could only be told between fall and spring.

Gonzales launched into the story she had planned for the class—telling it first in Kiowa, though none of the students knew it well enough to understand. Like many languages other than English, Kiowa marks "hearsay," or secondhand knowledge, within its grammar, so that stories are not told in the same tense as everyday statements—a small distinction that was lost in English.

When she got to the end, she told it again in English, interspersing Kiowa words for "meat," "knife," and "yes." She spoke in a deliberate but warm manner, looking kindly at the class. "It was about a couple of brothers," she began. In the story, one man's sister-in-law asked him to sleep with her. When he turned her down, the woman dug a pit for him to fall into. Later, he was rescued by wolves and went to live with them. When his people found him again, the wolves allowed him to return to them on one condition: The men had to give the sister-in-law to the wolves.

The class was silent as Gonzales finished the story. "And he went back to his family and told them. And the family said, Yes, what she did was wrong. They let the family make the just decision." She looked up as the baby in the class made a whirring sound. "And the chief wolf told him, We want you to get intestines and wrap her in intestines. With the consent of the family they did that. And then the chief wolf said to the wolves, Take her and tear her to pieces."

She looked up at the class calmly, waiting for a reaction.

"I knew that was going to happen!" exclaimed a woman in the front row, waving a hand in the air. I couldn't see much of her except her short, professional-looking wavy hair and her long, French-tipped nails.

This story could be used "to let young ladies know that [their] moral code has to stay clean. There are severe consequences if they don't," Gonzales said. But tonight she was emphasizing that the family's decision to let the woman be punished showed a harmonious example of a family bowing to the values of the tribe. "This tells us about the Kiowa way of justice. The family made the decision. You waited for the voice of the Kiowa, and the voice spoke, and this is how the judgment was made. *Khoiye-goo ha yah ah tdaen? Thau doy ahn tsaw ggah daw.* The word of the Kiowas when said *is.* Innately there are these rules for all of our standards or values that we have.

"I'm thankful for Glenna," she added, nodding to the smooth-faced young woman in the class. As people turned to look, the girl smiled slightly. "I don't have to tell her, Glenna, do this. Glenna, do that. Back then, they didn't have to be reminded." The rules for Kiowa life had once pervaded the community.

The woman in the front row spoke up again: "I liked that one. I think we've lost that kind of respect, and we need to go back to that." The woman, Johnita Haumpy-Williams, told her own story about tribal values. She'd grown up in Anadarko and was a teenager when her parents moved back to a small, tribal community called Carnegie. She said it was hard for her; she had been raised in the English-speaking mainstream with plenty of white friends, and at fifteen or sixteen she didn't understand the rules of Kiowa life. Indians now frowned on her white friends. On top of that, her parents wanted her to run for Kiowa princess, an honorary position given each year to a girl who embodied an ideal of maidenly behavior.

One night, she and her family attended a powwow. She decided to leave early with her friends, and when her father went looking for her at the event, she wasn't there. "When I got home that night, my father was waiting at the door with a horsewhip," she said. "I didn't understand what I had done then. But what I had done was shameful to him and the family: I had left the dance without his permission."

Haumpy-Williams had gone on to do well in white terms, excelling in college and holding down office jobs while raising a family. But it wasn't until now, in her mid-forties, that she had understood what happened. After she began taking classes like the Clemente course and studying her family history, she sensed a web of familial duties that she had never seen. "When I discovered my dad's dad was a medicine man, looking back on his humbleness and his kindness, I could see what his reputation was. Well, his father was a medicine man. I come from a blessed family. That opened my eyes. There were people praying for me before I was there."

Now, she said, she is starting to understand what it was to be Kiowa. She lives near her father, and he asks her when she returns from class, "What did you learn tonight?"

Gonzales commented, "Johnita knew these things but she didn't know the verbal connection to them. She never verbalized them."

Other students ventured their understanding of what being Kiowa meant: Each member of the family knew their role. Elders made decisions for the family. Younger people didn't interrupt elders. Men were served first. Children ate last. People thought of the community before themselves and were generous with material goods. People knew their relationship to each other; half the people in the class were second cousins of some sort, and they made jokes about each other's ancestors.

Jay Goombi, a middle-age Kiowa man who had helped found the course, spoke up from his place in the front row. He had a wide face, smooth, flowing hair, and sharp, watchful eyes. "When we started this project," he commented, "I was explaining that there's stuff I've seen our kids do—they would get people water or haul chairs for people—and they don't realize what they're doing *is* Kiowa."

In many ways, I found the discussion oblique. These rules were not entirely unique to Kiowa life. They seemed to reflect a brand of conservatism you could find in many tribal cultures, from Armenia to Nigeria. But I did sense that most Kiowas possessed a set of common understandings. There was a concept called the "speech community" that was helpful here: Some sociologists believe that a speech community doesn't have to speak the same language but only has to share norms for speech, rules, and concepts of meaning. The Kiowa culture consisted of a series of gestures that insiders could interpret.

Indeed, as I listened, I realized there was a lot I didn't understand. Huguenin, the white professor, tried to console me later by saying that in a small, tight community, a lot didn't have to be verbalized but could be communicated with a gesture, an expression. "It seems like there's a lot of subtlety here," he said.

But where did that leave the language? The professors and I were somewhat at cross-purposes, as I was trying to figure out why the language was important, and the professors were trying to shed light on the ideas that percolated into the culture without being articulated. The whole class was an act of translation, ferrying meaning across the borders of discourse.

The odd implication was that the culture could continue without its own language, as long as people kept behaving in Kiowa ways. It might be like many of the hyphenated American cultures—Jewish, Irish, Italian—which held on to a sense of identity without a common spoken language beyond a few words. They had mores, expectations, and mannerisms, and the culture survived at some level. The words were just trinkets, symbols of identity.

Every now and then I asked a Kiowa for a word we didn't have in English, and I found that even young people knew nicknames and little phrases like *ne ne ne,* the *tsk*-ing sound people made when other people were acting "too fancy," or the epithet *zaidl-bay,* which you could use to call someone "crazy"—one person said his family shortened it to *Z.B.* in a form of Kiowa slang. One man gave me *kaunende,* an exclamation for expressing derision at a person who does something one is unaccustomed to seeing him do, such as a man who finally executes a U-turn after many tries.

I emailed Brian Levy, who had left Anadarko by then, comparing the survival of Kiowa words to the use of Yiddish in New York. He wrote back, "I don't think that takes the pressure off those fighting to save these languages. The little bit of Yiddish . . . is just like sprinkling a little tandoori spice on your cornflakes and pretending you're living in Madras."

But I sensed a bigger role for language in the next Clemente class I attended, as we discussed the Kiowa family. Kiowas have more terms for the extended family than English, and each family role has a significance that's hard for outsiders to appreciate. In the protocol governing family relationships, most older family members require respect. But grandmothers and children have a joking relationship, allowing them to tease and confide in each other. Also, the grandparents are storytellers, making them the conveyors of moral authority in the family. (In a sense, Alecia was grandmothering the whole class.)

The mother's sisters are not called "aunt" but "the other mother." The father's brothers are not called "uncle" but "the other father." The father's sister has her own term, along with a special role: "to pamper and correct the kids," as Gonzales put it. All the children of the father's sister and the mother's brother are called brothers and sisters, not cousins.

"I'm a mother to my sister's children," Alecia said. "All the children are children in common. Kiowas never had orphans."

Lavert Autaubo, a stocky man in the back row, spoke up softly, and the class turned to look at him. He said, "My mom's uncles, I call them Grandpa, and at work when I ask for time off to take care of my grandpa, they say, 'How many grandparents do you have?' " A couple of students smiled and nodded, familiar with the reaction.

Autaubo said that when he'd worked at a previous job, one of his mother's uncles died. "I call them Grandpa on my dad's side, too. My dad's brothers call me son." He wanted to take time off to go to the funeral, but because the uncle wasn't considered immediate family, his bosses wouldn't let him go. "To us, that's a grandfather," he said. "I spend as much time with them as with my own grandparents." He said he took personal days to go to the funeral, venturing shyly: "That's kind of sad, too, because Kiowas love them just as much as their immediate family."

The class was silent for a moment. I thumbed through the Kiowa textbook, which Gonzales had written, and I noticed how the words carried reminders of stories, landscapes, and activities. Instead of June, July, and August, the Kiowa had words that meant: "picking plums time," "horse racing time," and "time when deer, antelope, elk shed their antlers." The word for winter, *siye-gyah*, "cold like it was in the north," referred to a migration in tribal history. One old word for Friday was "the day to go to the agency," when people picked up government food rations.

None of these words was essential. They were data points, stars, scattered artifacts at a village site. Even if you graphed them, connected the dots, you'd only create a sketch of what you were missing. And yet if you had them, then the transmission of such values was smoother. The language was a reinforcement of meaning; a handy conceptual basket; a marker of identity; and a wall that kept outsiders out. It wove in and out of the culture. When the language was there, the whole was more harmonious. Without the language, the effort to reconcile traditional and modern life was like Johnita's story: It involved perpetual transition and frequent dissonance.

As the professors let their students go for the night, I detained the Kiowa class leaders, Goombi and Gonzales, asking for one more example of an important Kiowa term.

Goombi seemed subtly disapproving. "There's concepts that you just can't translate."

I asked what they were.

"You'd have to explain the whole system," he replied. I felt somewhat defeated in my effort to gather examples, but I could imagine an English analogy: Try explaining the word *trespassing* to people without property; explain *sermon* to people without churches; explain *wilderness* to people who live off the land.

I tried to go into the world of Gonzales's story, to imagine a Kiowa world—to transpose all that I had gathered into a scene in the past: In the old days, Gonzales would have been a grandmother telling her story in a hot, smoky tent at dusk; as you approached from the outside, you would see the way the skin of the tent glowed as the fire came through. Inside, the listeners would have internalized the history, the spiritual significance of the landmarks they knew. They would already know when not to joke and the rest of the intricacies of relationships. She would tell a story about a group of young men who accidentally created a horse that turned into a tornado, and they would know it was a warning meant to tell young people—even the strongest, brightest ones—not to think that they were beyond the advice of the older people.

But I didn't know the system, and so I was at the limits of my form. This was not Indian City U.S.A.: It was a city I couldn't tour.

The difficulty of comprehending the Kiowa world pointed to one reason that small languages were so hard to preserve. Support for the languages depended on how Americans felt about ideas they couldn't understand. When I asked the professors how the Kiowa language was regarded in Oklahoma, Goombi shook his head and looked down. "People here don't really want others thinking outside of the box." Of course, he added slyly, "if we had a Kiowa world, I wouldn't be letting Western Europeans teach their stuff." Still, he said, the whole notion of making everyone alike—linguistically and philosophically—was foreign to tribal culture: "If you were a Kiowa, you were a Kiowa. If you were a Comanche, you were a Comanche. You wouldn't *convert* people to Kiowa-ness."

As we stood up to leave, I noticed there was a lot of leftover food sitting in the back of the room. On this night, the dinner consisted of cheese, a ham sandwich, popcorn, and celery. I had brought soda, and I decided to take it back home. "Who brought all this?" I said. Ms. Gonzales had. "Why don't you take it with you?" I asked her.

She smiled and articulated another rule. "You can't take back food that you brought." Dr. Huguenin and I wound up packing it up and giving it all to another man who worked in the center where the class was held, acting Kiowa without really knowing how.

"I Have Come to Cover You"

Listen! Now I have come to step over your soul. You are of the
(. . .) clan. Your name is (. . .). Your spit I have put at rest under
the earth. Your soul I have put at rest under the earth. . . .
            —*Cherokee spell for destroying life*

MY FIRST MEETING WITH Toby Hughes had elements of chance, whimsy, and counterintuitive fate. I had never gone looking for magic. Linda Jordan, a researcher in the Cherokee community, had offered to take me to a hog fry where she said everyone spoke the language. I wasn't sure how seriously to take it when Jordan warned me to beware of "conjuring." She emailed me detailed instructions on how I should protect myself. "Put the food in your mouth, spit it back into a napkin and say (Quietly!) 'I rebuke you, evil!' while dropping the food on the ground," she wrote.

Jordan was a sort of rogue researcher who had started out in a Ph.D. program and then decided to drop her academic distance and moved to Cherokee country. Raised in Tulsa, she had negligible amounts of Native American blood, but she had taught Cherokee at Oklahoma University and had a way of making friends in that community. She'd get everyone chuckling with funny stories about why she was late or why she thought a spider in her living room had to be old conjurer George Pumpkin; she raised goats. She went to a local store and said she thought her littlest goat had something called floppy-kid syndrome. "Now I walk in and people just start laughing," she told me. She was cute, with small features in a round face and long, girlish bangs. Her biggest asset, she said, was that unlike many white academics, she wouldn't dream of telling Cherokees how to do things.

I never had a chance to put her anti-conjuring plan into action. We met at her house in a quiet, overgrown pasture and drove out a few miles to a rural house where she supposed the event would be, but there was no one there. Then we went to another settlement, aiming to find someone to ask. We turned off the highway, climbed the hill, and turned down a red dirt road. As I was enjoying the big-sky feel of the hilltop and anticipating our arrival, Jordan stomped on the brakes. "Something's wrong," she said.

"What . . . well, why don't we go see—" I said, trying to hide my worry that she was about to back out of the trip.

"I can just tell. Something's wrong." She hit reverse, and I braced myself on the dashboard as we went scooting backward along the road. "I have a bad feeling."

She took me to see Hughes and his wife as compensation for our failure to find the hog fry. "Native medicine is dying because no one can find anyone else to pass it on to. Nobody else knows this stuff. They're it," she said.

It's hard to measure the loss of magic.

Most people don't even know when it's there. If you're going to have a shot at seeing it, you have to take the word of someone like Hughes, who sees it in the following places: the owls, a form favored by shape-shifters, settling on the lawn; a medicine tree root that grows eastward; and the tobacco smoke—a vehicle for conjuring—that drifts up from the bleachers at Little League games in Cherokee country and settles over the baseball field.

Hughes sees something else: that the magic is vanishing. He is a practitioner of Cherokee medicine—a blend of spells and herbology—and he says he can't find anyone who can inherit his tradition. Cherokee children now are on the whole too assimilated, more interested in Harry Potter's powers than Cherokee healers', and few speak enough Cherokee to utter the old spells.

As language goes, a thousand kinds of arts go with it—liturgies, poems, prayers, myths, hymns, and songs. The oral cultures of the Native Americans have literature, too; it is just more fragile. Of all these forms, magic is perhaps the hardest to preserve. Linguists and anthropologists record stories; old songs get taped. But it's harder to find a university academic who wants to preserve magic or a foundation interested in funding the research. Old sorcery traditions are hard to chart and count. They rely on a cohesive worldview that disintegrates along with tribal communities.

Look at magic around the world. It has stiff competition. These days, the big religions are globalized and multilingual. They have representatives on hand 24/7 waiting to answer questions. At the low end, superstitions like Wicca and astrology are cheap and easy to use. From Korea's shaman women to South Africa's witch doctors, local healers are aging or becoming National Intangible Cultural Treasure No. 272, spiffing up their costumes and doing their shows for crowds who don't believe in them. And in tribal communities, from the Creeks to the Kiowas to the Hopis, the last generation to know about spells, prayers, shamans, and magic traditions is dying. What's left is usually a handful of taboos, a scattering of splintered superstitions. Among the Lenni-Lenapes, "don't point at a rainbow. You might lose a hand," I was told by Jim Rementer, an honorary tribal member. He had been close to the last speaker of the language, but he didn't know the cultural tradition behind that aphorism.

I have a confused relationship with magic myself. For one thing, I don't believe in it. But I am plenty interested in it anyway. I often participate in what we call "wishful thinking," a combination of musing, hope, and intuition, and I'm not inclined to undermine the beliefs of others. Aren't we all entitled to our own indigenous flimflam? Along with traditional wisdom, don't we want to know about traditional irrationality?

I felt I was witnessing something rare as I sat in the store that Hughes and his wife, Valorie, owned. A middle-aged Central American man came in and looked around. It was easy to identify Hughes, lounging in a chair behind the counter in well-fitting jeans and a dark green T-shirt. At sixty-one, he was lean and magnetic, with thick, graying hair in a ponytail, a thick mustache, and lustrous brown eyes that gave him the look of a Cherokee Omar Sharif. He was a good advertisement for his magic. The customer said quietly that he was worried about his heart, and Hughes stood up and began asking questions. He asked the man to raise his arm, and the man explained that a nerve felt dead there. "Does your heart ever flutter?"

The man shook his head. They went into a back room and closed the door. It said PRIVATE on the back.

The magic of the Cherokees has a distinctive feature: With its potions go incantations, and they have been written down for a long time, in a rare marriage of Western technology (writing) and Cherokee tradition (shamanism). When the Cherokee alphabet invented by Sequoyah was adopted by the tribe, it strengthened the old culture. It gave Cherokees a new pride in their language and reduced English's competitive advantage—one could write a letter in Cherokee now. The adoption of a local alphabet often strengthens a language and gives it prestige, as it did for Armenian in the fifth century and Korean in the fifteenth.

The traditional healers quickly found a use for the Cherokee script. They started writing down their like recipes in what they called medicine books, using the books as memory aids and archives and passing them along to their descendants. The spells became a unique form; it's hard to know whether to call them doctoring, magic, or literature. But that's the point: In Cherokee culture, it all blurs together.

The Cherokee writer Jack Kilpatrick, who along with his wife published several defining books about the spells in the 1960s, said that when word got out that he was collecting old-time medicine books, he received ones that were written on pocket notebooks, ledgers, the backs of requisition forms of the Union army, and cardboard torn from boxes. Kilpatrick translated a number of the spells. The way he put it, "Recently I read in the *Encyclopedia Britannica* that no [N]ative American society north of Mexico had produced a literature: Yet during the past five years alone I have collected from attics, barns, caves, and jars buried in the ground some ten thousand poetical texts, many of which would excite the envy of a Hafiz or a Li Tai Po."

Most of the spells were for mundane uses. Their purposes included: placating people who were offended; ensuring success with girls; controlling weather; influencing courts and ball games; creating goodwill in a gathering; making a road seem short; and preventing frostbite or bad dreams. Some were to be spoken by a healer and others by a client. The following Whitman-style self-affirmation was meant to make the speaker more attractive.

In the very middle of the Rainbow I stand.
I am not lonely.
I am a man!

Ha! I have just sought quarry!
I am a great wizard!

My Provider ever remakes me daily.

In my beauty I go about.

A spell for restoring affection ended:

I will change you into a mere dog.
You will be yelping behind me as I go: "Gha?!
Gha?! Gha?! Gha?!"

The tradition has come down to Hughes, who has his own collection of Cherokee-language medicine books, some inherited from his ancestors and some that he has acquired. He has created more than forty spells of his own, too, "to fit the needs of nowadays," he says: "to help people along with finances," to sway a divorce proceeding in the husband's direction, or "to make a drunk quit drinking."

. . . I have come to cover you over with the black rock. I have come to cover you over with the black cloth. I have come to cover you with the black slabs, never to reappear. . . .

In Hughes's store, I kept an eye on the PRIVATE sign on the door after the Central American man went inside, and twenty minutes later the door opened and the man came out, carrying Ziploc bags filled with dried herbs. Hughes sat down with us, sighed, and picked up his beer.

I admired the necklace of bear claws that he wore around his neck, tight enough that the claws sometimes twitched when he talked. Hughes revealed that he had "doctored them up" with protective magic. "There's medicine in each one of them," he said, fingering a claw.

His wife, Valorie, leaned over and tapped her own bear-claw necklace. "That's one of them 'Don't leave home without it' things," she said.

Hughes talked about magical healing as if it were as homespun and ordinary as cooking or hunting or anything else people do to survive. He helped a woman find out what had happened to her four lost dogs; he made people stop drinking; and he shipped away "medicine bags" of herbs across the nation. He allowed that sometimes he tells clients to let doctors take care of the problem, if their kidneys or liver have gone bad, or if they aren't following his advice.

The store, called Cherohawk Trading Co., sells native crafts—beaded booties, baby dolls, baby carriers, and buckskin shirts. Hughes carves many of the wooden statues sold in the store. "He's part doctor part artist slash Ghostbuster," his wife said. The store is sparsely furnished and has the feel of a front for some other operation, which in a way it is. The couple told me they get more medicine clients than art customers, and from what I saw, that appeared to be true. As we sat behind the counter that first afternoon—Jordan, Hughes, Valorie, and me—talking and eating take-out from Taco Bell and subs from Wal-Mart, the doorbell kept tinkling, and customers came through. Most of them spoke Cherokee. In between appointments, Hughes sat with us, talking in his slow drawl, with the accent of his first language clipping the consonants. He smoked

127

short, hand-rolled cigarettes, sending wisps of unclear import winding into my face.

Some of his work is simply herbal healing. When I was there with Jordan, she mentioned her poison ivy, and Hughes got a plastic bottle of watery black-brown liquid out of the refrigerator and gave it to her to put on the sores. He said it contained aloe and roots, mostly.

Since so much of the healing was rooted in herbal remedies, I asked if anyone could use the recipes, and he said even amateurs got some benefit from herbs. But he qualified this quickly, leaning forward to emphasize his point. "See," he said, "you take your heritage, traditions, it don't *work* unless you got your religion to it."

"The plants themselves are hard to come by," Hughes went on. "It's got to be a root that goes to the east. You take a root from seven different trees. Then you pray for it to be a medicine and leave something in its place. That's the religion." The anthropologist James Mooney had written in the 1890s that in one spell the healer approached the plant, went around it four times, pulled the plant, and dropped a bead into the hole where it was left.

I asked what people came in for most. "Depression is the biggest thing right now," he said. "It gets people in their backs. It gets people down."

He gives them roots to make tea. "It takes care of tightness in your muscles. They drink this stuff before they go to bed, like a hot cup, and when they sleep their nerves loosen up." He was vague about what was in it. "There's a yellow flower that grows on the river and you gotta have a certain one. This one's got roots to it. When you dig 'em up, you scratch the skin on the root and it turns purplish and that's the one." What was the root? He thought for a moment. "In Cherokee it means 'that blooms in yellow,'" he said.

He also "fixes" tobacco at every new moon. The way he described it, he sits up playing his guitar until midnight, and then he prays over a pile of tobacco. When customers light or smoke it, Hughes explained matter-of-factly, "smoke carries the prayers to the man upstairs. I'll tell them, 'While you're using it, just put your mind to whatever you want.'" I asked him if the customer who wanted an advantage in divorce proceedings would smoke it when he went to court, and Hughes said, "Anytime it's bothering him, if it's on his mind, that's when he smokes." Other customers might smudge their houses with smoke or, if they were having problems at work, they could scatter the tobacco at the office.

Hughes said he didn't charge exactly but let his clients decide what to give him. He has received eggs, turnips, frozen meat, canned goods, hats, shirts, a jar of wild-plum jelly, and a diamond ring.

Some people, he told me, used the more sinister aspects of Cherokee magic—adopting the forms of animals or casting spells on their enemies. There were fearsome figures in Cherokee lore, such as the shape-shifters and the "raven mocker," a witch who robbed the dying of the last bit of life. But Hughes stressed that he did not do what he called "conjuring"—using magic to hurt people.

A running subtext in our conversation involved hospitals and doctors who wouldn't treat people or couldn't cure them, giving me an idea of why Cherokees might look for magic. Nationally, nearly a third of American Indians live below the poverty line, and almost as many go without health insurance for at least a year at a time. Hughes criticized the local Indian Health Service hospital in Tahlequah. "When [patients] run out of money, they drop 'em like a hot potato."

Like many Native Americans who retain traditional skills, Hughes was raised by his grandparents. His mother died when he was two, and his father disappeared from his life. His grandfather, he said, was "a strange person," with his own powers: "When I was little, he'd say, 'Follow me,' and we'd go out in the woods here and there and yonder through the fields and when we'd come home he'd ask me if I'd seen something along the way," testing Hughes's recall of his natural surroundings. One of his uncles was an "Indian doctor"—while Hughes used the term *medicine,* he winced at the term *medicine man*—and the gift went back a long way in his family. They lived in a rural area at the far eastern edge of Oklahoma, and his grandfather taught him how to write the Cherokee syllables at home. After Hughes graduated from high school, he won a scholarship to art school but decided instead to work on high-rise steel in Kansas City with his uncles. Later, he worked in quality control at a Cargill mill.

When he met Valorie, he said, she helped him market his artwork, and they opened the store. She is his second wife. In an earlier marriage, he had three kids: a daughter of thirty, and two boys, thirty-four and twenty-four. None of them is in the healing and conjuring business: The oldest son is a carpenter, the second son is a chef, and the girl works as a secretary in a school. "That's one thing you can't do for your children is pick their life for them," he said, shaking his head like any modern parent.

He had no other heirs. Most people simply weren't interested, he told me—but the ones who wanted to learn usually weren't qualified. An apprentice "has to be someone of good character. They'd have to read, speak, and write Cherokee." He had taught one older man who "had his great-uncle's books and didn't know what to do with them," but most of the other people he met weren't capable of getting the magic right. "They ask once in a while," he said. "I've even had, well, what you'd call white people, English, wanting to learn it. I say you couldn't learn it. You ain't got the upbringings, the heritage, the religion, or nothing, so best just leave it alone."

Valorie came over to us and put in: "If it *is* a kid, who's to say they're not going to get hooked on a Pacman video game and lose interest? Kids today are a lost generation." She was animated and emphatic. She touted her Mohawk ancestry on the store Web site, but she had clearly spent a lot of time in a white world, and her style was more can-do pioneer woman—ash-brown hair in a bun with a beaded bun cover, countrified accent—than anything else. She ran the shop for the two of them and spent most of the time I was there chatting up customers or working in her back office. She had a pale, heart-shaped face with broad, Ingrid Bergman cheekbones. When she spoke, her blue eyes lit up.

"Procedure," she said. "Hours or days go into preparing this stuff. My concern is to have it documented as this is the real proper true way, have it documented rather than having someone half-assed do it. People think, oh, you put your little hat on, wave your wand and it's done. We're talking hours of prayer. It's not like 'I can't go to the PTA meeting tonight.' You don't go to Wal-Mart and buy a book and learn how to be a medicine man."

I could see why sacred traditions are particularly hard to preserve. Often, they can be taught only to those who are qualified. Richard Grounds had evoked the idea when he'd told me that Euchee elders wouldn't put ceremonial songs on their CD. Similarly, a Caddo language-preservation group decided to exclude peyote songs, used in religious ceremonies, from a publicly distributed songbook: A Caddo has to apprentice himself to a master to learn the songs. The trouble with these restrictions is that a tribe can run out of insiders. Thus, like plants that can only survive in certain weather, cultural traditions can die for lack of places to emerge.

Gus Palmer, a Kiowa teacher and novelist, told me that his grandfather had known traditional doctoring, which involved taking on the power of various bird-spirits and using their feathers. Any one of a healer's descendants might have asked to inherit the gift, but no one thought of it before the healer died. Palmer said that he himself as a young man didn't understand enough of it to ask, and his grandfather didn't ever sit down and teach him. The doctoring skills, he said, "are not knowledge. They don't exist in that realm. They just are."

When people talked about these spiritual traditions, I felt I was dealing with a sealed envelope. I couldn't see these mysteries. The younger tribe members, not knowing their language or traditions, couldn't look inside, either. So the old people kept guarding those sacred secrets, waiting for the right novitiate to come along. Sometimes, the right person never arrived.

Hughes said he had spoken to an older Cherokee conjuror—the George Pumpkin of Jordan's spider story—about what was happening to the tradition. "What will I do when you're gone?" he said. "What will happen to the magic?" The way Hughes told it, Pumpkin said, "You're on your own. It's just going. I guess it's got ways of destroying itself."

Hughes wasn't averse to preserving some aspects of Cherokee culture. He was selling a series of Cherokee-language lessons on CDs, and he had created videotapes that he hoped would help teach the culture. One of his videos had been shown on cable-access TV, and Tulsa's Gilcrease Museum had bought a few copies. On the video, he carved a flute out of wood while narrating the process in Cherokee, "just like I'm talking to my uncles and brother." He took a traditional approach in his *Let's Speak Cherokee* CDs, combining language and content. On page 3, you learned the names for four different snakes. On page 6, you learned "great spirit." You wouldn't necessarily want to study this book at night, as he subtly evoked frightening scenarios. "Kill it." "I killed it."

"Someone is following me."

"Do you see him?"

"He's from the woods."

"He sure is fast."

By contrast, Hughes expressed a kind of fatalism about the loss of the magic. It seemed he had accepted that it would bow out of existence quietly. But when I mentioned it, he said, "We can't do anything, and I lived my life doing what I can to stretch it a little further. What else can a guy do? I am not supposed to worry about anyone else. I'd be in there, crying all the time."

A little later, Hughes stood up again as more people came in—a short old lady towed along her taller daughter, addressing him in Cherokee. Later, the ladies would leave the PRIVATE room, carrying brown bags. Some of the patients I saw were there for "nerves," he said; one simply wanted luck. He gave the old lady "herbs just to keep her going."

After we had hung out for a while, things got a little strange. I was used to hearing tall tales when I visited Cherokees. Here, the thing was that the people telling the ghost stories were all testifying to personal experiences. There were photos presented with spooky overexposed spots, theories involving an ancient Cherokee cure for AIDS, and moments when Hughes would say something like "I was talkin' to her ancestors face to face," and look at me for a response.

Valorie gave me some tips on how to tell if what looks like an animal is really a shape-shifting person. "You take a flashlight. They're a shape-shifter if their eyes are red. If their eyes are yellow, it's an owl." Sometimes, she added, "If it's a person they'll start laughing." She recalled that an owl once flew alongside her as she drove down the road. As she watched, it turned its head and she saw that it had a human face and—she remembers this particularly—hair combed and coiffed like Elvis.

Hughes told stories about his own successes. A broken-down, half-blind lady came to see him, he said, after a local hospital had sent her away. He assured her she'd recover. "I says, 'That walker you're usin', you're goin' to be drying hand towels on it soon.' She started crying. She said, 'Nobody ever looked me in the eye and said that to me.'

"Two months later, I talk to her sister, and she says, 'We can't keep up with her. She sees great.'"

"She's quilting by hand," Valorie put in.

He ran with it. "She made six quilts. I went to see her and she was out in the yard raking. And sure enough, that walker was sitting in a back room. She gets around real good, she's talkin'. I told her, 'Now, don't be flirting with me!'"

Some things were far-fetched. But no matter what I thought, Hughes had clients. I was unsure of the etiquette and found myself trying to behave like a polite apprentice, not wanting to close the door to the world I was glimpsing. I didn't ask for any demonstrations of magic—which they had stressed wouldn't work for unbelievers anyway and might even turn against them.

By 9 P.M., there were no more customers. As Jordan and I got ready to go, I made a joke about wanting to get home before it got too dark. I also remembered that I had originally meant to talk about language. Hughes commented that language, like medicine, is coming down to just a few people. "They say when the Cherokee language dies that will be the end of the world," he said.

. . . Toward the black coffin of the upland in the Darkening Land your paths shall stretch out. So shall it be for you. . . .

I looked up from a book of old Cherokee spells. My interest in Hughes had brought me to a stuffy little room devoted to obscure Oklahoma books at the public library in downtown Tulsa, where I had found a book of "love spells" recorded and translated by the Kilpatricks. The only other people in the room were old men passing the day. A pale, white-bearded man with a wizened little body announced, in a genteel, Kentuckian accent, "I just survived a rather classic accident in my pants." Another man cleared his throat.

"I Have Come to Cover You"

I returned to the spell:

Like the red lightning . . .
Like the fog . . .
Like the panther . . .
Like the red wolf . . .
Like you, you wizard, I have just come to make
my appearance.
I will be walking in the very middle of your soul.
Now! Now the smoke of the white tobacco has
just come to wing down upon you!

I read it over again. Back in college, I had conceived my thesis in the English department as a survey of American epics, though I quickly scaled it down to just one poet. These translated lines struck me as a deeply American brand of poetry. They were Cherokee in inspiration, and yet they were also born of a half-assimilated, nineteenth-century era in which the Cherokees recorded their compositions.

It's probably a Western bias to believe that a language must have self-conscious literature—preferably written—to be of aesthetic interest. Still, I was always hungry for samples of beauty in language, and these spells struck me as poetry in the same way as the Psalms. They were not intended to be read as poetry—they were not even meant for a "public" of more than one—but they were careful compositions that used their rhetoric to crystallize the speaker's intent—to make the magic happen.

This spell might have been used by a conjurer to inject power into tobacco, which a client would smoke, sending puffs in the direction of the woman he loved. Recalling an older system of animal worship, the speaker invoked the powers seen in nature, building image upon image of stealthy materialization and dazzling apparitions—the way love

135

strikes. Red is a positive color in the symbolism of spells, representing power and victory, while black signifies death. (Blue is longing, failure, disappointment, and melancholy, as it is in American love songs.)

Alan Kilpatrick, Jack's son, noted in his own book that many spells use a verb suffix that can be translated as "have just come to / has just come." The suffix, he said, is a "time-conflating device." "By declaring their intention . . . as a semi-completed temporal action, re-citers reinforce the illusion that metamorphosis has actually set in." Shortened words and archaic expressions added to the power of the Cherokee texts. Cherokee speakers came to recognize common ele-ments, like a "Now!" or "Listen!" to get attention.

Kilpatrick noted that the powers of the words he included in his books "have expired over time and have now been strictly nullified. Their inherent magic can only be revived by submitting the texts to certain 'Going to the Water' purification rites."

In a similar vein, Hughes had told me that the spells wouldn't work in English. The magic lay in the specific language: "The way it comes out, it's got more power to it." He also noted slyly that key lines had been omitted from published spells like the Kilpatricks'. "They left the punch line off, more or less."

Indeed, the spells seemed to represent an often overlooked aspect of language itself: that which couldn't be translated. The word *spell*, derived from an Old English word for "talk," has two meanings. Both refer to the form of communication: the right way to put together a word, and the right word's magic. The current academic thinking on language regards grammar as a code, a set of hidden instructions that tell you how to produce something, translatable and arbitrary; the sounds themselves have no intrinsic meaning. So if you can translate everything, you've lost nothing. But—particularly in sacred lan-guage—form and meaning are so linked that they lose much of their power in translation. The words matter.

"I Have Come to Cover You"

The spell represented language as an irreducible atom of meaning. It occurred to me that what Hughes was trying to tell me was that culture was irreducible, too. It had to be transmitted in a holistic way—or not at all. If it wasn't passed along, I thought, the best you would have was books that you could read in places like this little room at the library. The old man was resting his head on the desk now. The room was hot. I closed the book and laid it in the metal returns cart as I walked out.

> . . . *The clay of the upland has come. Instantly the black clay has lodged there where it is at rest at the black houses in the Darkening Land. With the black coffin and with the black slabs I have come to cover you.* . . .

A few weeks later, I went back to the store again. I waited out a few customers. Hughes's brother, a tall, slim man who wore khaki overalls and spoke to Hughes in Cherokee, came to get some mullein tea—a purely herbal treatment—for his emphysema. Later, a soft-spoken old man in a preppy striped shirt went into the office with Hughes, came out alone, and hung around for a few minutes, looking at the glass cases in the store, until Hughes emerged and handed him a pack of Marlboros. "Here you go," he said.

"I thank you, and I'll get on," the man said, tucking them into his pocket.

"Take care, now." Hughes watched him go, then took a moment to sit down with me. He turned on a fan, lit his own cigarette, and took a long, relieved smoke.

To do magic, he said, "I gave up a lot of stuff that I love to do."

"Like what?" I asked him.

"Like . . . play music in a crowd. And like talking to people. A lot of people I won't even talk to. You're just lucky." He turned his glowing eyes on me. Certainly, I had wondered why a true tradition-alist would reveal things to me.

He smiled, but he was serious. "Now you take other people that come in, a lot of them I'll reject. I can tell when a person ain't telling the whole truth or [is] holding back something."

I was emboldened to ask if I could see his office. He shrugged, got up, and opened the door.

My eyes went straight to a snake on a table. It was coiled up on a hide, head stiffly and permanently raised, and arrayed around it were other curios: a shell filled with odds and ends, including a big snake rattle; a giant peachy-yellow gourd that held tobacco; and a rough river rock with three regular holes in it, as if punched by small fingers. On the wall above it were knives, scabbards, and the fanned-out tail of a turkey. Toby walked up to the knives, pulled one out of its scabbard, and held it in front of a clip-on desk lamp. It was obsidian, and the light pushed through its translucent edges.

Toward the front was a bench covered with fleece where a customer might sit. I tried not to stare at the little bins and trays nearby, which were filled with dried herbs, twigs, and husks, like the leavings on a forest floor. I noticed an industrial-sized bottle of aloe vera gel. Seeing me looking, Hughes picked up a little wooden box and opened it for me. "Now don't touch this," he said. It was filled with the daintiest arrowheads I had seen. One was the color of coral; others were crystal pale. Then he closed it, laid it inside a metal suitcase, and closed the metal suitcase.

I asked where he got the prayers he used. "They're real old," he replied. "Some you can make up, but most of them were brought down through generations and written down when the Sequoyah syllables came around."

He had memorized most of them, but sometimes he looked spells up in his own book or in his library of medicine books. His great-uncle had given him some, and he had acquired others over the years.

I sat down at the table outside his office door, and he brought out a blue Mead folder filled with photocopies. He flipped the pages quickly, as if I could read what was on them. I could see tiny handwritten chunks of Cherokee syllables on each page—each group five to ten lines long, like the poems I'd read in translation. Some of them had dates—1906—and some even had prices—one said $4. Another book he had was an old herb seller's pamphlet, with spells jotted on the spare pages. Just as Cherokee has a variety of accents, it once had a variety of writing styles. To help decipher these old books, Hughes had made up a personalized syllabary, showing some of the forms that the symbols could take.

I took a guess on symbolic colors and asked if the blue of the notebook meant anything.

"No, that's just the cover I came up with," he said.

He went back to his office and brought out a neatly organized folder, saying, "And here's mine." He had collected forty-seven particularly useful spells in his own book. It had an index.

When I asked him to translate one, he initially said it wasn't possible, and then thought about it. He flipped to number forty, one of the shortest ones in the book. "Let's see, uh, okay, here's one," he said. "This was to get people to like you."

"Oh! I could use that!" I joked nervously.

He ignored that and roughly translated:

Tsa da nü do gv gi si	Your heart . . . I have got.
Tsa wa tsi li gv gi si	Your spit I have got.
Tsa gi ga gv gi si	Your blood I have got.
Tsa wo lï de da gv gi si	Your breath I have got.

(The umlaut is used for silent vowels. The *v* represents an *uh* sound.) He let the sound sink in and sat back: "You put that in, say that over and over four times, and then you blow on your tobacco, and then you repeat all of that four times. And then when you're done, you've got your tobacco fixed up."

I mused, "So does this make you more likable to a particular person or to everybody?"

"More likable to people that you know. Even the people that should hate you, you know, they'll come in and they won't say a word." He let out a raucous laugh.

"So what are you going to do with all this?" I asked, waving toward the books.

"Well, I'll use it until I die," he said resignedly. He gestured to Valorie's office. "I tell her she can set up a flea market somewhere. But I'm trying to get enough together that she could set up a museum."

Valorie put in, "It would be one of those time-capsule things. One hundred years from now when people are zooming around on their jet belts, they could say, 'This is what people used to dig for poison ivy.'"

The magic would be gone, Hughes said, but the memory of it would be "powerful." When he was a child, kids made fun of him in school for being poor, but he was able to identify with what he felt was his traditional strength as a Cherokee. "Look, I know who I am." He wanted the next generation of kids to do the same thing, to know that magic was once part of the Cherokee array of powers. "The Apaches have Geronimo," Hughes told me; other tribes had their own chiefs and warriors. "But what if all you remember of your old dad is a drunk. You don't get anything out of it." He paused. "Spiritually, that is what destroys a community."

I thought back to Parnell and the loss of her language at school. *At least they'll have the memory,* I thought, *of who they were.* That was also the point of the Cherokee Nation's camps where kids learned to make blowguns and bodark-wood bows: a way to connect with images of strength and power.

After I walked out of the shop, I noticed it was just a storefront in a mini mall. I could hear the pulsing sound of a big truck idling. On one side of the shop were Liz's Classic Curls and Nails and Miracle Laundromat, where a dour woman in a sweatshirt sat at the counter, watching the door. On the other side of the shop, an E-Z Mart emitted a blinding white light. Its walls said, MAKING LIFE EZR4U—modern magic. I watched as a couple of guys got out of an SUV and bought butter-roasted pecans and Cokes. Then I drove out and got on the road that led through Tahlequah to Tulsa.

It wasn't so surprising, in a way, that I had met a magic man through a search for language. Spells demonstrate the most dramatic power language has: to create the world by naming it.

I thought of another drive I'd taken, with Brian Levy on the highway near Anadarko. I was scared because we were going too fast in the dark, and at the same time I felt exhilarated, aware that this very fear was part of why I was traveling—the thrill of Oklahoma's highways, where I'd speeded so many times, watching dawn appear on the rim of the Plains after a Comanche powwow or watching the horizon glaze in the unrelenting heat of summer. Now, as we hurtled forward, Levy started telling me about a peyote trip he'd had in Mexico, and I wondered aloud how that had worked on his brain. He seemed a little deflated. "Do you mean it's only my neurons firing?" he said.

I said yes, and we started talking about life after death, a conversation that turned metaphysical very fast.

While I was playing a skeptical role, it seemed to me no accident we were talking about trips on our night drive. It reached to the core of what gringos like us wanted out of other languages—as Huxley put it, "to be shaken out of the ruts of ordinary perception, to be shown for a few timeless hours the outer and the inner world."

At some level, I realized, the other arguments I saw on behalf of endangered languages are faintly boring. It isn't enough to talk about grammar or even the altruism of saving endangered species. What people want out of language is nothing less than a mind trip: illuminations, spiritual revelations, better ways, understanding of the human condition, knowledge of "what the visionary, the medium, even the mystic were talking about," as Huxley put it. Some people go to mind-altering drugs, or mediums, or yoga, or Tibetan monasteries; others go to language. They want lifesaving philosophy. They want to rename the world. They want magic.

. . . Now your soul has faded away. It has become blue. When darkness comes your spirit shall grow less and dwindle away, never to reappear. Listen!

Seminole Rap

A KID IN A WHITE HELMET and gym clothes ran past me, lowered himself to the floor in a few dance moves, and began spinning on his head, flexing and extending his skinny legs, flexing and extending, until the people watching began to cheer. An emcee shouted, "You never seen Native Americans break-dance?" and the crowd cheered louder.

About nine months after I met Toby Hughes, I was in the gym at Riverside Indian School in southeastern Oklahoma, watching the brothers Brian and Quese Frejo DJ a Valentine's Day dance. This scene, with break-dancers spinning wildly on the floor, was about as far as you could get from linguists, language committees, and old men's magic. And yet some of the best hopes for Native American languages lay here, with the generation that wasn't ever around when I visited their moms and granddads.

I had heard that the Frejo brothers were working Native words into their hip-hop music. The notion appeared unlikely. But even the smallest manifestation of the languages here, the shortest sentence, would represent something powerful: an attempt to interact with both ancient and modern cultures at once, to reconcile the two worlds. That was the burden and the opportunity for all the Native kids here, in this high-school gym decorated with streamers and balloons in the red and white of the Riverside Braves. And where the kids went, so went the culture; so went the future.

Brian and Quese (pronounced *keess,* rhymes with *peace*) were some of the more creative players in this process. "Hey, you got Shock B, we are Culture Shock Camp!" yelled the emcee. Shock B was Brian, standing on the stage in headphones, nodding rhythmically as he spun records and lowered glow-in-the-dark needles onto two different turntables. As the DJ, he was doing most of the work tonight, while his brother Quese, whose birth name was Marcus, was there to add flavor, picking up the microphone occasionally and rapping in his sharp voice. They were a clean-cut, TV-ready pair with just enough contrast to set them apart: Quese, the rapper, slim and boyish at twenty-five, Brian, the DJ, muscular and handsome at thirty-five; Quese, pale and long-faced, Brian, darker, with a strong nose and high cheekbones that had once helped him get cast as a warrior in the movie *Last of the Mohicans;* Quese, quicksilver, light on his feet, Brian, rugged, anchoring the beat. Their father was Pawnee, and their mother was Seminole; they were a pan-Indian mix, like many of the young people here. Kids looked up at the stage and admired the guys, and some of them came over and tried to catch their attention. "What up, Brian," some kid called.

There were a lot of things that appealed to me about what they were doing. Using a Native language in hip-hop would show that the language didn't have to be tied too closely to a traditional lifestyle but could be compatible with modern life. It could potentially be a way of carrying forward an oral culture. It also represented the kind of spontaneous linguistic inventiveness that was missing from the language committees I had seen.

Yet the idea of putting Native languages into hip-hop—a form that has oratorical precedents in West Africa and an American urban sensibility—was problematic as well. Could Native American culture incorporate hip-hop, or was the opposite occurring, making the language merely a "sample" in a quintessentially American form?

To Brian, the notion of cultural purity was somewhat passé. "I can fancy-dance [at a powwow], and then start rocking as a B-Boy," he told me the first time we met, in a cavernous, empty sports bar in downtown Oklahoma City. He had grown up in the powwow culture, which evolved with the times—people could wear gold lamé and sell cotton candy, and yet the essence of a community gathering persisted. Sometimes he and Quese even performed hip-hop sideshows at powwows.

Most of his generation hadn't had the chance to speak a Native language, because their parents couldn't teach them. This was a post-loss generation, and so they had to make supreme efforts to get back to their languages. They had to steer between the "Indian" identity thrust on them from the outside and the known heritage they were able to gather from their relatives.

Brian and Quese had come far to get to this point. Growing up in a largely white Oklahoma City suburb called Moore, with parents who came from different tribes, the brothers didn't learn any language but English at home. Seminole was their mother's language. The Oklahoma Seminole dialect, counted together with the similar Muskogee-Creek language, has as many as six thousand speakers. (There are also Seminole speakers in Florida.) The brothers heard the language whenever they went to visit their mother's family. Their uncles and a grandmother spoke it, and even their mother used it with her older relatives. "We knew what they meant, but we wouldn't sit there and have a conversation with them," Brian said.

Pawnee, the language of their father's tribe, is almost lost, with just four speakers left. They heard elders who spoke it when they went to visit their father's side of the family, but it wasn't taught anywhere outside community classes. There is one young person who speaks Pawnee, a twenty-six-year-old named Adrian Horsechief who grew up with his grandparents near the town of Pawnee. But the classes Horsechief teaches, nearly two hours' drive from Oklahoma City, are some of the only ones in the world. "If it wasn't for Adrian, five or ten years from now, Pawnee would be an extinct language," Brian said. "I want to keep it going, but I have to make that effort."

It was hard for Brian to put in the time. He had a history of unusual achievement, but there was much he sought to escape in his home culture. "When I was eleven, I saw my cousin, an all-state basketball player, become an alcoholic the next summer. I had thought I wanted to be good like him. And when I saw him, he was drunk, and didn't know who I was. 'Who are you? Got some money?' He was like some old drunk, and I was like, 'Man, screw this.'"

Brian's father drank, too, and largely as a result, his parents got divorced. One summer, Brian said, his father insisted that he live in Pawnee, Oklahoma, to spend some time around the Pawnee side of the family. The life he saw there troubled him. "It motivated me not to want to drink, seeing my uncles and my dad drink and drunk and my cousins, the all-state basketball player, be alcoholics. My dad was drinking, and one time he was passed out on the bathroom floor. I remember picking him up and the smell . . . alcohol, sweat, cigarettes."

What bothered Brian the most is that his uncles jokingly accused him of drinking, and when they told his father he had been drinking, his father didn't believe his denial. "I was like, 'Man, you want me to be drunks like you,'" he said. "They wanted to categorize me like them. It was almost like they thought it was funny. It made me not want to be like them."

After a dispute in which he called his aunts and uncles drunks, he left Pawnee, went back to his old high school, and threw himself into basketball. He had a coach who tried to discourage him from playing, but Brian refused to quit the team. "I did it almost out of spite for the coach," he said. Eventually, he became a captain, taking his team to the state semifinals. By his senior year, he felt he had proved himself. One day, when Brian and his father were meeting for breakfast, they saw in the paper that Brian had been picked for the all-state team. "I looked at my dad, and I could tell he was kind of proud. Dad said, 'Someone was watching you.'" An outsider had seen something in him. "That was my motivation; no one's ever going to stop me from doing what I want."

After two and a half years at Oklahoma University, he began deejaying and acting, and he went to California, where he lived for five years. He got small, action parts in movies like *Last of the Mohicans* and *Under Siege*, but eventually he decided to leave Los Angeles; he was afraid of losing touch with his culture. "You're like a machine there," he said. "You have to be a machine to compete with other machines."

Back in Oklahoma he started a music festival called "Culture Shock" that was meant to showcase contemporary Native American musicians, and he joined a traditional drum group called Youngbird that wound up getting nominated for a Grammy in 2002. He also became a motivational speaker around high schools, talking about how he had turned negative emotions into the drive to succeed.

Brian said people weren't ready for whole rap songs in Native languages. "It's hard enough to accept a Native hip-hop artist." And in any case, he was at best "familiar" with the languages. Still, he hoped to incorporate drums, flutes, and other Native sounds into the music he produced. "We want to represent that," he said. The word gave me pause. *Representing* was a modern notion, a classic hip-hop mode in which one impressed the world with one's authenticity. I asked him the question that had plagued me: What was he representing? "If you don't have a language left and you weren't raised in the culture, what does it mean to be Native American?"

He paused. Not the stereotypes, he said. Not the braids and the ponytail.

I persisted: "What is it then?"

"Well, it's more . . . the message and the music and the lyrics." It was the spiritual way they lived their lives, he said.

Still, the question haunted me. How could you regain a culture you didn't know? How could you even respond to its loss?

At the hip-hop show, as I watched the kids clustering around the break-dancers, Brian's brother, Quese came up and drew me outside. He wanted to interview me. I wanted to interview him, too, but he had better equipment than my little tape recorder: a professional-looking video camera with a little screen that he watched as we walked out of the gym. He was making a film of his own rise to hip-hop stardom, deftly switching between microphone and video camera, in tune with the story and the meta-story.

As we stood by the gym, a flood of high-school girls came streaming onto a court and started playing an exuberant game of night basketball, and he nudged us over there, noting that the scene would look good behind us. He was stylish, in a pair of silver shield-shaped earrings that he described as Pueblo, a fresh white shirt, and corduroy cutoffs, his hair dyed red-blond. I admired his look, and he said, "It sets me apart."

We taped and filmed each other talking—me uncomfortable, him fluid in the cool night air, while the players went thundering up and down the court behind us. Riverside Indian School had once been one of the notorious boarding schools where children were stripped of their language. It taught kids from a number of tribes—from the Caddos to the Kiowas to the Wichitas—to speak English. Now it's a BIA-run boarding school that attracts Indians from around the country, advertising a sensitive environment and cultural programs. About five hundred kids were enrolled, with Kiowa and Cheyenne-Arapaho the largest groups. Kiowa was taught, though the vice principal, Milton Noel, had told me only four or five children were fluent in their native language. It was a good setting for our talk about what forms a modern Native identity might take.

Quese said he was trying to layer the Seminole language into his music. He had experimented by laying old Muskogee-Creek hymns from the Baptist church onto a hip-hop beat. "I played it for a bunch of these elders," he said, "and they were all just sitting there kind of nodding their heads a little bit, the beat was going, the hip-hop beat, and then all of a sudden here it came: *Hallelujah.*" He sang the rest of the song in a high, light voice. "And they started like laughing and singing with it, so what that showed me right there was what I'm going to do is use this, whether it be actual words or just chants, in a hip-hop song."

He rapped out a few lines of the soft Seminole that he had learned from his grandmother—it sounded to me like a long line of sibilant, multisyllabic Latin words, *quibus . . . urbibus*—and added, "I would say something like, 'In my tongue, my people, you know, we speak our tongue, and it's a powerful thing.'" He had tried it before at a hip-hop event. "I just started speaking my tongue, and all these people came up to me, asking me what are you speaking, and I told them I speak my native tongue, and it surprised them . . . I mean, they're so used to the melting pot, but the melting pot doesn't consist of Native Americans, so when I come into their world it kind of blows them away. Like that's dope. It kind of gives them a respect."

"What does that do?" I asked.

His warm brown eyes lit up: "What it gives is like this *ambience* of *power.*"

I asked how that ambience worked, and he went on. "It's like their heart will start beating and they'll get chills. And they'll be like, this guy's *spitting* something, that's *dope*. But he's not spitting something that's . . . culturally corny," he said, "like an Indian who says they're Indian, and they're like, 'My name is Chief Running Fawn.'"

He softened his voice. "There's nothing wrong with that. But there's a way to do it . . . A lot of people try to come up and want to be instant Indians and put on these little headdresses that look like carnival headdresses. To me it's cute, you know, it's harmless, but you can learn so much if you really opened up your mind and looked at the situation." He talked faster than most people, as if preparing to rap. I had to slow down my tape player later to play it back. "It's cultural; people love culture, and right now . . . it's cool to be culturally connected. That's just society," he added. "You can't do anything about it."

I didn't know how to look at this. It's easy—even advantageous—to be culturally connected when it's cool. But what happens when it's not cool? I wondered. Quese's *ambience of power* evoked *ambient music*—as if the language were a movie soundtrack, a special effect, or an accessory, like his Pueblo shield earrings.

Yet he had started with a Muskogee-Creek hymn—one of the thousands of Christian hymns composed in Native languages—and that reminded me how often compromises, adaptations, and acts of salvage have become conduits for tribal culture. The Christian church played a part in destroying the old cultures, harnessing the language to do so; missionaries translated Bibles into dozens of Native tongues. But later, the Cherokee-language Bibles and hymnbooks published by missionary societies in Philadelphia became primers for children; the Kiowa hymns are repositories of the language; and the churches are some of the last places the languages are heard. The powwow, too, offered a model of how to adapt while at the same time remaining within the life of the community, playing old songs, and enacting ancient rituals of giving. It made sense that Oklahoma could be the birthplace of another hybrid art form.

We talked until the wind blew cooler and the girls finished their game. As we walked back to the gym, some little boys said, "Hey, you're Shock B's brother, right?" Quese nodded and they said, "Cool."

Brian and Quese didn't use any Native American language on stage that night. But I did manage to find it in the audience. I had heard the best Native-language speakers at Riverside were the kids from the Mississippi Choctaw tribe. Like the Kickapoos, who had refused to talk to me, the Choctaws, descended from those who resisted the move to Oklahoma, tended to keep to themselves. In recent decades, the tribe had used proceeds from successful business ventures—it was among the state's largest employers—to fund schools and extensive cultural programs.

A teacher tracked the kids down for me. They were standing far from the stage, back by the food tables with carrots and dip. "Eric and Jerome," she introduced them. Eric looked at me through glasses, arms crossed across his chest. Jerome had the gray hood of his sweat-shirt over his head.

"What do you think of the music?" I asked.

Eric muttered something to his buddy in Choctaw, which impressed me, even as it excluded me. "What did he say—that was Choctaw, right?" I asked Jerome excitedly.

"It's all right, I guess." Jerome translated. The teacher tried to get another teenager to talk to us—a boy from the Santo Domingo Pueblo tribe in New Mexico. "Do you like the music?" I said lamely.

He shrugged. "Kinda. No." He drifted away.

I got Eric and Jerome to tell me they were seventeen and eighteen, respectively, but soon afterward they clammed up, shrugging or answering monosyllabically. Occasionally, they spoke to each other with words I couldn't understand.

"It's really cool that you have your own language you can use to each other," I said. They shrugged miserably. I was torturing them. Every now and then, when I talked to people, I felt as if I was catching a glimpse of myself in a mirror. Once was when a woman said that her father had told her a tall skinny white woman had asked him some questions; that was me. Another time, some Euchees remarked on my resemblance to a grad student who had visited them. I had met her, another tall skinny white woman, of roughly the same indeterminate grad-school age between twenty-five and forty. Tonight, I had on some earrings that had once been termed "phat" and the coolest T-shirt I could find, but I knew I bore an unwelcome resemblance to a teacher.

Still, I went on: "Do other kids think it's cool?"

They didn't even shrug this time. The fact that they were standing by the refreshment table was probably a bad sign. They stared out at the kids clustered around the stage. Girls walked by, their long ponytails bobbing, and paused to watch the dancers, crossing their arms shyly over their chests.

The music was deafening, and Eric asked if I might want to come back during the day. "Oh yes, the noise is bad," I said, and let them escape. I walked back to the teacher who introduced us and said, "They speak so well. They don't know how great that is."

"No, they don't know," she agreed flatly.

I watched the Mississippi Choctaws every now and then. I could always spot Jerome because he kept the hood of his sweatshirt on. They didn't move from their spot in the back for a long time; then they made a strategic decision to go sit on the edge of the stage, and

I didn't see them again. As I left, I found myself thinking about these two—not the pair I had come to see. They didn't seem to be benefiting from the idea that speaking your language is cool; perhaps they showed the limits of it.

A few weeks after the Riverside dance, I watched Quese rap at an Oklahoma City club called Samurai. Again, I hoped to hear him using his language.

I had expected to find a tough crowd at what was billed as an emcee contest, but people were friendly and easy to talk to. I approached a young blond girl wearing a feather boa—the only girl I've ever seen getting down on the floor to break-dance—and she told me she had heard Quese speak Seminole at a show. "What happens when he does?" I said.

"People get hype on it," she said enthusiastically. "It shows his uniqueness, who he is." I saw Quese working the crowd on his way to the stage. He was low-key on this night, in a long-sleeved T-shirt and pale cargo pants, mother-of-pearl disks hanging from his ears.

Aspiring emcees were jumping onto the stage and waiting for their turn. They were just kids bundled up in their protective ski jackets and hooded sweatshirts, nodding to the beat. One by one, two by two, people began gathering around the stage, and the crowd grew from five to fifteen to fifty. The scent of clove cigarettes filled the room.

At the back of the stage, I could see Brian behind the table deejaying, picking out beats. He liked to put in cool samples, trying to inspire the DJs. "Music is like these rhythmic vibrations that pass through the air and they hit people. When they hit you, you react," he told me. It reminded me of how people described the powwow drum, the heartbeat of the dance.

On stage, the rappers improvised rhymes and passed the mike around. Quese and his buddy Duo dominated the scene, handing it back and forth. Quese was fluid and frenetic. He rapped far faster than anyone else, sucking audible breaths into his small frame between his wrung-out phrases.

I had come with Seminole in mind; what I heard instead was English. Quese took on the typical rap subjects: how great the rapper is and how hyped up people get when they hear him. But individual lyrics stuck with me:

> It takes thoughts, abstract minds,
> To make a dope beat that comes in time.

Later, Quese's band, TuBass3, came on. They had drums, guitar, and (inspiring the band's name) a kid with a tuba. (If you thought it was hard to reclaim Native culture for hip-hop, try reclaiming the tuba.) They played jazzy tunes with Quese alternating between singing and rapping. Kids gyrated and break-danced in front of the stage.

> My vernacular
> comes out real spectacular.
> Over in the crowd
> Heads bobbing, y'all getting loud.

I found it contagious. I painstakingly composed a rap, just in case anyone put a mike in my face. "I'm an Oklahoma nomad, out on the highway, From the east to the west I do it my way. Just today I was in Stilwell, Cherry Tree, and Greasy. You say this is hard but I make it look easy." I sat back and said it to myself and made a considered judgment not to ever take the mike. It had taken me several minutes to compose. Why was I doing it anyway? I was responding to the culture around me, just like everyone else, trying to succeed in the contest at hand.

Quese was better at it. That was the point: He was beating all the rest of us at our English-speaking game. It occurred to me that Quese was—like Chibitty—a warrior, winning on the playing field of his generation (and reinventing the code in the process). He told me earlier that in his emcee battles, "People always come back, trying to put down Indians, but then I'll come back and reverse what they say and put it back on them in a wittier way. So they're like, 'Aw, dang, how did you think about that?'"

I thought of our interview by the Riverside gym: He out-taped, out-teched, and out-talked everyone. In hip-hop, you won by talking the fastest, communicating the most effectively. It's the game of the moment, the place where you want to win—and it's all about language.

> I'm courageous, Rock of Ages, I'm razors to faces,
> My paraphrases are mazes, contagious,
> I keep paces in rhyme races . . .

Brian and Quese sent their buddy Duo over to talk with me. Duo (short for "Duo the Sick Prophet of the Culture Shock Camp") was, at twenty-two, a deep-voiced, commanding rapper. He wore dreadlocks in various shades pulled back in a topknot, exposing his high forehead, and he had a kind of pirate flair, heavily decorated with big silver rings, tattoos, and a touch of dark nail polish, but his gaze was gentle. I asked him where he'd been born and raised, and he said he had grown up in an African-American community in Oklahoma City. "I'm an Okie," he said. I thought to ask if he was Native American at all, and he said, "Cherokee, yes, somewhere." He wasn't sure how much. He reflected the crowd; the majority of Oklahomans are mixed, reflecting whites, blacks, and a number of tribes in their makeup. Brian had described the Oklahoma City crowd to me as "black, Asian, Indian, white, bikers, hip-hop-heads, and hippies"—as if they were just a series of choices. The name of their crew, Culture Shock Camp, accurately described the melding of cultures that was occurring within the hip-hop scene around Oklahoma City.

During a break, I started to hail Quese and ask if there was a chance he would use any other language tonight. But as I faced him, I realized that the question was unrealistic in this club. If anyone spoke a tribal language, it was going to be a gesture, not an act of communication. Native-language rapping doesn't really make sense where there isn't a community to listen to it. I congratulated him on his rapping instead.

After the show, we—the band and about ten hangers-on—went to the local IHOP for big plates of pancakes. Everyone was so nice to me that later I would find myself missing them; I would go to sleep on a kind of summer-camp high, thinking about all the people I had met. People laughed and talked until three.

The young guy next to me at the table had a shy way of carrying himself, peeking out from under a Kangol cap and a straight fringe of hair, but he turned to me confidently and introduced himself as James. He was one of the break-dancers I'd seen around the stage, and he'd been at the Riverside dance, too. He was from Fort Cobb, near Anadarko and "out in the country," and he had found a kind of home in the Culture Shock scene. He was part Arapaho. His grandfather could speak the language, he said, "but he's passed." James was working on an associate's degree and trying to figure out what to do with his life. We talked about how he found it satisfying to study grammar, "direct objects, things like that," he told me sheepishly. "I always had an easy time writing. When I do a report, I like working with the words to make everything perfect."

When James got up to leave, Quese sat down by me, remarking, "Hey, look at James's profile. Doesn't he look exactly like the buffalo nickel? Perfect Indian features."

I told Quese I liked the scene, and he said he felt good about making that happen. I knew Brian had worked hard to get past the troubles of his community, and I asked Quese how he had gotten to this point and what the alternative would have been.

"Shit, sitting around, getting fat, doing nothing, being a couch potato, or drinking alcohol," he said. Later, when I got up to leave, Quese took my email address on his Motorola two-way and told me he would send me a piece he'd written, and that I should put on a song when I listened to it—"something somber," he said.

I read the story on email later, though I played Quese's demo CD, which was rather upbeat. Quese had watched his brother succeed, but he, too, faced specters of failure. It seemed his effervescent personality made it easy for him to get along. But at his predominantly white school, he said, Indians were at the bottom of the social ladder. "We're looked down upon as drunks, losers, dirty, savages, people that really don't mean anything."

In a high school dominated by whites, he hung out with a group of Latinos and Indians. He and some Indian friends made waves by walking out of a performance of *Annie Get Your Gun* that featured stereotypical Indians, "hand patting their mouths as they yell and holler 'hey! yaw! hey! yaw! hey! yaw!'" he wrote. "You hear corny, cartoonish stereotype drum sounds in the music and all the sudden the ol' holy cartoon indian actor says 'HOW!! my name is Running BEAR!'"

When confronted by the principal, they complained that the play was demeaning. "The crowd laughed at the indian actors as if they were clowns," he wrote.

Quese said the principal responded by telling him: "That's bull crap." Afterward, Quese and his friends got a Native activist to come to the school and back them up, but he felt that the incident tainted his relationship with school authorities. Like Brian, Quese had problems with a basketball coach, who told him to cut his braid and, when he didn't, demoted him from the varsity team. The best thing that happened to Quese in high school was a moment in his senior year when he learned that he had been nominated for homecoming king. He hadn't realized people liked him that much. "The girls on the basketball team were all giving my props," he wrote. "That made me feel good that they thought about me. I'll never forget the thought of them each thinking in their mind 'You know what, I'm gonna vote for Quese!' The thought sometimes brings tears to my eyes." He invited his family to see him honored; he said winning wasn't the point, but having been picked to compete in a school of "white suburban preppy kids" was a "victory" for American Indians.

Hours before the homecoming ceremony, a teacher drew him aside and said that he had missed a meeting that week—one his coach had never told him about—and that the teachers had given his nominee spot to someone else.

He wrote: "As i turned and looked through the gymnasium doors i could see my family, relatives, friends and grandma. They were all laughing and joking around as indians do when they get around each other. My head fell toward the floor and i backed quietly to the door . . . I cried and told myself 'one day Quese, one day . . .' I left the school and walked all the way home 5 miles."

After I read Quese's story, I read another email he had sent me from his pager.

"hey e. did u get my story. let me know. talk 2 u soon.—'Quese el sliknes' "

Instead of thinking about language, I found myself thinking about high school and about the Choctaw kids and about what it was like to be young. This wasn't a story about genocide; it was a story about pain. It was about excitement, fear, disses, crushes, and cool. It was also about not drinking and not being an outcast and not giving in to pressure. For most of the young people in the gym at Riverside School or on the dance floor at the Samurai club, this is the story. Such fears, hopes, and loves are what drive adolescents into their adult selves. They are what drive kids out of their communities toward hip-hop, toward English, toward America.

Listening to Quese's CD, I heard a line that went: "Cause I'm an orator from shore to shore, / I connect more than extension cords to a power source." Reading the story, I heard this as an assertion that Indians could say a lot more than *"How"*—that they were the best American talkers around.

This post-loss generation was still feeling shrapnel from the destruction in their communities. In a way, they were on the cleanup crew. The verses I heard elaborated on the theme of healing. "Okay, if you never heard of us, It's all good. / Cause we're bringing that medicine for your hood," one said. The word *medicine* was reminiscent of a stereotype but also of a genuine tradition. The sentiment was in line with the "positive" vibe the brothers touted. They were trying to heal culture shock rather than create it.

It was hard to say whether "representing" the language was just a show or whether it was the first step back inside a language. Quese and Brian were at a turning point. They had achieved enough balance to value the idea of Native American language, but it was going to take more to get them inside. Strong emotions drove Quese's urge to communicate and Brian's urge to succeed. What emotions could propel people like them farther into the language? Whose fears would chase them there? Whose approval awaited them there? Whose money? Whose fawning music writers? Whose love? Whose applause?

Before any young people would want to go, someone would have to construct a world in which people were rewarded for learning the languages. Someone would have to make one of these tribal languages a gratifying place to be, a place with a cool crew and a warm feeling like that IHOP where the crew hung out, a place that would draw in lonely kids and make them want to sit down and talk. Someone would have to build that place. I wondered if these brothers could help.

CHAPTER NINE

The Road to Ross Mountain

I HEARD ABOUT ROSS MOUNTAIN just when I was ready to give up the search for a community in Oklahoma where an American Indian language was spoken. Everywhere I went, it seemed I had come too late. Indeed, I had found many people working with the language but just a few who spoke it. By now I knew there were many individuals who used tribal languages at home—older Kiowas, Kickapoos, Choctaws, Cherokees, and Creeks, to list just a few. But I couldn't seem to find a community of people under retirement age.

Ross Mountain, however, sounded like a real lost city; Linda Jordan, the woman who had introduced me to Toby Hughes, said that young and old alike spoke Cherokee there. When I first started trying to find it, I called Beverly Leach from my apartment in New York. Leach lived outside Ross Mountain, but she was writing a grant to build a community center there, and Jordan had given me her number.

When Leach said "hello" in her cool, deep voice, I babbled for a minute about wanting to meet her, while she punctuated every pause with a flat "mm-hmm." I stopped speaking, and finally she spoke.

"Ah, Linda's supposed to set up a date," she said slowly, with an accent that was part southern, part something else. I felt briefly disoriented as I realized English wasn't her first language.

"Okay, all right, that sounds good," I said, finding myself starting to enunciate. When we got off the phone, I was no closer to meeting her, but the sound of her voice filled me with curiosity. I went to my computer and tried to find Ross Mountain with the Mapquest program that claimed to map everything in the world, but Ross Mountain wasn't there.

I soon found myself in a series of conversations and meetings with intermediaries, trying to make the right introduction to someone at Ross Mountain. After awhile, Jordan arranged for me to meet Frank Swimmer, whose late wife had come from the community.

We all met at the neutral venue of Raymond Vann's house. Vann was a Cherokee "community anchor," as his wife put it, who as far as I could tell ran a one-man think tank. He knew everything—who owned the leases on downtown buildings, who had spent the most years waiting for tribal housing, which grants the Cherokee government was missing out on. I appreciated the sheer volume of his ideas for the betterment of various communities: Why not raise catfish? Why not help people build greenhouses? Why not grow grapes or start a little store?

Vann had spent nearly thirty years away from the area, working for General Motors in Dallas. After he retired with a pension, he moved back with his wife, a Sioux, and they lived in a spacious, airy house in a picturesque river valley. They had a virtual museum of Cherokee crafts in their house. The kitchen was hung with various basket models, the washboard Mrs. Vann had inherited from her Cherokee grandmother, and other old-timey utensils, including a homemade corn grinder. Their living room was filled with paintings, pottery, pipes, terrapin-shell rattles, and that hickory whip made by Hastings Shade. In the living room was a bowl of cedar and sage that Vann burned after funerals to drive out any spirits that may have followed him home. Mrs. Vann suggested he had a touch of a gift, but later, when I blurted out the notion to Toby Hughes, he just laughed a deep belly laugh. It embarrassed me a little that I had tried to cross-check magic.

The Vanns were acting as diplomatic intermediaries: They wanted more people to know about Ross Mountain, and so their job was to coax Swimmer, the community representative, to testify and me to listen. Vann, a big fifty-nine-year-old man with a soft, jowly face and small amounts of hair in a tiny ponytail, welcomed us heartily and led us to their roomy kitchen.

As soon as we sat down at the table, Jordan and Vann began talking fast, laying out Ross Mountain's situation. Frank Swimmer and I looked at each other from across the table, but we kept fairly quiet at first as the conversation swirled around us. Swimmer, at about fifty-four years old, had thick black hair and could pass for younger. He sat back with his wide arms folded, his heavy-lidded eyes scanning over mine every now and then, though he didn't stare. He was waiting to see who I was. There was another good reason for him to stay quiet: He was more comfortable speaking Cherokee.

Ross Mountain was one of the traditional communities that had resisted assimilation for generations. "Cherokee life takes place in small, named communities of relatives," Albert Wahrhaftig wrote in the early 1970s, describing "efficient social units" of twenty to fifty households "knit by continual person-to-person interaction." Jordan and Vann reeled off some of the names of the other Cherokee communities in the area: Bell, Greasy, Chewy, Nicut, Cherry Tree, and Sally Bull Hollow. Ross Mountain was built around an eighty-acre Ross family allotment in a rugged area of the Oklahoma Ozarks, just a few miles from the Arkansas border. The Rosses said they were descended from Lewis Ross, the brother of old-time chief John Ross, a distinguished Cherokee leader who hadn't favored moving to Oklahoma in the first place. The community consisted of the extended Ross family. It was small; no one would tell me exactly what the size was—as small as thirty-five, as large as seventy, depending on whom you counted.

The people of the community had retained their language by keeping to themselves. Ross Mountain lay in Adair County, one of the two counties in the state with the highest percentage of residents reporting Indian ancestry. In a 2000 census survey, 1,724 respondents said they spoke something other than English, Spanish, or another European or Asian language at home. The Cherokee Nation survey, too, found that Adair and its neighboring Cherokee County had the highest number of fluent speakers in the area.

But Ross Mountain was facing a crisis. The isolation that had kept the language healthy for so long was hurting it. The backwoods existence was rough, and its young people were seeking jobs far away. "All the language programs in the world are useless if people are hungry," Jordan said.

Adair County is one of the poorest in Oklahoma, with nearly a quarter of the residents living below the poverty line. I had driven along its roads, and they were the places where you saw the most hand-lettered signs for churches and commerce: BACKHOE AND DOZER FOR HIRE; WOOD FOR SALE; EGGS $1.

The self-sufficiency of small communities had been eroding for decades amid the shrinkage of Cherokee landownership. In the first half of the twentieth century, many allotments passed out of

Cherokee hands amid widespread swindling, as well as the partitions that took place with inheritance. Hunting became harder. Over time, the forest habitats were logged, the hillsides were leased to cattlemen, and the hunting grounds constricted as properties were fenced off. Rural people came to rely on short-term jobs—picking beans and strawberries, cutting timber, or working at farms, canneries, and industrial plants nearby.

But even that way of life, always hard, was growing less viable. Now the Oklahoma economy was shrinking. To find work, people were driving an hour into Arkansas or nearly two hours to Tulsa. The absence of working-age parents not only divided the community but also fostered an atmosphere in which alcoholism, drug addiction, and teen pregnancies could become more common. The coutryside around Ross Mountain, always rough, had big-city social problems; other communities were making methamphetamine. Meanwhile, chronic illnesses like diabetes and asthma were decimating Swimmer's generation; his wife had died of complications related to diabetes less than a year before we met.

"The last generation, a number left because they had to," Jordan told me. "We have to do something so they can stay there." She said their first step was to start a community center where they would hold after-school programs, language classes, and a meals program for the elderly. Beverly Leach was applying for federal grants to do that. The next step would be economic revitalization and the launch of local small businesses.

The plight of Ross Mountain evoked a debate over the future of isolated language communities around the world. It was usually phrased: "Does a language die or commit suicide?" In other words, do languages die because their speakers have chosen to integrate themselves into the mainstream? And do speakers have to relinquish the economic benefits of assimilation to keep their language alive? That spring, a *Wall Street Journal* editorial had argued that language preservationists "apparently would like to see tribal members live in primitive bliss" at the cost of development. The author, John J. Miller, pointed to a book called *Language Death*, which described an Australian aboriginal language that preserved various names for grubs. The way Miller put it: "[The author is] trying to say that we may learn about biology if we preserve and study obscure languages—but he seems oblivious to the reality that most people would rather eat a Big Mac than a fistful of beetle larvae. . . . the most important reason some languages are disappearing is precisely that their native speakers don't regard them as quite so precious."

The article spawned a rather peripheral conversation in linguistic circles on the merits of Big Macs versus beetle larvae, but it also raised the idea that minority speakers face a harsh choice. When Cherokees moved to urban areas to work, they tended to lose touch with their Cherokee identity.

Of course, the idea that minority speakers have a language "choice" doesn't take into account the pressures they face. In the Cherokees' case, the disruption of their environment has made self-sufficiency nearly impossible. Furthermore, much of the misery of minority-language communities—bad health, unemployment, alcoholism—doesn't result so much from cultural isolation as from poverty: Even when people do adopt mainstream ways, there's no guarantee that they will find well-paid jobs.

Vann suggested that the notion of prosperity versus language was a false choice for other reasons. People could speak more than one language, and at Ross Mountain, he hoped that the alleviation of poverty would allow people to speak Cherokee at home. "If you want to keep the language in the community, then build that community. Bring jobs into it. Give the people something to look forward to," he said: "They know what they want. If we put them back together, then no matter what we bring in, it isn't going to affect them. We know some-where we're going to lose a kid. We can't keep everyone. But we can keep 90 percent in the community."

Swimmer looked down at his hands and nodded. Vann's wife, a tiny blond woman with the face of a porcelain doll, set a plate of taco chips and some hot cheese dip in front of us. Vann told me that if I wanted to look for the language, I would find it "still alive down there." He smiled. "You know, Cherokees have, I guess, a bad . . . people say don't go there after dark."

Swimmer gave a deep, throaty laugh but didn't say anything.

"But if you get off the road," Vann went on, "people out here are friendly people." He added, encouragingly, "But that's Frank's de-partment, language." He looked at Swimmer, who declined to run with it.

I asked Vann if he spoke Cherokee, and he said in the quietest voice I'd heard from him, "I don't." Then in his normal, polemical tone, he said, "See, that's what happens when you're gone and you don't have anybody to speak to. You're losing your culture if you lose that." He looked around at us and exclaimed: "It's true. If we lose our language, what have we got?"

"We've got brown skin," Swimmer said softly, but Vann went on: "You know, we're still making baskets, but is that the way baskets were made in sixteen hundred? How do you know if that lifestyle is the original lifestyle? See, you done lost that. We've done lost 90 percent of our culture, and if you lose the language, that's the rest of it, and we're just in the melting pot."

As we talked, Mrs. Vann kept refilling our coffee, and Vann kept smoking, letting the smoke follow a current out the door, and even-tually Swimmer got to talking about the language. I asked if children at Ross Mountain used it. He said slowly, "Some kids, yes, they could speak, but the thing is, they were laughed at when they started talking, so they shut themselves back down," he said. "You can go back, and twenty-five- or twenty-six-year-olds still speak. Down below that, they can speak, but they are afraid to speak."

Swimmer sat forward and went on. "Well, most of my dream is, I'd like to get these kids back into our language. Educate them and tell them a way to survive. 'Cause right now they can't survive. If somebody don't show them the road to get an education, they get twelfth grade and that's it. They say, 'Even if I go to so many years in college, I'll be right back in this yard. What's the white man going to offer? He'll make me go to school, but there's no jobs promised at the end of the line.'

"And the little ones, they don't speak hardly at all. If I speak in my language to them, they'll look funny at me. They go around behind my back and say, 'Mom, what did he say?'"

"When did all this start?" I asked. The Vanns and Jordan were silent, waiting.

"Well, I came back here around 'seventy, it was already getting like that."

"What changed?" I asked.

He laughed slowly. "I don't know. It just grew into their lives. They didn't study who they were. And it goes back to the leaders we have. They don't come around to the community." He talked for a moment about how little help was offered to marginal communities like his. "When I came back and applied to jobs, they said, 'We can't hire you. You're overqualified to have these jobs.' And I'm just a poor Indian country boy coming back wanting regular pay." Swimmer laughed again.

Mrs. Vann put in: "He was in the military. In Vietnam."

"That's another thing," Swimmer said. "I don't hardly open up. I just stay quiet." He looked back down at his clasped hands.

"Well, very good," Mrs. Vann said brightly. "He speaks from his heart."

The Road to Ross Mountain

We drank more coffee, and a little later we got up and crowded into Vann's study to find a Ross Mountain Web site Jordan had developed, and as Jordan pointed out its features on the computer, Swimmer leaned over and watched, hands in his pockets. As we broke up for the evening, I wondered if I'd see him again.

Back in New York, I noticed that one of my books on language contained a language lesson from *UKB News,* a newsletter put out by the United Keetoowah Band, the political group that tended to represent more rural Cherokees like those at Ross Mountain. It was about "Jay's Huckleberry Festival," and it told how to say the following things:

> Are you going to Jay?
> They will eat huckleberry pies.
> They will be selling beautiful necklaces they made.
> They will be singing. They will be dancing.
> They will be throwing horseshoes.
> Are you going to watch the parade?
> There will be lots of people.
> I will go there.

I got to know Ross Mountain better in a series of glimpses and quick visits over many months. A month or so after I met Swimmer, I got an email from Jordan inviting me to a community gathering at Ross Mountain. It was April when I arrived there for the first time.

Linda Jordan and her friends were driving there, and I somehow wound up in a car with another Cherokee couple, the Careys. It was April, and the hills already had a deep, shadowed verdancy. The green views all around refreshed, restored my eyes. I felt as if the natural denseness of the woods, the scarcity of signage, and the absence of people on the roads reflected an intense secrecy. It was a region full of people who didn't want to be found; down the road from Ross Mountain was Elohim City, a white survivalist compound.

We drove up and up until we reached a hilltop with sky on all sides and a view of blue peaks beyond, the real Ozarks. Cattle grazed on tilted fields. Mrs. Carey held up her lapdog, *U-s-di*, or "baby," to the car window, and said, "Sweetie, look at the *wacas!*" The Cherokee word for "cow" was borrowed from the Spanish, whom the tribe had encountered as early as the 1500s. The moment reminded me that the Cherokees' tribal life had been disrupted centuries before the Cherokees moved to what was now Oklahoma; cultural purity was a moving target.

After we drove along a red dirt road for a few miles, we turned down a bumpy driveway and parked near a flatbed truck where a small band of men were standing, playing and singing lively gospel songs. I glimpsed Swimmer, carrying a guitar. The strumming and singing carried out into the air. Nearby was a house with a long porch where a few older women sat comfortably, watching the players.

We settled into the grass among a small group of staring women as other people arrived, carrying Mountain Dew and big boxes full of bread. The audience was just a small group of two dozen or so, but I could hear that Cherokee was being spoken among the guitar chords and bursts of laughter. A few older women got up and harmonized to a bluegrass song in Cherokee. Jordan whispered that Swimmer's late wife used to sing with them, and we listened for a while. Then Jordan pulled Beverly Leach, the woman writing grants for the community center, over to me. Thin, with long, loose black hair, she looked younger than her age of forty-five. Her long jeans skirt and black boots gave her an interesting Patti Smith chic. Speaking terse, soft sentences out of the side of her mouth, she said Cherokee was her first language. She lived in Rocky Mountain, a nearby community, and of her six daughters, only the oldest could speak. But she said it was different here. "Little kids, from the time they speak their first words, they speak their language still. Ross Mountain's the only place like that."

A break came in the music, and Leach walked up to the front of the crowd to make a speech. It came mostly in Cherokee, though she embedded English words in it—*community center, application*—and people watched intently, nodding. She finished with an English flourish: "Them that can't get around, we're going to bring the center to them."

It was a wholly Cherokee-speaking gathering, from the musicians' patter between the songs to the conversation in the audience to the chitchat in the kitchen. Still, I noticed that most people there were of middle age or older. There were children running around on the lawn but I couldn't hear what they spoke.

The afternoon passed too quickly in a daze of music. I wanted to approach everyone, sensible of the time ticking by, the rarity of the opportunity. But I didn't want to disrupt the ease of the gathering. And—amazingly—I wasn't sure everyone would understand me if I spoke. Swimmer was elusive, greeting me quickly and then moving on to talk with other people. Jordan and I listened and whispered and during breaks in the music, we chatted to the middle-age women sitting around us. Much of the talk was about the United Keetoowah Band, which employed several of the people there, including Leach.

The Keetoowahs had a vigorous history of resistance to assimilation. The UKB has its origins in the Keetoowah Society, which was organized before the Civil War to counter proslavery influence and maintain traditional ways. The Keetoowah Society of the antebellum years was limited to traditionalists who spoke Cherokee. Only "full-bloods" were eligible—though the term in Cherokee country referred to people who hewed to tradition, not to actual blood. The Keetoowahs were reenergized in the 1890s to oppose compliance with the allotment of Cherokee land under the Dawes Act, and many of them went to jail rather than enroll for an allotment. They were among the last Native Americans in Oklahoma to resist the drive toward statehood; indeed, the Keetoowahs' refusal played a part in delaying Oklahoma's transition to a U.S. state in 1907. Now, it seemed, their political descendants included some of the last Cherokee speakers.

When the gathering broke up, I still hadn't met any young people. As it happened, I didn't return to Ross Mountain for a long time. Swimmer didn't seem to ever pick up his phone, and Jordan retreated from the community. Her father died; she moved to a new house; and she also admitted she was discouraged and was no longer sure the community could regain its old spirit. She planned to help Beverly Leach get language grants once the community center moved forward, but the effort appeared to stall on bureaucratic hurdles.

While I was waiting for my next chance to go to Ross Mountain, I went into the United Keetoowah Band's casino in Tahlequah and wandered around. Keetoowah Bingo (Oklahoma barred fancier casino games) was one of the UKB's big revenue sources, and, like all the casinos in eastern Oklahoma, it had a local clientele. I had passed the casino before, and I had always found it forbidding, with its black-glass windows—though it was wheelchair-accessible, like so many places in Cherokee country. But inside, it was a relaxing place, in a way, with skillful mirrors making the space feel endless and dim light coming as a relief from the glare outside. It was like a kinder, gentler video arcade, or a darkened nursery in which the toys came alive at night, an innocent, infantile pleasure zone full of soft pings and bells. People didn't look around as I walked by but kept their faces turned to the glowing game screens.

I wandered around in that fairy-tale world and then put a dollar into a machine that looked like a slot. Solicitous attendants approached and asked if I wanted coffee. The cherries and oranges and lemons spun around, and I won $1.50. I cashed out and walked around some more. It was not all retirees; in the heat of the early afternoon, old people and young played together in a long, mesmerized row. It was not all solitary; I saw a husband and a wife leaning on each other's shoulders, a mother drawing up a stool by her daughter. It was not all poor; I watched a woman in a suit ask where the ATM was. It was not all sad; the coffee girls smiled when they poured you a cup.

The following winter, Vann and I headed out to meet Albert Ross, a member of the community's core family. We had set up an appointment with Ross at the compounds of the Keetoowah housing authority, where he worked in housing maintenance. Vann drove me there and went in ahead to make sure we were welcome, while I sat in his truck cabin, wondering what would have had happened if I'd gone in on my own. In this unfamiliar country, personal introductions were important. People were hard to reach by phone— sometimes they didn't have one—and they tended to be suspicious of strangers.

Vann came out and waved me in. It was a wet winter day, and it was nice to walk into the warm cabin where Ross, a man with a ruddy complexion and wavy hair down his neck, was sitting at a desk in the corner. The Beach Boys were blaring on the radio. After a few seconds of awkward silence, Ross asked me what I was there for. I mentioned the language, and he said, "Yep, I speak it." When I said I hoped to meet more people who lived at Ross Mountain, he looked at me and said they weren't getting together much until the weather got better. There would be a "singing" on the third Saturday in September, a good nine months away.

I tried another angle: I wondered if anyone there could give me some Cherokee-language lessons. Ross seemed more confident that he could help me with that. He said he knew a guy who lived near

173

Stilwell. "Not in Ross Mountain?" I said. I wrote the name down: "Sonny." "Sauny?" Traveling around this country, I felt I was living in an oral culture again. My note-taking reminded me of the pre-diction-ary age that had left the English language with so many antique spelling variations—not excluding my own last name.

He dictated: "A L E X S A W N E Y."

"So there's no one actually in Ross Mountain who might be able to teach me?" I asked. Albert shook his head, saying that Sawney would be best: He knew the language well, and he had taught before.

Vann went outside to smoke a cigarette just as a couple of middle-age men entered the cabin, shook off the cold, greeted us in Chero-kee, and sat down in another corner. When Ross introduced me, they looked at me quickly and then never looked back again. Casting about for conversation, Ross and I talked about the weather, about animals around there—panthers, bears, and bobcats. Outside the window, I could see a steep hillside marching upward—the cabins of the hous-ing authority were set in a small, deep valley.

Vann returned, bringing a whiff of smoke, and said we'd better be moving on, and Albert got up with effort from his chair, went out to the car, and brought back a turkey feather that the artist Sawney had painted. A brown bird flew over the delicate quills. I liked the idea of it, the way the image depended on this fragile sur-face of tiny fibers.

Later, as Vann and I drove down the road in Vann's big, comfort-able pickup truck with a feather hanging from the rearview mirror, I asked him if he thought I'd ever get back to Ross Mountain. Was Al-bert Ross trying to discourage me? "Well, I think he's saying that there's nothing up there," Vann said, watching the road intently as we swung around big mountain curves.

Back by his house, I saw a sign that said KIDS—HORSEY-TIRE SWINGS FOR SALE. I glimpsed a set of tires cut and shaped into seats, with brightly painted horselike heads. I remarked to Vann that half the people I met seemed to be part-time craftsmen, from Sawney to Shade to a random secretary in a Keetoowah office who had looked up hopefully as Vann lifted a woven basket from her desk.

"People depend on it," Vann said. He began talking about how hard it was to make a living in Cherokee country. "It's the thing killing our language. That guy"—he gestured to the side of the road—"he probably starts selling tires each month around the fifteenth, when his Social Security runs out."

I kept in touch with the Keetoowahs periodically, and one day when the weather was better, I managed to reach Swimmer on the phone. He invited me to Ross Mountain for a visit and another gospel gathering.

This time, when I got to the hilltop, I took a different branch of the Ross Mountain road and drove to a pretty prefab house with a tiny porch built onto the front; two guitar players, a singer, and a drummer were crowded onto it. There were about seven trucks and a few dozen people there, though it was hard to tell. A bunch of skittish young dogs trotted around on a vast mowed lawn. It was evening, and from the hilltop you could see all sides of sunset, from yellow to indigo.

Soon after I arrived, Swimmer's sister-in-law Ollie saw me and smiled. She was a mainstay of the Ross family, a gentle woman in her fifties with a smooth, oval-shaped face, and she began assiduously introducing me to the rest of the family. She stopped Nancy Ross, the skinny, energetic old woman in jeans who owned the house, and as we looked at each other, uncertain what to say, Mrs. Ross's son, John Ross Jr., moved closer to us. He said he had grown up here "on the mountain," pointing across the road to a field where his grandparents' log house used to sit. Old Mrs. Ross stalked away through the crowd, greeting people in Cherokee.

As I spoke to John Ross Jr., every now and then I saw him wearing an elusive smile that encouraged me to keep asking questions. It took me a moment to identify his style—clean-cut, with cropped, gray hair covered with a baseball cap, a long-sleeved T-shirt, and well-fitting jeans—but it clicked when he mentioned he was a former baseball player; at forty-eight, he still had the look. It had been baseball that fueled his career; he was the first to get a college degree in his family, and had become a housing liaison officer for the Cherokee Nation.

He was fluent in Cherokee, but he believed there were hardly any kids who spoke it. His four-year-old girl, whom he called U-ji-las, grabbed at his legs, and he said, "She used to speak it, but her mom moved away." When he was raising his oldest children, now in their twenties, he said, he didn't teach them Cherokee because he thought "it would hold them back." He hoped that the programs at the Cherokee Nation would help change that.

"Nowadays, we need economic development," he said, gesturing around the land. His notion was to have a community marketplace up here; people could sell gift baskets with jams and native foods. When he was younger, he said, "that was my dream, to have a store for all the communities and a gas station."

"Why the past tense?" I asked.

He paused. "The funding part is hard."

The band kept playing and singing as we chatted. Most of the songs were in English, and I heard lines waft in: "With tears in his eyes, on the cross there he died," and "I will have a beautiful home someday." It was the kind of performance that would actually spoil me for other gospel music, because I had never before heard the music sung by people who actually meant it. (This was a land of small churches, from the Word of Faith Ministries to the Free Will Baptist Church to the Free and Full Gospel Church.) The singers confessed with songs like "My God Is Real"; their Jesus spoke in phrases like

176

"Son, I'm doing this for you." In between songs, they talked about how happy they were to be there (Ross translated for me) and gave testimony about how they had been saved.

It grew dark; fireflies and stars appeared. The grass was suddenly dewy, and crickets started up. Ross's child was getting impatient, and I let him go. Ollie reappeared and led me inside to a crowded kitchen to meet more people. We passed musicians taking a break to eat pie at the kitchen table, children running around, bedrooms with old women resting in them. Then we reached Frank Mink, a man who preached in Cherokee—he called it Keetoowah—at the nearby Full Vision Church every Sunday. He nodded his head as if he'd been expecting me, and I sat down with him at a table covered with pies and plastic forks. He was an old guy wearing a trucker cap, fair-skinned and mellow, and he kept a perpetual gentle smile on his lips as we spoke. As we talked about his daughter, who had taught the language at a community called Peavine until the school ran out of funds, I noticed Mink was presiding over an orange plastic bowl full of dollar bills. People kept coming over and putting folded dollars into it. I asked what they were doing.

"We're trying to help the lady who lives out here," he said, pointing to old Mrs. Ross. "Five hundred eighty-five dollars in income a month, SSI. She's got two other boys that live here."

There was something about the way he said it that got me asking more; I found out the boys were seriously disabled. The first had been in a car accident, and the other had been beaten around the head in a fight. I turned and took another look at old Mrs. Ross, who was walking by, holding a cigarette. She was small, lean, and athletic, with a long gray ponytail and lustrous brown eyes. The children settled in to watch TV, and she sat down by the open door to the porch and listened, rocking and tapping her foot vigorously. One of her sons was tossing a balloon around outside.

There was a reason that most people there were under twenty or over fifty: The middle generation, the generation of young adults and parents, was off at work. John Ross's two sisters worked the night shift at a factory in Stilwell that made frozen pies for Mrs. Smith's Bakeries Inc. Swimmer's sons were working in Arizona and serving in Kuwait. Ollie's thirty-one-year-old son was catching chickens, a term that struck me as odd until I discovered it referred to one of the most readily available jobs in the region. Chicken catchers go to poultry farms and capture the chickens to be taken to the processing plants. As contract workers, they meet vans that take them to a different place every night—Ollie said her son had been as far as Memphis. They don't receive benefits, though the men who've done it say it's hard on the knuckles. They tend to work at night, when the chickens are docile.

I had seen Ollie's son dropping by to pick up a daughter he'd left with her: A little black car bumped down the driveway, stopped, and sat idling for a moment. As Ollie and the little girl walked down to the car and spoke to him—in Cherokee—I just glimpsed his blue cap and ponytail, and then the car drove off—a typically brief appearance by his generation at Ross Mountain.

Before I left, I found myself talking with a handful of kids who were standing around in the grass, not listening to the band exactly but deciding what to do next. They all spoke Cherokee—a teenage girl, a nineteen-year-old man, and a goateed guy in his early twenties. Most Indian teenagers in Oklahoma would have to change their lives drastically to speak their language. But these young people could choose either Cherokee or English.

People called the nineteen-year-old Utan, or "big," referring to his height; he had thick, fluffy hair, fresh, pink skin, and a shy smile. I asked what he was going to do now that he was out of high school. "I don't know," he said. "Find a job, stay around here. I just stay around the house and take care of my mom." He had little desire to move far away. The guy with the goatee was Robert Hawkins, the son of one of John Ross's sisters. He had no trouble speaking Cherokee. "In second grade I had to take speech class to learn English," he told me. But he was at loose ends when it came to his future. He said he wanted to start taking some classes at a university branch in Okmulgee.

At 11:45 P.M., the band was still playing, and I began to take my leave. Mrs. Ross hugged me with her tight, skinny arms, a warm gesture, and we said *wa-do*, or "thank you," to each other. (I had brought some root beer.)

I looked back as I left; in the dark, I could see nothing but the players' silhouettes against the little porch light on the side of the house, but I could hear the singing and playing. It was a scene from the life of the old-style community, the last base of the language. I wondered if I had found what I was looking for. At Ross Mountain, plenty of people were still using Cherokee; the place was infused with the language. And yet, with the parents absent and most children switching to English, it was a fragile world, endangered even as I saw it. It was thin ice that would melt in a matter of time.

A little later, at the top of the mountain, I stopped the car and opened a window to see if the singing carried. It didn't; I heard only the steady hum of the bugs and the occasional night bird. I kept driving through Stilwell and passed the block-long mass of Mrs. Smith's Bakeries, with a glowing neon baking pin on the sign. A shift was ending. Perhaps they'd still be playing music, I thought, when the women who worked there got back to Ross Mountain.

CHAPTER TEN

Inside the Language

"CONVERSATIONAL CHEROKEE." There was something quixotic about the very notion. With whom, in this disappearing world, would I converse? Where would those conversations take place? Practical Cherokee! Everyday Cherokee! Cherokee you can use! I hadn't been entirely serious when I first broached the idea of learning Cherokee. But as I angled for another invitation to Ross Mountain, I wondered if the language might offer a kind of shortcut into the lost city that I sought. Before I could get to the place on the mountain, I would have to go to a place in the mind.

For a long time, the idea of learning an Indian language had intimidated me. Even as I lamented the failure of young people to study their languages, I was echoing their reasoning: I didn't have time; I wasn't sure which language to pick. But now, I felt I had reached a limit to my understanding as an outsider. In addition, I had developed a small crush on Cherokee: its magic, its mysterious syllabic script, and its habitat in the rolling countryside. I wanted to know what it felt like to think in a language so different from my own.

Raymond Vann drove me to Stilwell to see Alex Sawney, the man Albert Ross had recommended as a teacher. Overall, our elevation rose only slightly—about 250 feet—between Tahlequah and Stilwell as we headed farther into the Ozarks. It felt like more, though, as we dipped in and out of flood valleys cut by the creeks. There were a lot of animals there, judging by the roadkill-per-mile index, and I noticed a couple of funeral wreaths set up in the ditches.

On the way, I worried that Sawney would be unwilling or unable to teach me. I had already made one false start; Vann had introduced me to another teacher he knew, an old weaver named Lucille Hair. As I stepped forward from her doorway onto her shiny, spotless living-room floor, wondering if I'd wiped my feet hard enough, she peered up at me suspiciously. She was small and wiry, with tightly curled gray hair and a little, hooked nose, and she shook her head negatively even before she invited us to sit down.

As I explained that I wanted to learn the language, she sat down in a rocking chair and began moving back and forth quickly. "I've kind of quit," she said. "I kind of forgot the language. My kids, they all speak English."

Lucille looked at me again, piercingly. "Maybe if it were a kid," she said to Vann.

She switched off her TV, which was blaring *The Price Is Right* from the corner of the room. "I always did say you can't forget Cherokee," she went on. "People used to tell me they had and I never understood that. But I'm getting to where I forget it. With kids, I try to say some words. They don't want to learn. They're learning Spanish! I tell you, our Cherokee, it's just going away."

Vann asked her if she knew anyone else who spoke. He mentioned the name Alex Sawney, and she said, "Yes, he talks Cherokee." She thought for a while and then threw out another name. "James Foster, of the Echota church, near Titanic."

Vann laughed. "Titanic."

"They used to call it Rabbit Trap," she said. "Well, he talks Cherokee, but I don't know if he *would* or not."

She mused about the Echota church. "Sometimes I want to hear some Cherokee preaching," she said. The neat line of pictures that headed around her living-room walls, festooned with ribbons and plastic flowers, included the "Footprints" story about being carried by God through hard times.

"It's just getting away, that's all it is," Vann said, nodding. "But the thing is, we need it."

We sat silently, while she tried to think of more teachers. "Might have been more," she said. "But they're all gone. It's getting hard, it's just gone." Her eyes grew evasive.

"Well, we'll talk to a few more," Vann had said. He'd thanked her in his kindly manner, and we'd gone on out.

Now Vann and I climbed Highway 51 back out of the Illinois River valley where we'd been and followed it over big, roller-coaster hills toward Stilwell. The countryside was hopelessly plain in winter, painted in drab shades: beige for the fields and the modern buildings; red-brown for the rusty propane tanks, the cars in the yards, and the fallen leaves; gray for the gravel heaps and tangles of barbed wire; black for the skid marks on the road and the wandering, endangered stray dogs. The only colors lay in the dissonant brights of trash in the yards and beside the road, and the only order was the reproachful, close-mowed severity of the farmers' brick houses. Still, the country rolled pleasantly into hills, and we drove toward a pearly sky.

"First trailer on the left," Vann said to himself as we pulled off a highway onto gravel at a scattering of houses and stopped in front of a little trailer with a porch built onto its front. It was just off the highway, backed up against a big, snowy hill. Beside the house was a red truck with a UNITED KEETOOWAH BAND sticker on it.

We stepped up onto the porch, knocked, and stood there, listening to soft, high wind chimes, until an old man with neatly combed black hair, dark eyes, and a thin mustache opened the door and looked up at us.

Vann introduced us, and the man moved back so we could enter the warm, dry box of a living room. His wife stood up silently. She seemed to recognize Vann's name, and as he started talking to her, the old man invited me into his office, a room less than seven feet wide lined with painted feathers and shelves of miscellaneous crafts. I explained what I wanted, and he said, slowly, "That'll be all right."

"So. Okay," I said. "I can just come over, then, next week?"

"All right," he said in a calm, friendly way. As we worked out a schedule, Vann and his wife squeezed into the doorway and watched us. After a while, Mrs. Sawney began silently handing me little objects her husband had made: feathers painted with simple eagles or American flags; rocks painted to look like little animals—a yellow dog, a monkey's face suggested by the shape of a wrinkled surface; elaborate peace pipes with beads around them; canes carved in sumac. As I admired them and handed them back to his wife, it occurred to me that she might not speak much English. Perhaps she thought I was a customer.

As Vann and I left, we stood on the porch for a moment, saying good-byes, and I felt the wife come up behind me. She held a peach-pit mouse under my nose. "It's cute?" she said. It had little turned-out shells as ears.

On the way out, Vann kept pointing things out—with the kind intent, I suspected, of ensuring I would notice the landmarks and not get lost when I went there alone. "So it was the first trailer past the bridge," he said. "There's the Chalk Bluff grocery. And Fourkiller church, a graveyard . . ." We passed a house with about five people on a porch. I could see someone turn and watch us drive by. "Full-bloods having a big dinner," Vann said.

I called Sawney and canceled our first class. There was an unusual snowstorm, and the thought of those hairpin curves and little funeral wreaths on the road frightened me. But I also was nervous about the unfamiliar community, the close-aired trailer, and the possibility that it wouldn't work out, either because he couldn't teach or I couldn't learn.

But the next day, when I did manage to skid up in the snow beside his trailer, the class went well. Without much preliminary conversation, we sat down at the worktable in Sawney's little office and began saying Cherokee words. He spoke them; I repeated them, trying to learn the sounds.

I drew on every language I'd ever heard—the Frenchy nasal sound of *ng* hanging around the ends of certain vowels, the grunt in the *uh* vowel, the *u* that seemed to slide between the short *u* of *umbrella* and the long *u* of *blue,* the soft-sounding *l,* and the way some words seemed to end with a sharp little exclamation point. There was a new syllable that it seemed to me was *tla.* Then he repeated it, and it became equally clear to me it was *cla.* And he leaned over and wrote it: *hla.* I couldn't even hear it, let alone say it. There was also a sound written as *hna;* the best way I could see to approximate it was by exhaling through my nose as I said *na.* We sat facing each other, saying words, until the office smelled like our breath.

I thought of my first impressions of Comanche—"harsh"; and of Cherokee—"rippling." That first kind of attention you pay to the sound of a language seems superficial, because it's not about meaning—and perhaps even harmful, in that it's tempting to load the listening with preconceptions about "pretty" and "ugly" languages. But it's actually a basic first step in learning a language, a productive kind of listening that's somewhat akin to what infants do before they can talk. Their "babbling" is an exploration of the sonic landscape they hear: the exploration of sounds, rhythms, stress distinctions, and rising and falling tones.

Cherokee is a soft, drawling language that you don't have to open your lips too wide to say. It's the opposite of Italian or some other explosive, emphatic, language. The up-down cadences are there, but subtle, so that the sound flows, legato, like a creek.

I was devoting the freshest hours of my day to the lesson, and so it went well. At the end, I asked him how to pay. He said, "Whatever you think is appropriate." He added, "I don't expect nothing. I like doing it." I gave him two twenty-dollar bills, and then he handed me back one, saying that was too much.

Afterward, I walked out, smiling to his wife, who as far as I could tell had spent the whole time at the kitchen table, looking out a window and warming herself in front of an open oven door.

When I left, I decided not to head back west, where I'd come from, but to turn east, just to see what I'd find. I was in a good mood. What was it about learning new languages that made me so happy? Perhaps it reminded me of high school, when I'd always enjoyed learning languages (I wouldn't find out for years that real French people couldn't understand my French).

But it was a stronger pleasure: The language seemed to open up a new place. I could remember having the same feeling once when I looked at a map of Mexico's states—Durango, Sonora, Michoacan—and realized how much more there was to learn. It was a kind of explorer's high. I had initially thought of the language as a kind of business necessity, but I realized that it was going to be deeply engaging.

The road climbed the hill that stood behind the Sawneys' house. It rose steeply into a zone striped with thin, wintry evergreens, as if I'd entered a different climate. We'd said the word for "wilderness"—*i-na-ge-i*—and Mr. Sawney had commented, "That's the countryside, like we are right here." Birds dipped, surprised, in front of my car. I passed a hand-lettered sign for a fur dealer. It was less than four miles to the state line; Arkansas began in the swell of the Ozarks. That was it: I'd reached the outer border of the Cherokee counties, the end of the tribe's little dominion, as well as the state's. After a mile or so of Arkansas, I turned the car around and headed back, and going this way, I passed a sign decorated with an Indian shield: WELCOME TO OKLAHOMA / NATIVE AMERICA.

Mr. Sawney and I began setting the rhythm of our lessons. I had brought a primer written by Levi Carey, a friend of Linda Jordan's, and we started by learning its sprinkling of vocabulary and simple grammar. Every day, too, Mr. Sawney taught me a few common phrases. I wanted quality, not quantity; I wanted to know a few colloquial things that would make people say, "Wow, you really speak it well."

Mr. Sawney conducted the lesson with a kind of grace, from his careful attention to hanging up my coat at the start to his gentle encouragement: "Just like I'd say it, that's right." He seemed to find easy pleasure in teaching. A lot of things we said seemed to make him giggle a little "hee-hee." Once he explained it was the sound of us saying "me!" in Cherokee—"a-ya!"—like children. But there was more to it. He mentioned to me he had taught a class once, and it tickled him to hear white people speaking Cherokee. It wasn't that he was making fun of them: It just seemed so incongruous.

The first thing I found was that it was hard to represent all of the language in English. Take the word for "family." Written down, it looked like *su-da-ne-lunh-i*. But which syllable was accented? *SU-da-ne-LUNH-i? su-DA-ne-LUNH-i?* Did some of the letters get swallowed up, the way the family in English often sounds more like *fam-ly?* Were the sounds clearly separated—staccato—with the glottal stops found in Cherokee, or run together? Did the tone rise or fall, the way the last syllable of English's *this is my family* is often distinctly lower than the first?

187

Cherokee has as many as five distinct tones, and though they aren't as necessary for comprehension as in Chinese, they can be as important as the difference between "salt"—*a-ma*, with a long, scalloped initial *a* and a light, high *ma*—and "water"—*a-ma*, with short, low tones for each syllable. I drew crude musical scales to mark tones and used dots and dashes to mark how long I held each syllable. I also gave Mr. Sawney a blank tape so he could record some words.

In one of our early lessons, I arrived at his house to find a car parked in front. Mr. Sawney's stepson and daughter-in-law were inside with their little girl. At the door, I tried my Cherokee greeting and glimpsed the ends of smiles on their faces as I walked in. I ventured to ask the man, who was about thirty, if he spoke Cherokee, and he said yes in a tone that suggested he was surprised I might have to ask. What about the daughter, I said. They shook their heads. "No, not much," he said. "She's just a young one, just playing." Mr. Sawney didn't react to that but politely led me into his office.

Later, as he was teaching me a mini dialogue—"Are you tired?" "Yes, I am tired"—I noticed his voice sounded a little bit hoarse and said: "Really, are you tired today?"

He smiled and told me in his calm way that he had woken up at midnight and come in here to read ahead in our book and think about what we would talk about. "That's how I do things," he said.

"I'm really glad you're learning," he added. He had taught Cherokee classes to both adults and children before, and at seventy-three, he was determined to become a teacher again. He had been raised in Salem, a community not far from Ross Mountain. Juanita, his wife, was a cousin of the Ross family, and he liked to play music there. He had a guitar pick on his desk with a little alien face painted on it. He said, "Summertime, we're going to be getting together a lot. Then you can come. We play music. At Ross Mountain, with that long porch, they built it just for that."

188

There were two black-and-white photos on the wall. Both of them showed Mr. Sawney proudly posing with a car—lounging coolly on the trunk in one, striking a pose with a foot on the running board in the other. (He used the old-fashioned Cherokee word for car, which he said meant: "big eye.") The younger Mr. Sawney had a macho, dapper look, with thick, shiny hair; he wore it the same way now, combed back from his widow's peak, and he had the same small features and heavy brows.

He was dressed up in both shots, wearing a natty tie and dark new jeans in one, a shiny jacket in another. I told him he looked like an entertainer, and he said he used to like dressing well. "I don't know why," he added. After high school, he played his guitar in bands around the region. He said he'd liked country music since he listened to the Grand Ol' Opry on the radio as a child. He still composed songs, but only in English. "I have tried to make it in Cherokee," he told me, but he had trouble with "too many words" and the fact that "it just doesn't rhyme."

He'd spent the bulk of his work life in brick masonry, working as a laborer and as a small-business owner with his own equipment. By the end of that career, he had been away from this area for almost twenty-seven years. I wondered if he would teach with the Cherokees, but he had quit the Cherokee Nation to join the Keetoowahs, who he felt were more community-minded and open to using him to teach. If Ross Mountain ever got a school going, he said, he would teach there.

"But here you are teaching me!" I said, laughing at the idea that the only student he'd found lately was a white girl.

I asked him if he knew any kids who spoke the language. He looked at me with a tight little smile around his mouth. "Not really," he said. "That girl you saw"—his granddaughter—"she doesn't speak it." Even though his son spoke it, that generation wasn't fluent. Mr.

Sawney said that among the children of his seven siblings, there were just a couple who really knew it.

Initially, Mr. Sawney and I decided to advance into the spoken language without studying the Cherokee alphabet, thinking its eighty-five characters would be too hard to learn. But I found myself studying it between lessons.

It was a looking-glass world, a madman's fantasy alphabet, with a font that you would use for a Gothic horror title and an overabundance of curlicues and flourishes. To an English speaker, it appeared that someone had tossed all the Roman letters in the air, randomly assigned them to sounds, and then hung a few decorations on them.

Like Russian, it had some letters that looked like English but made utterly different sounds. I had seen **G W Ᏹ**, or *ja la gi*—the word for Cherokee—on signs around Tahlequah. Similarly, a Cherokee letter that looked like **D** stood for the sound *ah*. The shape **S** stood for *du*. Then there were all the unconventional-looking letters, which I dubbed with names that sounded like Texas ranches: Slash S and Funky S; Radioactive H and Flaccid H; Big Theta, Lightning Theta, Upside-Down 4, and Electrified C **Ꮪ Ꮥ Ꮂ Ᏺ Ꮒ Ꮎ Ꮵ Ꮯ**. There were also flat-out mysteries like Ꮷ. I traced their shapes and tried to copy them well enough to write, discovering another talent I didn't have. Still, their strangeness inspired me; deciphering them, I felt as if I were reading the secrets of the world.

Sequoyah was a Cherokee blacksmith in early-nineteenth-century Alabama who noticed that white men had a kind of competitive advantage in their ability to convey messages in writing, and he spent as many as twelve years tinkering with ways to represent his own language. After rejecting the idea of using a Chinese-style pictograph for each word, he systematically divided the sounds of the Cherokee language into syllables and came up with a letter to represent each one. While Sequoyah had seen other alphabets—certainly English, as well as missionaries' Greek and Hebrew texts—he did not know English, and his own handwritten letters looked less like English than the ones we see today in books. The language underwent a remodeling when Sequoyah and a missionary designed a font to print the language.

The resemblance of the letters to ours is distracting to an English speaker, but our "Roman" alphabet would have seemed oddly familiar to the Etruscans, Greeks, Phoenicians, and other predecessors going all the way back to the ancestral Semitic people who created the forebears of our letters (and they in turn had likely seen Egyptian hieroglyphics). Indeed, nearly every alphabet in history has spread through a similar process: Someone catches sight of another culture's writing and decides to create something like it—sometimes copying it outright with a few modifications, sometimes redesigning it completely. Many scientists believe writing hasn't been independently conceived more than a few times in history—by the Sumerians in ancient Mesopotamia, possibly by the American Indian civilizations in Central America, and possibly by the Chinese.

In any case, after Sequoyah proved the usefulness of his invention to the Cherokees by showing he could write letters to his young daughter, the alphabet spread widely. The Cherokees established the first American Indian newspaper and did their own translation of the Bible. Sequoyah created numbers, too, but the ones we know (called Arabic, but actually originating in India) were already in use.

Now it's hard to find the syllabary used outside the old Cherokee hymnbooks, Bibles, and a few symbolic street signs in downtown Tahlequah. While nearly 95 percent of Cherokees knew the syllabary in the nineteenth century, these days fewer than 5 percent of Cherokees can write their language.

Like Toby Hughes and most other Cherokee-literate people, Mr. Sawney had learned the syllabary at home as a child. His mother gave him lessons, using a Bible and a songbook. He'd started by writing his name: Alex. *E li gi.* **ᎡᎵᎩ**. "It didn't take me long," he said.

"That was every day and every night," he told me. "Every evening I'd come home and do that." Newspapers were no longer published in the syllabary, but people still used it for correspondence, and later, when Mr. Sawney moved away from home, he wrote letters home in Cherokee, because his mother could read it better. He pulled out an old Cherokee Bible, opened it on the table in front of me, and pointed to a word. "See," he read upside down. "*Je-lu-se-le-mi*—Jerusalem."

English sentences consist of a group of stand-alone words. In Cherokee—as in many Native American languages—sentences often consist of a verb nucleus and particles attached before and after the verb. The particles don't stand alone but can be snapped on or off as needed to create a complex and often long word.

We combine words in English when we fold the word *book* into *handbook*. We use prefixes like *pre-* and suffixes like *-able;* we have drive-thrus, love-ins, and phone-athons. I once saw "orange-sicles" advertised on a sign along an Oklahoma highway. *Sicle*—an ungrammatical morsel of *icicle,* derived via *Popsicle*—can be joined with a flavor word to describe ice on a stick. But in English, we combine word parts only occasionally, like when we want to create a new word. By contrast, verbal flexibility characterizes Cherokee speech. Cherokee sentences are formed around verbs linked to prefixes, suffixes, and even infixes—additives that go in the middle of the word, a phenomenon that almost never occurs in English (with the exception, linguist John McWhorter noted, of "fan-fucking-tastic"). These additives show not only tense but also how the action is done—slowly, for the first time, deliberately, etc.

Ruth Bradley Holmes, author of the textbook *Beginning Cherokee,* put it nicely to me. "It's sort of like when you're creating a certain color in paints; if you want a light blue, you put in just a few drops of color. Each infix is like a drop that changes the color of the verb slightly. The verb to [Cherokees] appears to be more of a living thing than our verbs." By contrast, she said, quoting the Cherokee spell translator Jack Kilpatrick, the English language is made up of "dreary little walls of word-bricks."

There are other ways you have to open your mind to learn Cherokee. For instance, it has more pronouns. English has one *we,* while Cherokee has four separate ways to express the concept, depending on who's included. Perhaps a story will illustrate how that works. I once went on a long camping trip with a group of strong-minded women. One of us, Georgie, got a concussion while bounding into our van, and we took her to the hospital. In the parking lot, we found ourselves undecided about how many people needed to go in with her. My friend Solange and Georgie got out of the van, and I followed them with my friend Heather close behind. Solange turned around and told me "We should go inside."

In English, that was an ambiguous sentence. By *we,* did she mean herself and me? Herself and Georgie? Herself, Georgie, and me? Or herself, Georgie, and Heather, but not me? Cherokee has a specific pronoun for each of these groupings. Of course, in English, Solange could and did clarify her meaning by adding proper names and gestures, but the example illustrates one kind of specificity that is possible in Cherokee.

During one lesson, I learned a verb for "coming toward me" and used it successfully to say a cow, a man, or a dog was coming. But Mr. Sawney laughed when I used it for a snake. Cherokees tended to use verbs that referred to animals' way of approaching. What I had learned as "come" was only used for things that walked. Most animals didn't just approach—they walked, ran, hopped, flew, crawled, or swam.

I felt that having studied French, Latin, and a morsel of Korean made it easier for me to learn Cherokee—even though none of these languages was related to it. The other languages had expanded my thinking. They had opened a few auditory pathways, which was why I heard certain sounds in Cherokee as "French," and heard the softness of consonants as "Spanish." People kept warning me that Cherokee was "backward," but the construction of Cherokee, with the verb at the end of the sentence (instead of *I-see-a-dog*, it went *a-dog-I-see*), didn't faze me as much as it might have if English had been my only language.

Still, the more I learned, the deeper the complexity grew. Cherokee tends to represent pronouns like *I* and *he* with prefixes on the verb, and I found they weren't as regular as I might have hoped. No sooner had I learned to say "I" with *a-gi* and *a-ge*—repeating them until they *felt* like "I"—than I found some verbs took *ji* and other sounds. There was also a troublesome *s* that often marked a question: It seemed easy enough to add it to the end of a verb, but sometimes it showed up at the end of another word—and sometimes it was absent, while some other question particle showed up instead.

I wrote to Linda Jordan, who had studied Cherokee, to tell her what I was doing, and she commented to me in an email that "Cherokee really IS a shining example of what linguists like to call 'the infinite complexity of language' . . . just thoroughly amazing stuff, words with three verb roots combined just to get a very specific meaning across, *chunks* of words flying across sentences to reattach at different places, etc. REALLY cool stuff!"

When I was young, we used to have a game in which we threw Velcro balls at a cloth dartboard. In time, the balls deteriorated, and if you threw them too hard or too softly some of them would bounce off and roll back. That was what memorizing lists of words felt like: You'd toss out a bunch of words and hope that some of them would stick. *Sa-gwu, ta-li, jo-i, nv-h-gi, hi-s-gi,* one through five. *Su-da-li, ga-hl-gwo-gi, cha-ne-la, so-hne-la, sgo-hi,* six through ten. Whether we were talking about verb endings or vegetables, there was little substitute for brute memorization. This was the other side of the arithmetic of cultural preservation: In a limited life, how many words can a learner take in per day?

Having worked as a writer, I was all too familiar with the psychological methods of failing at a task: the trick where you decide it's too hard at the outset and stop; the trick where you take a few steps and stop to rest; the trick where you realize you're almost done and get so happy at the thought, you stop working; the trick where you work on a small, trivial task to avoid having to do a big, hard task. In learning a language, I found, I faced the same temptations.

To cut down on the work, I was constantly prioritizing what I needed to learn—for instance, Mr. Sawney told me very few people used the Cherokee names of the months. I didn't know why I should bother learning all of them, so I learned only the spring ones, so I could talk about the immediate future. I even skipped several verb conjugations for "you (two people)," since it appeared unlikely I'd ever talk to two people, much less a group of people, in Cherokee.

I realized later that I was unconsciously simplifying the language—one of the stages in language decline—but at the time, I felt I had to focus on what was most important to know.

When we had repeated enough phrases and studied enough words, Mr. Sawney said I should start putting it all together and using the language. He encouraged me to try to form sentences. "Go ahead and try 'em anytime."

"On who?" I said. I couldn't just walk down the streets of Tahlequah and find people to speak with. There were no restaurants where I could practice on the waiters.

He smiled and didn't say anything.

I didn't follow his suggestion right away. My secret: I wasn't good at actually speaking languages. As well as I could learn verb tenses from books, I had trouble conversing. For one thing, it was scary. Even when I knew a textbook answer, I tended to freeze up when someone looked me in the eye and asked me a question. And when it came to holding a conversation, the tones and accents that I could parrot in lessons deserted me. My accent needed constant reinforcement or else it slid back into English sounds. I remember that in middle school, the trick to the long jump or the perfect dive was to get off on the right foot. Step, step, step, and you're in the right spot for the leap into space. I never did that well. The physical act of speaking felt the same way: too fast. My mouth couldn't launch the sentences properly.

Once, outside of class, a Cherokee teacher I was interviewing asked me if I'd been exposed to any Cherokee. I launched into my prize Cherokee phrase: "I am learning Cherokee." I didn't stumble, but afterward, he just looked at me solemnly. "It's best to learn these words one syllable at a time," he said. "You get each syllable right before you learn longer things." I felt my face heating up.

Real conversations sounded different, too. When Mr. Sawney spoke at a normal pace, the words he'd carefully sounded out were unrecognizable. Once a conversation got started, I felt like I was sledding down a steep slope without any way of stopping, headed for disaster.

As a first step, we had little, unreal dialogues. "What do you want?" he'd ask in Cherokee.

"I want gold," I answered, drawing on an odd vocabulary word in an effort to surprise him.

"Use *a-se-hno* ["but"] in a sentence."

"I want to learn Cherokee, but I'm tired."

"What do you see?" he said, pointing out the window.

"I see a giant snail." I liked to make him giggle.

196

We both enjoyed our lessons. What started as two-hour sessions stretched into three as we got hyped up on the coffee that Mrs. Sawney brought us silently every day, and the approach of spring boosted our spirits; the sun began slanting into the office in the afternoons. Mr. Sawney taught me to say: "It's a beautiful day." I was living mostly at the Holiday Inn Express in Tahlequah then, while taking road trips around the state; driving toward Tahlequah around that time, I actually got lost on a route I'd driven a dozen times, because the new brightness of the season made the fields look unfamiliar.

Late in the lesson, we talked about how the teaching was whetting his appetite to start leading a class again. "I want to do what I can," he said in English, "because our language, it's going."

Sawney asked if I thought he could teach people. "I'm really sure I'm teaching the *right* way," he said. "I believe I can teach anybody, because I know all of it." I felt sure he could, but I didn't know where he would find more students.

Cherokee grammar emphasizes different thought categories from English. I was learning how to mark my location spatially as I spoke, not to say that someone is walking but that someone is walking toward me or walking by or walking away from me. In French, you have to always be aware of what's grammatically feminine, what's masculine. Things to keep in mind in Cherokee: the shape of objects; their relationship to you in space; whether they are living or dead, human or inhuman; the way they move.

Linda Jordan described the words as "data-laden, dense with information concerning the speaker's perception of, attitudes toward, and proximity to actions, events and objects." Cherokee used a different word for "have" depending on the object you had: different ways of having something flexible, something alive, something solid, something solid and long, and something liquid. Cherokee also marked possessives in several different ways. You possessed your car in a different way than you possessed "your" parents, and Cherokee accounted for that by describing a relationship rather than a possession.

I wanted to find heightened differences among languages; there lay a justification for saving them. But the reality was subtle; differences in thought weren't so much embedded in language as shot through it, angling here and there through semantic categories. The meaning of the language remained personal, imprinted by the moments of use, the bonds with the other people who spoke it.

It was at the end of one of our sessions that Mr. Sawney told me about a Keetoowah Band meeting that was to be held at Ross Mountain. "Umm, can I go?" I said, trying not to sound too eager.

"Sure," he said.

They were planning to talk about teaching; the meeting would start at six-thirty on Friday night. He said, "Don't be shy. Use the language. If you have questions, feel free to ask." We ended with a lesson on how to say, "Mr. Sawney is a good teacher." Somehow it made sense that I had needed to learn the language before I would get a chance to visit the place again.

After class, I did a dress rehearsal to make sure I'd be able to find Ross Mountain again. I followed Mr. Sawney's directions there, omitting only the last half mile. I drove down Highway 59, went around the bend of a big hill, noticing the signs, and took the Ross Mountain road that slanted up to the left. Then there was a little curve and an intersection, and half a mile later a dirt road turned right. For now, I paused and turned around, admiring the blue hills on the way out.

Before the meeting at Ross Mountain, I muttered phrases to myself as I drove: "Hello. How are you? Good. And you? Pretty day. It really is. My name is Li-si." Mr. Sawney had told me that was how Cherokees rendered *Elizabeth.* "I am from New York. Do you speak Cherokee? Yes, I am learning Cherokee."

I was still hearing them in my head as I walked up to the house with the long porch and waited at the open door. I could see people inside; no one approached, so I walked in and recognized Albert Ross, who was talking with a cluster of men in the sparsely furnished kitchen. He said something to me in Cherokee—I couldn't make out what it was. He repeated it. Another man helped me: *"O-s-da,"* he muttered. "Good." So Ross had been asking me how I was. I felt a shadowy sense of futility, as if I had just failed my first test.

Mr. Sawney looked up from the crafts he was displaying on a table and caught my eye. He welcomed me and found me a seat at the edge of a room. His wife, back with her family, was more vivacious than I'd ever seen her, hanging out and giggling and chatting in Cherokee. In almost no time—as if they'd been waiting for me—people stood up, and Mr. Sawney began a long, flowing Cherokee prayer. There were about fifteen of them, mostly men, lounging on chairs around the edges of two sparsely furnished rooms decorated with pictures of children, of Jesus, and of praying hands. On the wall was a certificate proclaiming the Ross Mountain Community Foundation a 5013C nonprofit.

I nodded to Frank Swimmer as he took the floor, standing beside a big stove on one side of the room. Swimmer was also vice chairman of gaming commissioners for the United Keetoowah Band, chairman of the housing board, and a councilman. He began speaking about the importance of language, switching back and forth between Cherokee and English. He seemed more animated than I'd remembered. He preserved the same mood—calm, straightforward, with a leavening of jokes—in both languages. I hadn't heard Cherokee spoken at such length in a while, and I watched how Swimmer spoke his Cherokee out of the side of his mouth. Even after the lessons, I could only pick out words.

Swimmer switched into English: "You look around and another generation don't speak the language no more." The youngest people there were a pretty, sleepy-looking woman in a T-shirt from a local bar chain called Eskimo Joe's and her four-year-old boy, who was sprawled in extreme boredom on her lap.

"We do really need to keep our language going," he added. Otherwise, "the inside is a white man. That's the way the white man figured to get rid of Indians, get rid of their language." That was why he hoped they could construct the community building and hold classes there. "Even myself, I mispronounce my language," he joked, saying that one old woman had laughed at him when he said the wrong thing.

In formal style, other Keetoowah Band officials made reports on their membership and fund-raising activities in English. They exchanged English and Cherokee easily, because the crowd understood both. Julie Moss, a younger, more assimilated official, spoke entirely in English, but when Swimmer commented on her speech in Cherokee, she nodded and said "All right."

Archie Mouse, the deputy chief of the Keetoowahs, stood up and joked for a while like a stand-up comedian, with a cigarette in his hand. He had a smooth, unlined face with slightly protuberant eyes and a thin ponytail. He was a rapid-fire talker, a former lobbyist who seemed to enjoy matching wits in English. He had bought a pipe from Mr. Sawney. "Hey!" he said. "Where's my pipe?" He jokingly accused the men on the couch of stealing it.

"Someone was witching you with it," one of the men said.

"One thing I cherish a lot, in my age group, we were taught how to read the language," Mouse said, turning serious. He said he thought he might know fifty people who could read and write in the syllabary. As Mouse spoke, I looked at Mr. Sawney and noticed he was sitting forward in his chair, attuned and anticipatory.

I was beginning to feel a numbing realization that I would have to say something to the group. My heart started to beat faster, and my hands felt shaky. I began writing myself a little speech that strung together everything I knew I could say in Cherokee. Before I could finish, Mr. Sawney stood up and said in English that he had taught me some lessons and it was going really well. He said, "You just ask her anything in Cherokee, and she'll give you an answer." I emitted a laugh of modesty and fear and slumped into the beat-up leather chair I was sitting in.

"Ask her anything you want," he said. "See, for example—"

"Excuse me, Mr. Sawney," I broke in. "Can I say something?" I flipped my notebook to the section with my little speech and read it. "*Lis-i da-gw'do-a.* New York *di-je-nv-sv. G'de-la gwa-a jalagi a-ge-wo-ni-hi-s-di-i.* Mr. Sawney *os-da di-de-yo-hu-s-gi.*" I picked up in English. "And while I came here as a journalist, writing about what's going on with the language, I'd like to support the project any way I can."

There was an encouraging nod from Swimmer and then polite applause.

Mr. Sawney insisted on quizzing me anyway, but it was easy enough. "What do you want?"

"*Ka-hwi?*" I guessed, "*a-gwa-du-li.*" I want coffee.

"And say if she's selling strawberries I'll ask her, 'What are you selling?' "

"*A-ni ji-na-de-ga.*"

"That's it," Frank said with a small smile. He said ceremoniously in English that he would like to invite Sawney to come and teach a class at Ross Mountain on Saturday afternoons, and he hoped, with a significant look at Archie, that maybe the Keetoowah tribal council could find some gas money.

Through the rest of the speeches, I mused about what had happened, half afraid to look at Sawney. I was gathering belatedly that

Ross Mountain was moving its language program forward, and that I was unwittingly providing a spark of entertainment for the announcement. I was accustomed to watching, but now I was part of the action.

Still, it was hard to tell who would take Sawney's lessons at Ross Mountain. As the meeting ended and people began lining up at the kitchen for portions of chili, I chatted with the pretty young woman who had brought her four-year-old boy. I asked if he spoke any of the language. "No," she said sheepishly. Nor did she. She had married into this community, after growing up at Line Switch, not far away. I said, "Oh, so your parents didn't speak it?"

"No—they spoke it," she corrected me.

"But they didn't teach you?"

"Oh, they wanted to teach me," she replied with a smile. "But I didn't want to learn." Her boy hid behind her legs and looked at us with bright, round eyes. We played a brief game of peek-a-boo, and he smiled silently.

People started dispersing, and I followed Mr. Sawney out with a few Cherokee good-byes. As I drove away, I watched people walk off the porch into the darkness, heading for the houses down the hill. Once I had gone about five hundred feet down the road, I poked my head out my car window and looked up at the sky, which seemed to hang low here: more stars than I had seen in a while, and a bright sliver of a moon.

A lot would depend on Sawney's classes. I was not sure the place could remain a haven for the language. But my worry was tempered by excitement over something unexpected: The language was entering me. Instead of witnessing the language, I was becoming part of it.

In fact I loved it: the deciphering of the alphabet, the pleasure of sounding out words, the discovery of deep structure in the grammar. It wasn't just the code breaking; I don't enjoy crossword puzzles or acrostics. Maybe the difference is that languages promise something bigger. The reward is not the feeling of completion one gets at the end of a puzzle; completion is what I don't want. What drew me instead was the promise of endless absorption in the problem, the promise that there would always be more to learn, the promise of a descent into order and meaning. Yearning for harmony, I found it inside the language.

There was some kind of escapism in the studying, a sensation of merciful obsession. Eventually, it occurred to me that learning the language distracted me from having to think about losing the language; it was my balm for that loss, my riposte to the questions. And so they alternated, a sense of loss and a search for order, and drove me forward into the language.

Sawney and I continued our lessons after the Ross Mountain meeting. The next time we met, the office window was open; the temperature was seventy-five degrees, and we could hear the wind chimes tinkling on the porch. In Oklahoma, seasonal change is instantaneous. The light snow melts away to reveal flowers already blooming.

I waited for him to say something about the meeting, but he didn't. When I asked him how he thought it had gone, he said it was all right. "Those things we're learning," he said, "it's time you put those together." He wanted me to start making longer sentences. "Just line 'em up, and one of these days, maybe we'll talk Cherokee together."

Mr. Sawney said he knew now that he could teach the language, and he wondered whether there was some way I could help.

"How?" I said. "I don't speak it well."

"I speak this language, and you can pronounce it, and if there's any problem, we put our two heads together." He noted that I had a college degree and knew how to write things down.

I asked him if people would object to the idea that a white person had anything to teach them, and he said he didn't think that would be

203

a problem. "In high school and grade school, they come, they just know that someone is there to teach, to help, to do whatever, and they usually accept anybody. It means that you've learned and you are sharing with them what you learned."

I found myself wondering how I could help. I loved this language, this alphabet, this teacher. I found myself aspiring to speak better than anyone, to please Mr. Sawney, to be the person who could keep the language going. I thought of Brian Levy in Anadarko. I was beginning to better understand the relationships I had seen between other older speakers and younger learners, between Kionute and Levy—the fine strands of affection and obligation that sprang up between people. This relationship delighted me.

But it also scared me, because I wasn't sure I would be able to fulfill my part. I wasn't sure I wanted this lonely identity, half inside, half outside a rare culture. It seemed a ridiculous position: the white hanger-on, the eternal outsider. I was aware, too, that my learning a few phrases wasn't going to help the community at Ross Mountain or change the future of the language.

Back in Tulsa, I had allowed my parents to drag me to a lunch some of their friends were having. The Cherokee immersion school came up, and one woman said: "Isn't that a hoot. Immersion school in a dying language. It's like . . . an immersion school in Latin!" She wasn't saying this dismissively but making a point that anyone in pragmatic, businesslike Tulsa might make. In a time of recession, when the last Fortune 500 companies were leaving Oklahoma and the schools were shrinking, and unemployment was rising, why would anyone spend money on a language?

I was beginning to understood in a more visceral way the challenge of learning a Native American language. It's not only hard to learn. It's hard to believe in the learning. It feels crazy to imagine living in one of these languages.

I had come late this day, and we talked until five, when the rare sun of spring had left the little window. We talked about the lessons Mr. Sawney was planning at Ross Mountain. "I just hope someday that you and me will be speaking Cherokee together," he added. "And I know . . . *ni-da-ga-l-s-da-ni.* It's going to happen."

The weather got warmer; wherever I drove, I smelled smoke as people went out and started barbecuing and burning things; more vendors came out—a pottery maker, a birdhouse maker by the side of the road in downtown Tahlequah. One day, we had class outside on the porch, as trucks and cars growled by on the highway and the chimes jingled. Off in the distance I could see blue hills, one of which was Ross Mountain. Sawney's classes there hadn't started yet. As Mr. Sawney tested me with a few phrases, his wife listened for a while, covering a smile with her hand. Once, she corrected me when I said "New York."

"It's *Nuyoki,*" she said. "That's how Cherokees say it." Then she wandered off to check her pots around the trailer: She was growing roses, begonias, tomatoes, peppers. I learned "it's hot" this day; the heat made me sleepy. I was hungry, so I pulled out a couple of cookies I had in my bag and offered one to Mr. Sawney. His eyes lit up. "I'm a real cookie monster," he said, making me giggle.

I wondered if it was the innocence of new-language world that attracted me to it. In new-language world, everyone is so nice. In new-language world, people focus on the basics, like eating bread and drinking coffee and talking about their parents and children. It's like being in summer camp: a natural world with trees and sun and rain and earth and nothing more complicated. No one condescends or obfuscates; no one cheats on his girlfriend or takes cheap shots. People sometimes can kill each other in new-language world, after they've been there for a while. But even that is pretty simple. No one goes on life support or has a panic attack or gets hooked on medications. (Not unless they're precocious, anyway.)

They can't and they won't talk about these things; even if they can describe such feelings, it's against the culture of the lesson. It's as if the teacher and learner must revert to childhood. There is a wonderful ease to it—the innocence, the learning, the discovery. The new language allows everyone to start over.

But of course, you can't live in new-language world for long. You can see why many people in their teens and twenties don't like it there; it doesn't express the full complexity of their emotional lives.

Not long afterward, I revisited Hastings Shade, who was about to end his term as deputy chief. I told him about my Cherokee studies, adding that I hadn't learned very much. "It's hard," I said offhandedly.

"That's how we limit ourselves," he said reprovingly. "All the time I hear people say, 'I'd like to learn this or that.' I say, '*Do* you?' And they say, 'Maybe.'" He looked at me: "They want to learn only what they want to learn. They don't want to learn what *has* to be learned. The world is full of choices. Do you *want* to learn? It's a choice."

As the spring wore on, I looked halfheartedly for a house to rent around Tahlequah, but I couldn't commit to the idea. Since I had started looking for language two years before, I had been gradually coming to accept that I would be using the word *home* for sites in both New York and Oklahoma. I would have to work out a life in two places, as I flew back and forth from New York. Already, I was commuting. I had even run into Archie Mouse, the deputy chief, in the Tulsa airport once; he was heading off on some tribal business. I told him what I was doing. "Wish I was rich like that," he joked.

I had a ticket to New York at the end of March, and before I left I brought a tape player to Sawney's house and taped him saying a compendium of phrases I'd selected. I said I wanted to make sure I didn't forget the pronunciation, but he suggested a deeper reason: "That way, you'll have someone to practice with."

I had a bunch of other words that I wanted to run by him. First, I asked him about a phrase that I had heard referred to Lost City, but he didn't know it; indeed, he'd never heard a Cherokee name for the place. Then I ran some of Hastings Shade's words by him: *anidolido.* He knew it: "a person that roams here and there." I tried *anihiya:* He looked at me quizzically and said: "That's for people that was already here when everything was there, or you could use that for people that live there all the time. People who were born and raised all their life in their own community."

I remembered that Mr. Sawney's lessons at Ross Mountain were supposed to have started. I told him about a handwritten syllabary I had seen. "Maybe you could use that at Ross Mountain," I said.

He replied, "Well, I made something like this." He reached behind a file cabinet and pulled out a big piece of posterboard with a calligraphic syllabary drawn on it in thick pen lines.

"This weekend—you made it just now?" I stuttered, a little ashamed that I had been telling him how to plan a lesson.

He nodded with the small, reticent smile he had when he wasn't going to give anything more away.

I asked how the first lesson had gone. "Well, hardly anybody showed up," he said. "Three of 'em. We'll try again Friday evening. Saturday people usually go places."

"I hope it works out." As I helped him slide the poster back behind the cabinet, I was infatuated with admiration for his work, and at the same time my heart sank at the thought of him sitting in his office at night, drawing away in preparation for a class that might never find students. Still, he said, someone else from the Keetoowahs had asked him about teaching another course.

When it was time for me to go, I gave him a pen I had brought. "For all that teaching and writing you do," I said. He looked at it and used the fanciest Cherokee expression of thanks we had learned. "I'll be using it a lot." I hoped he would.

Now I said, "Well, I have to go," and I took a cheating glance down at my notebook and said it in Cherokee, too.

"Did you know I'm going to miss you?" he said in his straightforward way, catching me off guard. We hadn't learned that phrase in Cherokee yet.

"I'll miss you, too," I said, standing up. He stood up and gave me a hug, and I bent way down to hug him back. Then we walked out to his living room, and he proudly tested me in front of his wife, asking me in Cherokee where and when I was going. "When will you come back?" he asked.

"In the month of April I will come back," I said in Cherokee, though as usual I fumbled a little.

It was a gray day, and the gentle chimes on his porch seemed sad. I had never noticed before that their chord was in a minor key. As I drove away, I glanced at him, standing in his small doorway, and I wondered that I had ever found the house strange or foreign.

Of all my travels in Oklahoma, this was my favorite: into the outer precincts of the Cherokee language. Surely I had learned no more than a high-school student in one semester, and I had no illusions that my lessons were changing the plight of Ross Mountain: Sawney needed young students. Leach continued to plan for a cultural center, but we wouldn't know for years how successful it would be.

But this journey touched me in a different way. When I first was taking Cherokee lessons, I occasionally had language dreams, full of spurious connections and lost poems and unnamable yearnings. I dreamed of a recognition that there was a common American word for storekeeper, a familiar word, and that it came from the Cherokee word for "are you selling," *hi-na-de-ga*. I later realized that I was likely making a false association with the Spanish word *bodega*. Another time, I dreamed that someone had given me some kind of little-known password I could use to enter a Cherokee conversation. "What if I don't use it?" I asked. "They'll speak English if you don't," a woman said to me.

Then there were generalized language dreams, like the dream in which you're reading a text—or, even more tantalizing, writing it—but the more you try to grasp it, to memorize it, the more it slides, melts away, until what's left is just a sensation that you can no longer put into words. And then you wake up and the words you use to write down that sensation feel like a rough skeleton of a half-built house.

There is the dream of being lost, surrounded by people who don't speak your language or understand what you're doing. It is the flip side of cultural diversity—the potential for finding yourself among strangers who don't understand, cut off from your background, alienated, alone in America.

There is another dream, too, that there is a place where you can use your language. It might be hill country full of birds and spirits and colors and trees. You wander over its hills. You walk through its forests. You arrive in glades where strangers are sitting around a fire, and you listen like a ghost as they joke with each other.

That place where you can use your language must exist; you know it must be out there. What, after all, is the idea of learning a language? What is the point? When do you know you're done? It's a road without an end. Along the way, you hope the scenery's all right. You hope it will lead you to some interesting people. But the destination is always obscure. Really, the end is for the road itself to disappear beneath you; the end is that you find yourself in trackless woods and you realize you can turn any which way, and it won't matter; you're home.

Epilogue

THE BRONZE INDIAN shone on the top of the state capitol dome as a group of people gathered on the steps below. Several dozen protesters were holding up signs, trying to attract the attention of a few media cameras. They were rallying against a bill that would declare English the official language of Oklahoma.

Ron Kirby, the Oklahoma legislator who was sponsoring the measure, strongly denied any intent to devalue Native languages in the bill. "This is a cost-saving measure," he told me. "It just makes common sense. You walk in and you want a copy of a death certificate in Italian. Now we have to figure out your dialect . . . Think of the expense of that. Hey, if you want it in Italian, get one of your friends to speak a little English."

He conceded that no one had ever asked for multilingual documents in Oklahoma, but said the bill was preemptive. The measure came at a time when Oklahoma was undergoing a severe budget crunch. School funding was in a crisis; the legislature was cutting substitute teachers, increasing class sizes, and asking the remaining teachers to sweep floors.

Though the bill was a mainly symbolic measure, the scene demonstrated the continued relevance of the argument about how much value to assign to diversity—and the need to define the value of minority languages. The issues that the English Only bill raised are being debated all over the world. And they will continue to simmer as long as the frontier of modern culture continues to move across the globe, reducing language diversity.

Babel can be costly, whether it means finding Cherokee-speaking nurses for health clinics or translating documents. Reviving small languages—from writing textbooks to funding classes to improving communities' viability—is even more expensive. Voters have not expressed a consensus that minority languages are worth saving; trying to nurture them is seen as a quixotic waste of resources.

At the Oklahoma rally, many people argued that there was a broad societal interest in preserving the languages. They made an analogy between biodiversity and linguistic diversity, noting that languages and animals are subject to similar forces of extinction. As Quese Frejo had once put it to me: "It's almost like these languages should be looked upon as an endangered species. But now when you look at species, you have all these people, organizations, that come together and say 'We have to do something to save this animal. We have to save this pet. We've got to save this bird.' But when they look at Native Americans, it's like, 'Well, you know it's going to die anyway.' "

The analogy to biodiversity is imperfect, because it relies on a view of ecological interbalance in which the loss of some species affects the larger ecosystem; languages aren't like that. Humans evolve new languages faster than earth evolves new species, so variety in language will be with us longer than variety in species. And languages look less likely to provide future scientific and medical advances than rare plants.

Yet there are practical reasons for keeping languages around. Old languages are a rich source of information, not only for linguists but also for cognitive scientists and students of human history and culture. Linguists use them to understand the universal rules of grammar and the origins of language itself. Anthropologists learn about the history of human migrations and ancient people's contacts with each other. One linguist is studying languages spoken in Chechnya, Georgia, and Azerbaijan to understand the culture of the first farmers of the Fertile Crescent. Other scientists have analyzed Celtic languages to explore who inhabited the British Isles before 700 B.C. and used languages to study how universal spatial concepts are. The information contained in the vocabularies of tribal languages, which reflect intimate knowledge of plants and animal habits, may contain many useful insights about the natural world. And the variations that occur within languages could help philosophers explore the boundaries of human thought. "We have to know about human language, because we want to know what it is to be human," said Alice Anderton, the head of Intertribal Wordpath Society, who was leading the rally.

Also, the languages are connected to broader philosophical traditions, from the Navajo sense of the sacred within daily life to the Cherokee interconnections with nature to the Kiowa primacy of social relationships. One man named Quinton Roman Nose got up and said that his mother had dreamed in Cheyenne. "When you think in other languages, you have a different perspective on things," he added. "This bill could prevent new ideas from coming to Oklahoma."

As I watched, though, it occurred to me that there was no winning the debate on utilitarian grounds; proponents of languages would never be able to prove their value to outsiders. The life of the languages would have to depend on Americans' ability to value other cultures' ideas and creations. Some speakers agreed. "Language is a fundamental human right," said Harry Oosahwee, a Cherokee speaker who was coordinating a language curriculum for the Cherokee Nation. "We shouldn't even be talking about this in the state of Oklahoma."

Ross Mountain and the other small communities I had visited were on my mind. The bill would not pass through the legislature that year. But its movement forward—and the scanty media coverage— were signs of how little clout the languages had, and the main threat to the languages was not active discrimination but a lack of action. Maybe, I thought, this state would go the way of the rest of the country, where the old names are entirely alien to their places. Oklahoma simply represents the last stage in the long destruction of these cultures—lost cities, a lost continent. If that happens, why not take down that flag with the crossed peace pipes? Why celebrate a past that runs no continuous line to the present? Let nothing remain but the names on the map.

But before that happens, there are steps policymakers could take to support the languages, not only in Oklahoma but also in New Mexico, Arizona, California, and all the other places where people still speak Native tongues. Federal and state education authorities could encourage schools to offer American Indian languages and raise the standards for classes. Often, Indian-language courses are taught at basic levels with rudimentary textbooks. Presenting short word lists for a few minutes a day has some symbolic value but won't bring back any language. Immersion schools like Hawaii's are more effective.

At the same time, the schools could make better use of the remaining fluent speakers. Some elders want to teach more—but if they don't have the credentials to teach in public schools, they are limited to as few as ten hours a week. Other elders need to improve their teaching skills, but they have neither the money nor the time to enter university degree programs. Some teachers fear that the No Child Left Behind Act of 2001 will be particularly hard on Native-language programs, because it links school funding to a narrow set of tests, leaving schools with no incentive to offer tribal languages. Plus, it requires teachers to have more of the kinds of college degrees that are difficult for older, poorer people to get.

To help bring more qualified teachers into the schools, state universities could establish specialized teacher-training programs aimed at fluent speakers who are older or lack academic backgrounds. Meanwhile, states could create alternative teacher-certification processes. For high-school children, schools may want to focus on improving the quality of teaching and textbooks; for preschool and Head Start programs, which are less academically oriented, the focus would be on quickly getting fluent elders into classrooms with children, whether that means easing requirements or pairing a fluent elder with a young, English-speaking teacher. Meanwhile, both states and the federal government could provide grants for establishing language programs.

The tribes themselves could do even better by starting their own schools and immersion programs. Very few tribal governments in Oklahoma even fund a language program every year; hardly any have a teacher-certification process. Most of the language committees I encountered were founded outside of tribal governments, sometimes because they feared political interference and sometimes because the leadership was simply uninterested in the language. This is worrisome, because tribal governments are in the best position to help by starting immersion schools, as the Cherokees have; by developing curricula; and by funding more positions for teachers.

Private donors and foundations could raise money for language materials, for the recruitment, training, and support of teachers, and for community centers that protect elders from poverty and disease. One organization, Anderton's Intertribal Wordpath Society, is already working to train teachers, to advise Oklahoma's tribes on alphabets and curricula, and to raise awareness about Indian languages through a cable-access TV show and an annual festival. Anderton, its founder, is one of the few people in Oklahoma who have long recognized the plight of the languages there. A number of other organizations, such as the Oklahoma Native Language Association, the American Indian Language Development Institute, the Indigenous Language Institute, and the Endangered Language Fund are already helping train teachers and assist language committees, among other projects.

All these efforts need not be limited to academic programs. It's easier to preserve a community that still speaks a Native language than to try to revive the language among nonspeakers. This suggests a radically different, more holistic approach: identifying the few communities where Native languages are spoken and preserving them. One step might be identifying the Ross Mountains and honoring their speakers the way the Comanches honor the code talkers— as the standard-bearers for a tribal tradition.

Ultimately, though, the languages' fate will be up to the people who speak them. Some plants bud at the onset of drought; in the past decade, there has been a desperate flowering of programs from Canada to Mexico, as tribes try to ensure that their languages will continue to be spoken. In recent years, Oklahomans have started classes in Cheyenne, Shawnee, Wyandotte, Choctaw, Muskogee-Creek, and Osage, among others. But it is not an easy task. If language occasionally seems beside the point, it is because other values—community, identity, culture, success—are so entwined with it that it is hard to pick out a single strand.

Before I left Oklahoma again, I needed to go to one more place. I followed the rolling ranch countryside—cows, woods, curves, little hills—back toward Lost City. Something unexpected was happening there: The Cherokee Nation was planning another immersion classroom at the Lost City school.

The catalyst, it seemed, was the local school superintendent, Annette Millard, who was not Cherokee but liked the idea of an immersion class. Her kindergarten group wouldn't start until the next school year, but in the meantime, Lost City was hosting a night class in Cherokee, and I decided to attend. I wanted to take stock of what had changed since I had first visited.

I drove past the dark windows of Toby Hughes's shop, and visited the Vanns, too, on the way out. I drove past little churches. In the countryside, there were spots of pretty things—a stain of clover on a field, bunches of daffodils along a lawn, and the bud trees that were so prevalent in Oklahoma—redbuds, white buds, slipping their mists of color sleevelike over the branches. You could almost miss them when you stared, but the colors were there in the corners of your vision. "Redbuds bloom in early spring . . ." said the poet Robin Coffee, who had written about "a scar upon our voice." The twilight vision reminded me of all the communities I'd hoped to see, the ones that were there half seen, the ones that had faded away.

The fields that looked so plain in the glare of full day gradually turned gold in the afternoon light, the trees' shadows deepened and brightened, and the sky had more shades of lavender than any language had words for. As I drove, the colors flowed without distinction toward blackness.

I liked the idea that even Lost City might get its language back. But as promising as the immersion class was, I was aware of all that it was not. Lost City had always been a romantic notion. Since I had first driven these roads, I had learned that the past was ever-receding, that language was intertwined with culture, that preservation was nearly impossible, that perfect order was reserved for heaven and alphabets, and that the children were already out of elders' reach, spinning spells even I couldn't decipher.

The gravestones by the school stood tall under a streetlight, and a big, pink moon hung low in the east. As I got out of the car, it was very quiet on the road. All I heard was the twittering, sniggering frogs and insects of the countryside. Hastings Shade would know their names, I thought. He was not involved in the immersion school, but it was what he had envisioned.

When we had driven by, the school had been empty. This time, I was meeting people in a large, bright classroom. The walls were lined with classroom icons—a map of the United States, the Bill of Rights, a poster that said BUILDERS OF A NEW SOCIETY, and pictures of various great moments—a train coming around a bend, a bunch of horses with Plains Indians on them, the Statue of Liberty, the Iwo Jima flag raisers.

This was a beginner-level class—and only the second in the series—but the teacher, Jim Carey, was serious about teaching Cherokee. He had taught for years at Sequoyah High School—I had stood outside his classroom when I was there—and he had an easy, self-deprecating manner: He clowned, joked about his handwriting, and worked Cherokee lore and history into the lessons.

"A lot of people here don't speak anymore because the elders didn't teach them," Carey explained as the class got under way. Two mothers were there to study Cherokee that night, each with a light-

218

haired daughter. They were part of the substantial mixed-blood community in the area. The two women watched him respectfully. Much of this was new to them. "People wanted everyone to assimilate," he said.

"Why would you want everyone to be the same?" exclaimed the woman to my left.

Carey didn't reply but got the class under way by reviewing vocabulary from the previous lesson: "What's *su-li?*"

Both women looked blank; both little girls said "buzzard." He went on: "*We-sa*. Cat." Water. Salt. Bread, meat, bird, fish. The girls slouched back in their chairs. They knew most of the words. Flower, goose, little, milk, children.

Carey then stood up and went to the blackboard for a lesson in drawing the syllabary. "You'll have to excuse my penmanship," he joked. "I was asleep during that class in school." I relaxed: Back in class.

I watched them learn the shapes of Sequoyah's letters—Ꭸ *(ge)*, Ᏻ *(yu)*, Ꮭ *(tlo)*, Ꮃ *(la)*, Ꮭ *(tso)*. I had never watched anyone actually make the strokes for each character: For Ꮭ, he said, "Come down, go back up, make a little loop, and go back across," and they all reproduced his moves, down, up, loop, across. I tightened my grip on my pen and drew the sign again. I could see that the woman to my right had done her homework, rewriting each syllable a dozen times across the pages of her notebook. Carey wiped off the blackboard and started again.

As the students in the class practiced speaking and writing, I listened, saying the words to myself, too. To learn, you had to inscribe the language in the muscles, train them to recombine the sounds with ease. It felt like too little to bother with. The syllables went into the air and faded. Speech is brief. But extra practice never hurt, even if it felt sometimes like the art of losing.

I recalled that many years ago, when I took a trip to China, I saw a man who painted Chinese characters in water on a sandstone path every day in the park. He used a brush so long he walked sideways as he worked. A line of calligraphy trailed in the sun, disappearing behind him like a comet's watery tail. He went there every morning to practice his writing, the way others went to the park to do tai chi or jog.

I watched him for a long time, and I never forgot him. The image stuck with me, because it showed how language lived in the muscles; because shaping the letters with wisps of hair and water, the swish and turn of the brush, was the closest thing I could think of to making love to the alphabet; because words in water practiced impermanence so gracefully, unlike our printed, indented pages; and finally because any letter could be a clue, and we couldn't afford to neglect anything that might tell us what to do with our lives.

Author's Notes

Introduction

I BASED THE INTRODUCTION on a variety of sources. The origins of Oklahoma town names are described in George H. Shirk's *Oklahoma Place Names*.

The Micmac language anecdote comes from *Vanishing Voices*, by Nettle and Romaine. *They Have a Word for It: A Lighthearted Lexicon of Untranslatable Words and Phrases*, by Howard Rheingold, contains a delightful list of words from other languages that includes the Iroquois word cited here. The Muskogee-Creek words were described in the author's interviews with Margaret McKane Mauldin, co-author of *A Dictionary of Creek Muskogee: With Notes on the Florida and Oklahoma Seminole Dialects of Creek*, in January 2002, and the Comanche word comes from interviews with Alice Anderton and Richard Codopony. The notion of "the great forever that was" was cited in interviews with Sequoyah Guess, a collector of old Cherokee stories.

A list of words that come from Indian languages can be found in *America in So Many Words: Words That Have Shaped America,* by David K. Barnhart and Allan A. Metcalf, and Charles L. Cutler's *O Brave New Words!: Native American Loanwords in Current English.* Edward Gray's *New World Babel: Languages and Nations in Early America* is one source for the speculations about Native American origins. Thomas Jefferson wrote about his speculations on Native American sources in a letter to Ezra Stiles Sept. 1, 1786.

More information on the history of Native languages in North America can be found in *The Voyages of Jacques Cartier,* as well as in *The Languages of Native North America,* by Marianne Mithun, *Indians and English: Facing Off in Early America,* by Karen Ordahl Kupperman, *American Indian Languages: The Historical Linguistics of Native America,* by Lyle Campbell, and the *Languages* volume of the *Handbook of Native American Indians,* edited by Ives Goddard.

The anecdote about a village in Papua New Guinea that chose a new word for "no" comes from D. Kulick's *Language Shift and Cultural Reproduction: Socialization, Self and Syncretism in a Papua New Guinean Village* (Cambridge: Cambridge University Press, 1992) and is cited in the book *Vanishing Voices.* Roman Jakobson's insights on language can be found in his 1959 essay "On Linguistic Aspects of Translation," published in the book *On Translation,* edited by Reuben A. Brower.

Edward Sapir's comment on Algonkin sentences, from *Language: An Introduction to the Study of Speech,* is quoted in *O Brave New Words!* by Cutler. The evolution of languages is described in John McWhorter's *The Power of Babel,* which is quoted here. Aldous Huxley's quote is from *The Doors of Perception.*

Chapter 1: "Where Do I Find Lost City?"

Hastings Shade's book *Myths, Legends, and Old Sayings* was compiled in 1994; he was interviewed in August 2000 and June 2003. Joshua Fishman commented on the "indexical" relationship of language to culture in "Maintaining Languages: What Works? What Doesn't?", an essay found in the book *Stabilizing Indigenous Languages*. Information on California languages comes from Leanne Hinton's *Flutes of Fire: Essays on Californian Indian Languages*. Robin Coffee's poem, "A Scar Upon Our Voice," appears in his collection, *The Eagle and the Cross*, published in 2000 by Whitebird Publishing Adventure, P.O. Box 124, Tahlequah, OK, 74465. This Cherokee font, created by the Cherokee Nation, is found at www.cherokee.org.

Chapter 2: Lost Causes

Michael E. Krauss assessed the state of Indian languages in an article called "The Condition of Native American Languages: The Need for Realistic Assessment and Action," published in *International Journal of the Sociology of Language* 132 (1998), 9–21. Lyle Campbell's chart of Uto-Aztecan languages is found in *American Indian Languages: The Historical Linguistics of Native America*. The Comanche Language and Cultural Preservation Committee Web site is http://www.comanche language.org.

Washington Irving's *A Tour on the Prairies* and Thomas Nuttall's *A Journal of Travels into the Arkansas Territory During the Year 1819* are still in print. Fort Sill history was drawn from http://sill-www.army.mil/tngcmd/tc.htm.

Interviews with Ron Red Elk took place in March 2000 and March 2001; Richard Codopony was interviewed in March 2000 and

June 2003; Carney Saupitty, Barbara Goodin, Ken Goodin, Billie Kreger, Vernon and Gloria Cable, and Lucille McClung were interviewed in March 2000; Margrett Oberly Kelley in March 2001; and Rosalie Attocknie in March 2001.

Anthony Woodbury analyzed Cup'ik suffixes in "Documenting Rhetorical, Aesthetic, and Expressive Loss in Language Shift," *Endangered Languages: Language Loss and Community Response*, edited by Lenore A. Grenoble and Lindsay J. Whaley, 234–258. Information about the Comanches' history is derived from: *Being Comanche: A Social History of an American Indian Community*, by Morris W. Foster, and *The Comanches: Lords of the South Plains*, by Ernest Wallace and E. Adamson Hoebel. Joshua Fishman is quoted from his essay, "Maintaining Languages: What Works? What Doesn't?" in *Stabilizing Indigenous Languages*, edited by G. Cantoni, pages 186 and 198.

Chapter 3: The Code Talker

Interviews with Charles Chibitty, August 2000, January 2002, and May 2003, provided the bulk of the information. Hugh F. Foster, a retired major general of the U.S. Army in Furlong, Pennsylvania, provided valuable background. Comanche language use in 1940 was described by Joseph B. Casagrande in "Comanche Linguistic Acculturation III" in *International Journal of American Linguistics* 21 (1955), pages 9–10, and was cited in Morris W. Foster's *Being Comanche*.

Other sources were: Jonathan Gawne's *Spearheading D-Day: American Special Units of the Normandy Invasion*, and William C. Meadows's *The Comanche Code Talkers of World War II*. Another resource is *Comanche Code Talkers: The Last Comanche Code Talker "Recollections of Charles Chibitty,"* a video made by Hidden Path Productions, P.O. Box 248, Mannford, OK 74044.

Chapter 4: Orphan Child

Author interviews with Sadie Parnell took place in January 2002, April 2002, and May 2003; author interviews with Don Franklin, in January 2002. He possesses copies of *Oklahoma Indian School Magazine* from the early 1930s, where comments were drawn from the Seneca Indian School and the Jones Academy editions.

Information on Indian boarding schools is drawn from *To Change Them Forever: Indian Education at the Rainy Mountain Boarding School, 1893–1920,* by Clyde Ellis, and David Wallace Adams's *Education for Extinction: American Indians and the Boarding School Experience 1875–1928.* Estelle Reel's comments in the 1901 Annual Report of the Commissioner of Indian Affairs are cited in *To Change Them Forever.* The anecdote about the code talkers is drawn from Meadows's *The Comanche Code Talkers of World War II.*

A wealth of information about Sequoyah can be found in *Celebrating Sequoyah: Meeting the Needs of Native Youth for 125 Years,* a 1997 compilation of history and memories put together by Don Franklin.

Information on the biological foundations of language is drawn from *The Biology and Evolution of Language,* by Philip Lieberman, and *The Secret Life of the Brain,* by Richard Restak, as well as an author interview with Marilyn Monnot in January 2002.

General information on the Cherokees' and the Keetoowahs' origins can be found in *After the Trail of Tears: The Cherokees' Struggle for Sovereignty, 1839–1880,* by William C. McLoughlin. The latter is the source of the suggestion that Keetoowah resistance delayed Oklahoma's statehood. More information lies in *The Cherokees: A Population History,* by Russell Thornton, as well as United Keetoowah Band handouts on their history.

Information on Cherokee Nation efforts to promote the languages is drawn from interviews with Diane Woodard, Barbara Littledave, and Sandra Turner in January 2002, as well as interviews with Gloria Sly, Dusty Delso, and Harry Oosahwee in March, April, and May 2003.

Chapter 5: Plan B

Author interviews with Brian Levy took place in October 2000, December 2000, January 2001, and January 2002. More information on Kiwat Hasinay Foundation, a Caddo-preservation organization, can be found at http://ahalenia.com/kiwat/ or Kiwat Hasinay Foundation, Box 305, Binger, OK 73009. Charlene Brown Wright was interviewed in January 2001; Richard Grounds in October 2000, December 2000, and January 2001. Linguist Akira Yamamoto spoke at an Oklahoma Native Language Association Conference in October 2000. Data on Anadarko's biggest employers stem from the Anadarko Chamber of Commerce. The contents of the Smithsonian's archives were described in "Now Hear This," an essay by Alan Burdick published in *Harper's Magazine* in July 2001. Information on Cherokee possessives is drawn from Linda Jordan and her paper, "The Effects of Place and Animacy on Possession in Oklahoma Cherokee."

Chapter 6: The Kiowa Rules

Interviews with Kiowas took place in February and March 2003; with Alice Anderton, in spring 2000. Gus Palmer, Jr., a Kiowa professor at Oklahoma University, is the source for the term *kaunende*. Whorf's *Language, Thought, and Reality* is quoted. Parrish Williams and Alice Anderton worked on Ponca color terms in January 2000. Louise Erdrich wrote about Ojibwe in "Two Languages in Mind, but Just One in the Heart," an essay published in *The New York*

Times on May 22, 2000, page E1. Oliver Wendell Holmes's aphorism comes from his ruling in Towne v. Eisner, 245 U.S. 418, 425 (1918). Speech communities are discussed in Wick R. Miller's "The Ethnography of Speaking," in the *Languages* volume of the *Handbook of Native American Indians*.

Chapter 7: "I Have Come to Cover You"

Interviews with Luther "Toby" Hughes took place in April 2002 and March 2003. The spells quoted here are from *Walk in Your Soul: Love Incantations of the Oklahoma Cherokees*, by Jack Frederick Kilpatrick and Anna Gritts Kilpatrick. The extended spell for destroying life comes from James Mooney's *The Sacred Formulas of the Cherokee*. More information on Cherokee spells is available in the following books: *The Night Has a Naked Soul: Witchcraft and Sorcery Among the Western Cherokee*, by Alan Kilpatrick, and *Run Toward the Nightland: Magic of the Oklahoma Cherokees*, by Jack Frederick Kilpatrick and Anna Gritts Kilpatrick.

Information on writing systems can be found in *Language Adaptation*, edited by Florian Coulmas, and *Advances in the Creation and Revision of Writing Systems*, edited by Joshua Fishman.

Chapter 8: Seminole Rap

Interviews with Brian Frejo took place in summer 2001, January and February 2002, and February and March 2003; interviews with Quese Frejo, in summer 2001 and March 2003. Background on Riverside High School came from Milton Noel, vice principal. Quese's lyrics appear on a Culture Shock Camp CD, *TuBass3 Live*, created in 2003.

Chapter 9: The Road to Ross Mountain

Interviews with Raymond Vann and Frank Swimmer took place in January 2002, as well as March and May 2003; interviews with Beverly Leach were in April 2002, February 2003, and March 2003. The Keetoowah language exercises are from the *UKB News*, July 1994, page 6, and are reprinted in the Native Writing Systems chapter of *The Green Book of Language Revitalization in Practice*, edited by Leanne Hinton and Ken Hale. John Miller's essay, "How Do You Say 'Extinct': Languages Die. The United Nations Is Upset About This," appeared in *The Wall Street Journal* on March 8, 2002, page W13.

Chapter 10: Inside the Language

Interviews with Alex Sawney took place in February through May 2003. Author interview with Ruth B. Holmes was in January 2002. The "fan-fucking-tastic" quote comes from John McWhorter's *The Power of Babel*. The book used in the Cherokee lessons was Levi Carey's privately printed *Language of the Cherokees*, which comes with tapes. For more information, contact Levi Carey, P.O. Box 2168, Tahlequah, OK 74465-2168 (918-456-7745). Information on the development of the Cherokee syllabary comes from Holmes and Bradley's *Beginning Cherokee* and from Willard Walker and James Sarbaugh's article "The Early History of the Cherokee Syllabary," in *Ethnohistory*.

Epilogue

Alice Anderton provided guidance on language policies in conversations during January 2000, January 2002, March 2003, and June 2003. Information on her organization, Intertribal Wordpath Society, which helps Oklahoma tribes promote their languages, can be found at http://www.ahalenia.com/iwf or at 1506 Barkley St., Norman, OK 73071.

Bibliography

Adams, David Wallace. *Education for Extinction: American Indians and the Boarding School Experience, 1875–1928.* Lawrence: University Press of Kansas, 1995.

Baker, Mark C. *The Atoms of Language.* New York: Basic Books, 2001.

Barnhart, David K., and Allan A. Metcalf. *America in So Many Words: Words That Have Shaped America.* Boston and New York: Houghton Mifflin Co., 1997.

Basso, Keith H. *Wisdom Sits in Places: Landscape and Language Among the Western Apache.* Albuquerque: University of New Mexico Press, 1996.

Brody, Hugh. *The Other Side of Eden: Hunters, Farmers, and the Shaping of the World.* New York: North Point Press, 2000.

Brower, Reuben Arthur, ed. *On Translation.* New York: Oxford University Press, 1966.

Cameron, George. *Sequoyah Orphans Training School.* Tahlequah, Okla.: Heritage Printing, 1994.

Campbell, Lyle. *American Indian Languages: The Historical Linguistics of Native America.* New York: Oxford University Press, 1997.

Carey, Levi. *Language of the Cherokees.* Tahlequah, Okla.: privately printed.

Cartier, Jacques. *The Voyages of Jacques Cartier / With an Introduction by Ramsay Cook.* Toronto: University of Toronto Press, 1993.

Coulmas, Florian, ed. *Language Adaptation.* Cambridge: Cambridge University Press, 1989.

Crystal, David. *Language Death.* Cambridge and New York: Cambridge University Press, 2000.

Cutler, Charles L. *O Brave New Words!: Native American Loanwords in Current English.* Norman: University of Oklahoma Press, 1994.

Debo, Angie. *Oklahoma: Foot-Loose and Fancy-Free.* Norman and London: University of Oklahoma Press, 1949.

Ellis, Clyde. *To Change Them Forever: Indian Education at the Rainy Mountain Boarding School, 1893–1920.* Norman: University of Oklahoma Press, 1996.

Fishman, Joshua, ed. *Advances in the Creation and Revision of Writing Systems.* The Hague: Mouton & Co., 1977.

Fishman, Joshua. "Maintaining Languages: What Works? What Doesn't?" In G. Cantoni (ed.), *Stabilizing Indigenous Languages* (Flagstaff: Northern Arizona University, Center for Excellence in Education, 1996), 186–198.

Foster, Morris W. *Being Comanche: A Social History of an American Indian Community.* Tucson: University of Arizona Press, 1991.

Gawne, Jonathan. *Spearheading D-Day: American Special Units of the Normandy Invasion.* Paris: Histoire & Collections, 1998.

Goddard, Ives, ed. *Handbook of Native American Indians,* Volume 17:

Languages. Washington, D.C.: Smithsonian Institution, 1996.

Gray, Edward G. *New World Babel: Languages and Nations in Early America.* Princeton, N.J.: Princeton University Press, 1999.

Grenoble, Lenore A. and Lindsay J. Whaley, eds. *Endangered Languages: Language Loss and Community Response.* New York: Cambridge University Press, 1998.

Hinton, Leanne. *Flutes of Fire: Essays on California Indian Languages.* Berkeley, Calif.: Heyday Books, 1994.

Hinton, Leanne, and Ken Hale, eds. *The Green Book of Language Revitalization in Practice.* San Diego: Academic Press, 2001.

Holmes, Ruth Bradley, and Betty Sharp Smith. *Beginning Cherokee.* Norman: University of Oklahoma Press, 1976.

Holt, Marilyn Irvin. *Indian Orphanages.* Lawrence: University Press of Kansas, 2001.

Huxley, Aldous. *The Doors of Perception.* New York: Harper & Bros., 1954.

Irving, Washington. *A Tour on the Prairies.* Norman: University of Oklahoma Press, 1956.

Kilpatrick, Alan. *The Night Has a Naked Soul: Witchcraft and Sorcery Among the Western Cherokee.* Syracuse, N.Y.: Syracuse University Press, 1997

Kilpatrick, Jack Frederick, and Anna Gritts Kilpatrick. *Run Toward the Nightland: Magic of the Oklahoma Cherokees.* Dallas: Southern Methodist University Press, 1967.

———. *Walk in Your Soul: Love Incantations of the Oklahoma Cherokees.* Dallas: Southern Methodist University Press, 1965.

Krauss, Michael E. "The Condition of Native American Languages: The Need for Realistic Assessment and Action," in Teresa

McCarty (ed.), *International Journal of the Sociology of Language*. 132 (1998), 9–21.

Kroeber, Karl. *Artistry in Native American Myths*. Lincoln: University of Nebraska Press, 1998.

Kupperman, Karen Ordahl. *Indians and English: Facing Off in Early America*. Ithaca, N.Y. and London: Cornell University Press, 2000.

Lassiter, Luke E. *The Power of Kiowa Song: A Collaborative Ethnography*. Tucson: University of Arizona Press, 1998.

Lieberman, Philip. *The Biology and Evolution of Language*. Cambridge, Mass.: Harvard University Press, 1984.

Malcomson, Scott L. *One Drop of Blood: The American Misadventure of Race*. New York: Farrar, Straus & Giroux, 2000.

McLoughlin, William C. *After the Trail of Tears: The Cherokees' Struggle for Sovereignty, 1839–1880*. Chapel Hill and London: University of North Carolina Press, 1993.

McWhorter, John. *The Power of Babel*. New York: Perennial, 2003.

Meadows, William C. *The Comanche Code Talkers of World War II*. Austin: University of Texas Press, 2002.

Mithun, Marianne. *The Languages of Native North America*. Cambridge and New York: Cambridge University Press, 1999.

Mooney, James. *James Mooney's History, Myths, and Sacred Formulas of the Cherokees: Containing the Full Texts of* Myths of the Cherokee *(1900) and* The Sacred Formulas of the Cherokees *(1891) as Published by the Bureau of American Ethnology*. Asheville, N.C.: Historical Images, 1992.

Nettle, Daniel, and Suzanne Romaine. *Vanishing Voices: The Extinction of the World's Languages*. New York: Oxford University Press, 2000.

Nuttall, Thomas. *A Journal of Travels into the Arkansas Territory During the Year 1819.* Norman: University of Oklahoma Press, 1980.

Philp, Kenneth. *John Collier's Crusade for Indian Reform, 1920–1954.* Tucson: University of Arizona Press, 1977.

Powers, William K. *Sacred Language: The Nature of Supernatural Discourse in Lakota.* Norman and London: University of Oklahoma Press, 1986.

Restak, Richard. *The Secret Life of the Brain.* Washington, D.C.: Joseph Henry Press, 2001.

Rheingold, Howard. *They Have a Word for It: A Lighthearted Lexicon of Untranslatable Words and Phrases.* Los Angeles: Jeremy P. Tarcher, Inc., distributed by St. Martin's Press, 1988.

Shirk, George H. *Oklahoma Place Names.* Norman: University of Oklahoma Press, 1965.

Statement in U.S. Senate, Native American Languages Act Amendments Act of 2000 (S. 2688): Hearing Before the Select Committee on Indian Affairs, July 20, 2000.

Stille, Alexander. *The Future of the Past.* New York: Farrar, Straus & Giroux, 2002.

Strickland, Rennard. *The Indians in Oklahoma.* Norman: University of Oklahoma Press, 1980.

Thornton, Russell, with the assistance of C. Matthew Snipp and Nancy Breen. *The Cherokees: A Population History.* Lincoln and London: University of Nebraska Press, 1990.

Wahrhaftig, Albert L. "Making Do with the Dark Meat: A Report on the Cherokee Indians in Oklahoma." In Sam Stanley (ed.), *American Indian Economic Development* (The Hague: Moulton Publishers, 1978).

Walker, Willard, and James Sarbaugh. "The Early History of the Cherokee Syllabary." *Ethnohistory* 40.1 (winter 1993), 70–94.

Wallace, Ernest, and E. Adamson Hoebel. *The Comanches: Lords of the South Plains.* Norman: University of Oklahoma Press, 1952.

Whorf, Benjamin. *Language, Thought, and Reality: Selected Writings.* Cambridge: Technology Press of Massachusetts Institute of Technology, 1956.

Wilkins, David E. *American Indian Politics and the American Political System.* Lanham, Md.: Rowman & Littlefield Publishers Inc., 2002.

Wright, Muriel H. *A Guide to the Indian Tribes of Oklahoma.* Norman: University of Oklahoma Press, 1951.

Index

INDEX

INDEX

Acknowledgments

IT IS A PLEASURE for me to acknowledge the generosity of many people in Native American communities who used hard-won moments of free time to help me. They are the heroes of this book, and I am humbled by their inspiring example.

I owe a great deal to Alice Anderton, a tireless worker in the cause of preserving the languages. I'd like to note the outsize hospitality of Raymond and Sioux Vann and the patient kindness of Alex Sawney. For taking the time to talk with a long-winded lady, I'd like to thank: Hastings Shade, Ron Red Elk, Richard Codopony, the Comanche Language Committee, Charles Chibitty, Hugh F. Foster, Sadie Parnell, Don Franklin, Sandra Turner, Diane Woodard, Barbara Littledave, Gloria Sly, Dusty Delso, Harry Oosahwee, Brian Levy, Richard Grounds, Alecia Gonzales, Jay Goombi, Sanders Huguenin, Toby Hughes, Valorie Hughes, Linda Jordan, Brian Frejo, Quese Frejo, Frank Swimmer, Archie Mouse, Beverly Leach, and the families of Ross Mountain.

I am also deeply grateful to a number of people in New York, without whom this project wouldn't exist. Many thanks to Lis Harris, who saw promise in a few pages, and to Ken Wells for his crucial encouragement and wise guidance. I couldn't be more grateful to Kris Dahl for her unfailing support and Ann Treistman at Lyons Press for her editorial insight and enthusiasm. I thank Nancy Agabian, Catherine Kapphahn, Brenda Lin, Laura Carden, and Jen Uscher for their caring and thoughtful criticism, and Patty O'Toole, Richard Locke, Michael Janeway, Karl Kroeber, Stacy Schiff, Colin Harrison, and Robert Isaacs for smart comments along the way. I also appreciate the help of my early readers in Lis's workshop, my supportive writing buddy Christine Larson, and teachers John McPhee and Alice Price.

Finally, thanks to my parents and Peter for their provision of essentials, particularly love.

Elizabeth